# Fundamentals of Supply Chain Management

## AN ESSENTIAL GUIDE FOR 21ST CENTURY MANAGERS

*Kenneth B. Ackerman* ▪ *Art Van Bodegraven*

*To Gene and Phyllis, who have been wondering*
*what we've been up to down in the basement*
*but have stuck with us nonetheless.*

# TABLE OF CONTENTS

# FOREWORD

A growing number of publications directed to a wide range of audiences embrace the rapidly emerging topic of Supply Chain Management. While Supply Chain was rarely discussed as recently as the 1990s, today it has become a common topic on the nightly news and in our morning newspapers. Consumers, most of whom have no idea of what constitutes a Supply Chain, regularly hear or read about Supply Chain Management.

Advertising messages abound as global enterprises such as UPS, FedEx, IBM, Dell, and others promote their Supply Chain competency. Business seminars regularly address a broad array of Supply Chain topics, and several different professional and trade associations compete for leadership in the Supply Chain space.

Likewise academic institutions have significantly expanded their commitment to research and teaching the fundamental, and emerging, theories of Supply Chain Management. This first decade of the 21st century may well be described by future business historians as the beginning of the Supply Chain Age.

Of course, the roots of today's Supply Chain were seeded long ago at the inception of commercial enterprise. While the basic need to move products to the right place at the right time is very old, the newness and popularity surge surrounding Supply Chain Management are directly attributed to the rapid and widespread adoption of Internet-based information technology.

While many of the needs for effective and efficient supply chains are time tested, the emerging 21st century performance models are new, challenging, and very exciting. In his updated and expanded *The World Is Flat,* Thomas L. Friedman has identified "Supply-Chaining" and the closely related trend toward increased Outsourcing as two of the 10 fundamental forces that are reshaping the very world we inhabit. We are thrust into what Friedman refers to as "The third stage of Globalization."

Yes, things are truly different than they used to be, and they continue to change rapidly. However, something is missing: information to help us understand what's really taking place.

Most of today's senior management completed their formal education prior to the advent of all this new understanding of the importance of contemporary Supply Chains. Where do they turn to get up-to-date information about new developments? Where can they get answers to their questions, no matter how basic they may be?

In a world characterized by a growing array of acronyms, how does one find out what works and what does not? How does one see the big picture without losing sight of the most elemental details?

The answers to these important and fundamental questions are found in *Fundamentals of Supply Chain Management.* Authors Ackerman and Van Bodegraven, each having over four decades of practical experience, have collaborated to present, in straight talk, the information needed to understand 21st century Supply Chains.

Both authors became involved in the fundamental work of supply chains early in their careers. They individually performed and managed work at all levels of the supply chain. This widespread experience became the foundation for successful consulting careers. Along the road, each became a doer, leader, and, most of all, a mentor to many of today's most successful Supply Chain practitioners. In recent years, they have teamed as teachers to present an introductory executive education seminar, under the auspices of the Council of Supply Chain Management Professionals. These seminars have helped countless people new to the profession better understand supply chain fundamentals.

Now the duo has once again made a notable contribution to a stronger, more informed, Supply Chain future. *Fundamentals of Supply Chain Management* brings to students of all ages a basic and factual description of this emerging discipline. Basic terminology is defined and illustrated in a meaningful way. Concepts are positioned and linked in a manner that makes it easy for readers to use this book as their Supply Chain reference. In a world increasingly operating with information overload and message clutter, Ackerman and Van Bodegraven offer a no-spin, hard-hitting look at the fundamentals of Supply Chain Management. This book is a must for the library of today's business leader.

*Donald J. Bowersox, Ph.D.*
*University Professor and Dean Emeritus*
*Michigan State University*
*2006*

# ACKNOWLEDGMENTS

Light is the task when many share the toil.
*Homer*

Life is to be fortified by many friendships.
*Walter Winchell*

It is not once nor twice but times without number
that the same ideas make their appearance in the world.
*Aristotle*

I am part of all I have met.
*Alfred, Lord Tennyson*

There is a host of people from whom we have drawn inspiration, illumination, insight, input, and information in the construct of this supply chain management primer. A number of them are no longer with us, a few for some centuries now. We salute their memories, each and every one. Attempting to list all those whose thoughts and actions have made a direct impact on our thinking is extremely dangerous, in that we'll surely forget someone. Nevertheless, we'll take a stab at it.

Our heartfelt thanks go, in no meaningful order whatsoever, to: Bruce Abels, Jim Apple, Dick Armstrong, Shawn Barnett, Jeroen van den Berg, Rick Blasgen, Joe Bockerstette, Don Bowersox, Mike Branigan, Clif Burns, Martha Cooper, Henrik Danford-Klein, Mike DelBovo, Ralph Ehmann, Tom Freese, Gene Gagnon, Bill Gates (no, not *that* Bill Gates), Craig Hall, Remko van Hoek, Bob Hribernik, Bud LaLonde, Chuck LaMacchia, John Langley, Larry Lapide, Cliff Lynch, Vin McLoughlin, Scott McWilliams, Paul Marshall, Steve Mulaik, Phil Obal, Bob Ouellette, Paul Peoples, Terry Pohlen, Elijah Ray, Donna Richmond, Emily Rodriguez, Herb Shear, Yossi Sheffi, Tom Speh, Dave Stallard, Jim Stock, Bruce Strahan, Stephen Timme, Kate Vitasek, and Walter Zinn.

For further inspiration, illustration, and example, additional thanks are due to: Aberdeen Group, Affiliated Warehouse Companies, Jeff Bezos, Michael Bloomberg, Larry Bossidy, Sir Richard Branson, John Browne, Ram Charan, Stephen Covey, Michael Dell, W. Edwards Deming, Chris Denove, Mike Eskew, Ken Evans, Henry Ford, Frank and Lillian Gilbreth, Sir James Goldsmith, Richard Harrington, Jeff Immelt, Steve Jobs, Joseph Juran, Robert Kaplan, Herb Kelleher, Hugh Lockhart, John Maeda, David Norton, Taiichi Ohno, Michael O'Leary, David Packard, H. Ross Perot, Laurence Peter, J.D. Power, PricewaterhouseCoopers, Ronald W. Reagan, Ivan Seidenberg, Fred Smith, Stern Stewart & Company, the Supply-Chain Council, Frederick Taylor, Diana Twede, Sam Walton, and Jack Welch.

Finally, the work would most assuredly have suffered without the unique contributions of: Richard Adler, Lucille Ball, William Blake, Calvin Broadus, Edmund Burke, Alphonse Capone, Thomas Carlyle, Charles Chaplin, Ethan and Joel Coen, Tom Cruise, Tino De

Angelis, David Dickinson, Walter Elias Disney, Charles L. Dodgson, Albert J. Dunlap, Fred Ebb, Albert Einstein, Billy Sol Estes, Jasper Fforde, Tom Friedman, Mark Geragos, Malcolm Gladwell, Albert Gore the Younger, Warren G. Harding, Wayne Woodrow Hayes, Homer, John Kander, Larry the Cable Guy, Jerry Leiber, Willy Loman, Phil McGraw, Moshe ben Maimon, Whitney Massengill, Rebecca de Mornay, Alfred E. Neuman, Bob Newhart, Jack Nicklaus, the Nitty-Gritty Dirt Band, Louis Pasteur, Charles Ponzi, Giacomo Puccini, Amanda Reckinwith, George Romero, Jerry Ross, Laura Schlesinger, Rod Serling, William Shakespeare, Don Siegel, Russell Simmons, Anthony J. Soprano, Martha Stewart, Mike Stoller, Joe Tacopina, Vivian Vance, Kurt Vonnegut Jr., Meredith Willson, Tiger Woods, and Bill Watterson and Marge Inovera.

Our illustrations are a mixed bag. The line drawings and cartoons have primarily come from material originally commissioned by the late Gene Gagnon, which are used with permission, and from a series developed for Kenneth B. Ackerman, also — probably obviously — used with permission. Art Van Bodegraven provided some new illustrations and enhancements as well, as did Cathy Avenido.

Other images, charts, tables, and drawings include: materials handling equipment drawings taken from sources in the public domain; an example DuPont Model; sample Johari Windows; and Maslow's Hierarchy. These latter three are interpretations of original concepts by Art Van Bodegraven. The Johari Window was originally a psychological tool first presented by Joseph Luft and Harry Ingham in 1955's *"The Johari Window, a graphic model of interpersonal awareness,"* Proceedings of the Western Training Laboratory in Group Development; Los Angeles: UCLA. The contemporary business adaptation of the window was created by Art Van Bodegraven. Maslow's Hierarchy was first presented by Abraham H. Maslow in 1943's *A Theory of Human Motivation;* Psychological Review, 50, 370-396. The DuPont model was initially employed for internal analytic purposes in 1919 at E. I. du Pont de Nemours and Company, Inc. It has since experienced countless adaptations and variations in a spectrum of applications in numerous companies and consultancies; this latest illustrates only one possibility for application.

The quotations introducing each chapter had many sources, the principal of which was *The Harper Book of Quotations,* edited by Robert I. Fitzhenry. The Internet has become a wellspring of quotations, as well, and we went often to bartleby.com (and also drew from other sites too numerous to list). All Whitney Massengill material was taken from the as-yet-unpublished *Massengill Speaks* by Art Van Bodegraven.

Also, many thanks to those who made physical production possible, notably Cathy Avenido at the Ackerman Company and our doggedly determined editors, Karen Bachrach and James Cooke. And, finally, to all of our colleagues at *DC Velocity,* whose continuing support kept us going long after the coffee had run out.

We are particularly grateful to Mitch Mac Donald and Peter Bradley there, who grabbed the vision early and have worked with us to make *Fundamentals of Supply Chain Management — An Essential Guide for 21st Century Managers* a reality.

Even with all this help, we're almost certain to have placed some number of errors of fact in front of you. For these we apologize and take full responsibility. You may regard some of our conclusions and observations as being erroneous, as well. For these we also take full responsibility, but most certainly do not apologize.

# ABOUT THE AUTHORS

Writers seldom write the things they think.
They simply write the things they think other folks think they think.
*Elbert Hubbard*

Every compulsion is put upon writers to become safe, polite, obedient, and sterile.
*Sinclair Lewis*

Neither man nor God is going to tell me what to write.
*James T. Farrell*

What is written without effort is in general read without pleasure.
*Samuel Johnson*

## Introduction
Who are these guys, anyway? What gives them the crust to think that they should be writing about the fundamentals of supply chain management? For starters, this effort is only their latest joint venture; they've been working together for over 25 years, consulting, teaching, writing, and training. Without getting into their entire life stories, the following will tell you a little about where they've been and what they've done.

## Ken Ackerman
Kenneth B. Ackerman is President of the Ackerman Company, the warehousing and logistics management advisory service in Columbus, Ohio.

Ken is a past President of the Council of Logistics Management (CLM), now the Council of Supply Chain Management Professionals (CSCMP). A founder of the Warehousing Education and Research Council (WERC), he is the only recipient of the highest award from CLM, WERC, and IWLA (International Warehouse Logistics Association).

Ken has been a practitioner, writer, speaker, and educator in the field for decades. Earlier in his career, he built Distribution Centers, Inc. (DCI) from a small family business into a multi-city public warehousing network, finishing his tenure there as Chairman. Subsequently, DCI was acquired by Exel as its entrée into the U.S. market.

The author of a number of standard references in the industry, Ken has been writing books since the '70s. His most recent works include *Auditing Warehouse Performance, Warehousing Tips, Warehousing Profitably — A Manager's Guide, Warehousing Profitably — An Update* and *Words of Warehousing*, a unique reference work. He edits and publishes *Warehousing Forum*, the monthly subscription newsletter. His latest book is *Lean Warehousing*, published in 2006. Ken's independent writing has appeared in numerous journals, including the *Harvard Business Review*.

Always in demand as a speaker, Ken has appeared on five continents, and he's a perennial favorite at the major events in the supply chain management field. He has led countless seminars and workshops both domestically and internationally, with "Fundamentals of Supply Chain Management" for CSCMP, followed by "Fundamentals of Supply Chain Management II" as his latest efforts.

Ken is a graduate of Princeton University and received his MBA degree from Harvard. He has consulted for companies around the world since 1980.

Contact information: (614) 488-3165; ken@warehousing-forum.com; www.warehousing-forum.com

## Art Van Bodegraven

Art Van Bodegraven wears a number of hats as a Partner in The Progress Group LLC, President of Van Bodegraven Associates, and the five-term Chairman of The Supply Chain Group AG.

Art has been a management consultant for 38 of the 46 years in his business career. He has also been the accidental tourist of consulting specialties. After a series of incarnations in Information Systems, Manufacturing, Organizational Performance, and Consumer Products during his 25-year stint with Coopers & Lybrand (subsequently PwC Consulting, now IBM), Art focused on Supply Chain Management and Logistics. In his dozen years with The Progress Group, he has been Executive Vice President, Supply Chain Management Practice Leader, and Director of Marketing, but has mostly been a dirty-fingernails working consultant, and loving it.

Art's consulting experience includes assignments with more than 150 clients in over a dozen industry groups, ranging from small family businesses to multibillion-dollar multi-national enterprises.

Other experience has included work with Inland Steel, Hirsh Company, Household Finance, and the National Security Agency, very little of which he is willing to talk about.

A prolific author, speaker, and teacher, Art has written articles that have appeared in *Warehousing Forum, DC Velocity, Modern Materials Handling, Material Handling Management, Inbound Logistics, Transportation & Distribution, Journal of Business Logistics, WERCSheet, Logistics Comment, Progress Report*, and others.

He is a frequent speaker, track chair, and topic chair at the CSCMP and WERC annual conferences, and has also appeared at IIE, SES, SCMIS, APICS, and AMA.

The co-developer of "Fundamentals of Supply Chain Management" and "Fundamentals II," the CSCMP workshops, he has also developed programs for events at Clemson University and the University of Louisville. Art has been the co-producer of Georgia Tech's "Supply Chain Short Course" for nearly 10 years.

Art's international experience includes working and teaching in: Guatemala, Colombia, Canada, Brazil, Argentina, Cuba, Vietnam, Germany, Mexico, Greece, and the United Kingdom.

He is a long-time member of CSCMP and WERC, and a graduate of Purdue University.

Contact information: (614) 336-0346; avan@theprogressgroup.com; art.van_bodegraven@the-scg.com; www.theprogressgroup.com, www.the-scg.com

# INTRODUCTION

## IN THE BEGINNING

All this will not be finished in the first 100 days.
Nor will it be finished in the first 1,000 days, not in the life of this Administration,
nor even perhaps in our lifetime on this planet. But let us begin.
*John F. Kennedy*

There will come a time when you believe everything is finished.
That will be the beginning.
*Louis L'Amour*

In my beginning is my end.
*Thomas Stearns Eliot*

## The Clarion Call — The World Needs This Book

Do we really need another business book? In particular, do we need another book about supply chain management (SCM)? Hasn't that been done to death? Doesn't everybody know all about SCM by now?

Well, SCM has not been done to death, in our not-very-humble opinion, and not everyone knows all about it, either. In fact, it's hard to find writing on the subject that covers the full breadth of the field and concentrates on the basics, the fundamentals — what we've been calling the ABCs of SCM.

As we wend our way through the maze of conferences and seminars offered each year, we see lots of attention being paid to the "next big thing," to "best practices," and to new and advanced concepts in supply chain planning and execution. That's fine. But there's also a crying need for a coherent discussion of the bare fundamentals of SCM.

## Taking the Long View

To be blunt, we've been watching — and participating in — the evolution of this thing called supply chain management from before the beginning.

We've carefully chosen the term "evolution." What began as Traffic Management and Warehousing became Physical Distribution, and then Logistics. Logistics morphed into Supply Chain Management. (The leading professional organization has periodically changed its name to reflect how the scope of practice has evolved, both physically and linguistically.) Whatever the terminology, basically, we're talking about moving stuff and storing it.

But there's more at work here than just a change in nomenclature. The days when the

Traffic Manager was second only to the Purchasing Agent when it came to gifts of spirits received on holidays and the people who couldn't do anything else were dispatched to the warehouse are long gone. Today's savvy managers have a more significant role to play — they have problems to solve and challenges to overcome, and they have sophisticated new tools to help them do it.

We don't believe that the field has emerged as the result of intelligent design; the current incarnation has too many flaws and shortcomings for a divine being to have been involved. We have concluded, therefore, that more evolution lies ahead of us. Whether that will lead to yet another name change (for the field or for its leading professional association) is beyond our ken.

## Who Is This Book For?

Why a fundamentals book? you may ask. Well, there are loads of reasons. First, we believe that 'most everyone can benefit from periodically revisiting the fundamentals. The phenomenal successes, in different generations, of golf greats Jack Nicklaus and Tiger Woods are testimony to their dedication to the fundamentals — to practicing the basics over and over and over again.

But there are many people, both inside and outside the supply chain world, who can benefit from understanding more about the basics of SCM. Begin with senior managers and executives, whose careers began before supply chain management was an acknowledged field of endeavor. They now sit in judgment of supply chain strategies and investments — and deserve to have an understanding of what SCM is all about.

Close behind are those managers who wake up one morning to discover that they are now in charge of supply chain management and who need a crash course in its scope, definition, and language. Such things happen in companies in which executives circulate through a series of postings on their way to the top.

In other cases, individuals who have spent their careers in singular aspects of the supply chain need to know more about the "other" links in the chain, either to prepare for expanded responsibilities or to gain a better understanding of upstream and downstream supply chain functions.

Then there are all those folks who are colleagues and co-workers of the supply chain practitioners. Management and staff in such corporate functions as Sales and Marketing, Finance and Accounting, Engineering, Information Systems, and Human Resources all need to know about the functions and motivations of supply chain practitioners. Armed with empathy and understanding, they will be better positioned to serve and support — and collaborate — effectively with the supply chain team.

Finally, there is the army of newcomers — people who are brand new to the field and who have arrived without the benefit of formal education in logistics and supply chain management. Early exposure to the basics of the field can keep them from learning too many lessons the hard way.

There are other reasons for putting this collection together as well. In his book *The World Is Flat: A Brief History of the 21st Century,* Thomas L. Friedman selected "supply chaining" as one of the 10 fundamental flatteners in the new global economy. We'll go a step further and suggest that supply chain management is the engine that makes globalization even reasonably feasible.

Without supply chain management, there isn't a global economy in modern terms. And every manager in every sphere of business activity needs to understand that, as does anyone who wants to think about how the world economy works at the operating level.

## Meanwhile, Back at the Oasis

While we were contemplating these factors, it became clear that the pace of change and development in globalized supply chain management (as in all fields of modern endeavor) is enough to give a body whiplash. It was not that long ago that the term "20th century" connoted the pinnacle of achievement. The *20th Century Limited* was the last word in transcontinental passenger train travel; now the notion seems quaint. *20th Century Fox* implied the height of cinematic sophistication; today it's a unit of a media conglomerate owned by an Australian-born tycoon. And "dragged kicking and screaming into the 20th century" was a term of derision reserved for the most reactionary of managers and employees.

Then we experienced Y2K, in which the world's computing resources were sidetracked into the most non-value-added project ever experienced by contemporary human beings — and all before the new century dawned. Today, concepts and events from only yesterday are "so last century." The 20th century has come to signify yesterday's news, yesterday's thinking, and yesterday's technology, all in just the snap of a finger, cosmically speaking.

## Getting It Together

So, with all these constituencies and developments in mind, we have assembled our thoughts on the essentials of supply chain planning and execution, written them down, and packaged the essays as a book, *Fundamentals of Supply Chain Management*. This arena is the one that managers, in all fields, must get their heads around in order to survive, let alone succeed; this book is meant to be their essential guide through this new frontier.

## What Has Moved the Authors to Do This?

Possibly greed and a desire for notoriety have played roles, but there are other motivations. The principal driver for the effort is our contention that the supply chain community needs more attention to the basics. This core contention has motivated each of us to chair the "Fundamentals" track at recent Council of Supply Chain Management Professionals (CSCMP) annual conferences and to present a topic in the track in non-chair years.

As we thought about the groups of people who might benefit from a better understanding of the basics, we conceived the notion of a two-day workshop, centered on the fundamentals of supply chain management. CSCMP adopted the seminar and has sponsored its presentation from 2004 onward. The following year, *DC Velocity* magazine, the premier logistics and supply chain journal, approached us. The magazine, which had been looking to include some "basics" material along with the more topical coverage it's known for, asked us to prepare summaries of some of our presentations from the workshops (and others that extend beyond the two-day workshops' scope). These have appeared in the magazine since September 2005 as a monthly column called *BasicTraining*.

## The Bottom Line

The seminar series has proved successful beyond our expectations, with enthusiastic reviews from course attendees. Based on that level of response and on the acceptance from *DC Velocity*'s readers, we decided that our collected writings on the fundamentals of supply chain management could fill a need in the marketplace. So here they are.

The material that follows represents a collection of highly personal views of core issues in supply chain management. Structurally, we've attempted to assemble the pieces into some more or less logical sequence, but the subject's diversity and breadth defy precise arrangement.

Each segment or chapter is preceded by a set of notable quotables. Often, these quotes relate directly to the subject matter at hand. Other times, the connection won't come clear 'til later in the day. But it's fun for us, and we hope for you, to reflect on how the wit of the sages and the wisdom of the ages can apply to Supply Chain Management.

A word or two of caution — these chapters are about the basics, the fundamentals, the ABCs. They are intended to constitute a primer on the subject. This is not about best practices, bleeding-edge solutions, or the last word on any of the topics.

Nor does this book profess to provide absolutely everything you need to know about Supply Chain Management. It doesn't, though it might be everything you need to know to get started. At the same time, it might also help you become familiar with the entire range of SCM's fundamentals.

Yet another word — we do have points of view that can run counter to the prevailing wisdom. Occasionally, we even display a little attitude. So what?

Now, let's get started on this adventure.

# OVERVIEW

## SUPPLY CHAIN DEFINITIONS

Definitions are like belts. The shorter they are, the more elastic they need to be.
*Stephen Toulmin*

This is it. There are no hidden meanings. All that mystical stuff is just what's so.
*Werner Erhard*

The world is not to be put in order, the world is order incarnate.
It is for us to put ourselves in unison with this order.
*Henry Miller*

A rock pile ceases to be a rock pile the moment a single man contemplates it,
having within him the image of a cathedral.
*Antoine de St. Exupery*

## What's It All About, Alfie?

What's this Supply Chain Management (SCM) thing all about, anyway? Put five experts in a room and you'll get six opinions. It seems that this profession we find ourselves in — some of us by accident — won't stop morphing into its latest incarnation, while we're all still trying to master the last version. Time was, when our world consisted of transporters, of various stripes, and warehousemen (gender diversity was yet to come). Back in the day, we defined ourselves by our specific functionality.

Then industry leaders began to apply organized thinking to the process, and the notion of Physical Distribution was born. And, in 1963, we formed a professional organization around ourselves, the National Council of Physical Distribution Management (NCPDM).

Enter Logistics, a term we first became aware of in the '40s and '50s through its military application. But it involved a broader scope of activity — more integration and planning. In 1985, NCPDM became the Council of Logistics Management (CLM).

In the late '80s and '90s, consultants — and practitioners — began to talk about supply chains, demand chains, and value chains, and the management of the same. Once again, the shift was more than linguistic, as the scope of activity, the degree of integration, the level of planning, and the role of information technology were all escalating to new levels. Then, in 2004, CLM became the Council of Supply Chain Management Professionals (CSCMP).

## The World Discovers SCM

Which is a little like saying that America discovers Columbus. But SCM has gone mainstream; it is no longer the purview of specialists and visionaries. When the *Harvard Business Review* devotes space in three consecutive issues to a topic (as it did in 2004), you know that discipline has finally arrived. And if there were any lingering doubts, they were dispelled when *The Economist* published a special insert titled "Logistics — The Physical Internet" a scant 18 months later.

In academia, the pace has gone from a trot to a full gallop. Time was, when only a few schools were brave enough to deal seriously with the dirty-fingernails world of logistics. Ohio State, Georgia Tech, Penn State, Michigan State, and Tennessee come to mind, and there were selective efforts at Northwestern in transportation and Arizona State in purchasing. Today, it's tough to find an institution that doesn't have some supply chain management faculty, if not a full-blown curriculum.

It's borderline gratifying. For the longest time, we felt as if we were latter-day buskers, shuffling and scuffling in the streets and hoping for a little spare change from passers-by.

The profession has even, in the collective, begun to gain boardroom access, with all of the pressure and expectations — and pay — implied in working relationships at the C level.

## But What Does SCM Mean?

Dr. Bernard J. ("Bud") LaLonde, professor emeritus at The Ohio State University, has described SCM's evolution as a passage through three stages of integrated logistics: from Physical Distribution, through the inclusion of Procurement and Operations, to the end-to-end view encompassing Vendors and Customers.

In the world of Supply Chain Management, though, what goes on *within* the boxes is as important as what goes on between them. The end-to-end view now, appropriately, includes suppliers' supply chains, along with those of an enterprise's customers. The need for visibility, synchronization, and integrated planning far surpasses anything we have needed in the past.

Rick Blasgen, a longtime leading supply chain practitioner who was named head of CSCMP in 2005, maintains that Logistics is to the Supply Chain as Planet Earth is to the Universe — that Logistics is a matter for Science, and that Supply Chain is a matter for Theology. To understand the aptness of that analogy, consider some of the attributes of each:

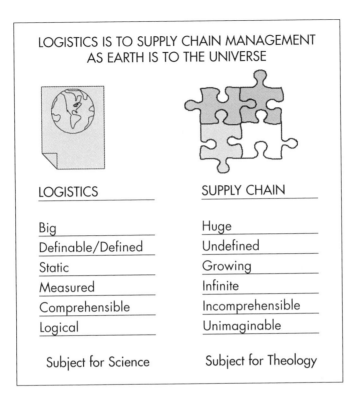

## LOGISTICS IS TO SUPPLY CHAIN MANAGEMENT AS EARTH IS TO THE UNIVERSE

| LOGISTICS | SUPPLY CHAIN |
|---|---|
| Big | Huge |
| Definable/Defined | Undefined |
| Static | Growing |
| Measured | Infinite |
| Comprehensible | Incomprehensible |
| Logical | Unimaginable |
| Subject for Science | Subject for Theology |

## Taking a Stand

CSCMP invested many months — and untold person-years — in committee time to come up with the ultimate definition of Supply Chain Management as a prelude to staking its claim as *the* professional organization for Supply Chain practitioners. That definition reads as follows: "Supply Chain Management encompasses the planning and management of all activities involved in sourcing and procurement, conversion, and all Logistics Management activities. Importantly, it also includes coordination and collaboration with channel partners, which can be suppliers, intermediaries, third-party service providers, and customers. In essence, Supply Chain Management integrates supply and demand management within and across companies."

CSCMP went on to redefine Logistics, as well. Know what? We think there's an important omission, and that is the *execution* of all those planned and managed activities. Oh, well — five experts, six opinions again.

## Yet Another View

Another school of thought talks about Supply Chain Logistics — that is, Logistics in the context of Supply Chain Management. Its followers make the point that our world is characterized by the dynamic tension between the demands of the marketplace and the capabilities of supply mechanisms. These are exemplified by the gaps — sometimes chasms — between:

- When and where products are desired, how many are wanted, and in what mix; and

■ When and where products are made, how many are produced, and in what mix.

Logistics, then, consists of the processes and techniques used to bridge the gaps. Supply Chain Integration is the sum of efforts — strategic and tactical — to shrink the gaps between market needs and supply capability. And Supply Chain Management would include a collective of processes, technology, and decision-making to simultaneously plan, manage, operate, and improve the performance and cost of supply chains.

A tall order, to be sure. And one that makes leaping tall buildings in a single bound look easy. But it may come close to describing the business world's current expectations of Supply Chain Managers.

## Such an Easy Game to Play . . .

In the early days of supply chain thinking, it did look like an easy game, even considering needs for greater integration, enhanced information, and planning, planning, planning. The concepts were relatively straightforward. We could talk endlessly about substituting information for inventory, responding to demand signals.

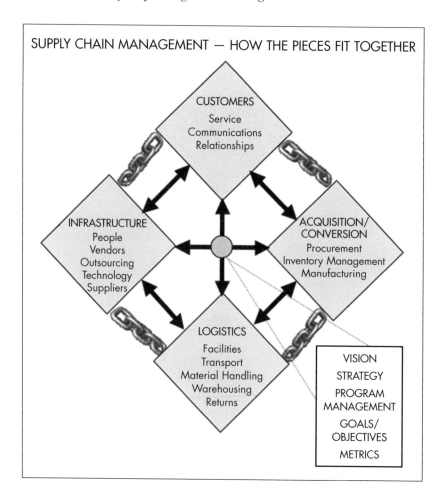

SUPPLY CHAIN MANAGEMENT — HOW THE PIECES FIT TOGETHER

Then we discovered some sobering realities. One was that there's no such thing as a single supply chain, no matter what it's called. Any enterprise operates or takes part in numerous supply chains. Ohio State's Dr. Martha Cooper presented ground-breaking thinking in the field, comparing supply chain(s) to a tree, with myriad roots, even more branches, and a trunk made up of pathways linking each and all. So much for the simplistic pictures.

Another was the need for all the partners in a supply chain to be on the same conceptual page. The hoary, but marvelously effective, Beer Game was devised at the Massachusetts Institute of Technology (MIT) in the late '60s to illustrate how traditional (read: dysfunctional) supply chains go wrong through the simple failure to share information. As anyone who's ever played the game (http://beergame.mit.edu) knows, the one player in the middle who just doesn't get it will destroy the best efforts of the rest of the players. The lesson is even more compelling in real life.

A third was that information technology wasn't even close to what was needed to optimize the simplest supply chains. That condition has mightily improved since, and the capabilities of today's systems are genuinely impressive. But the road from there to here is littered with dashed hopes, broken promises, and budget-buster solutions that didn't pan out.

Despite it all, we'll submit that, in the realm of supply chain systems, the promise is getting closer to the reality, in both planning and execution dimensions. The technology future is bright for supply chain managers.

## The Ultimate Objectives

However we define Supply Chain Management, it has a few fundamental missions in business life, and it's vital for supply chain managers to understand — and believe in — these objectives. Ultimately, it's all about increasing shareholder value, improving profitability, and supporting revenue and market share performance. Supply chain integration involves product flow, information flow, and cash flow — it's not just about moving boxes.

That's at a high level, but it's all got to translate to the operating level. Face it: the supply chain challenge — in management, in operations, in administration — is to:

*Deliver more customized products/services*

*... With faster order turnaround*

*... With smaller and more frequent (and perfect) orders*

*... With higher fill rate*

*... With higher quality*

*... With less inventory*

*... At lower cost.*

And don't forget to leap tall buildings in a single bound, while you're at it.

# THE ROLE OF INFRASTRUCTURE(S)

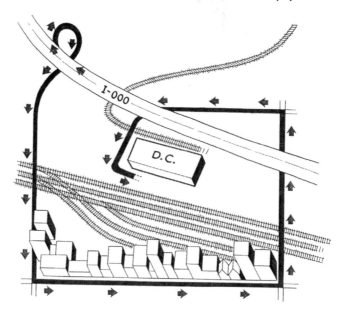

And the first little pig built his house of straw ...
*Traditional*

One only needs two tools in life: WD-40 to make things go,
and duct tape to make them stop.
*G. M. Weilacher*

If we work upon marble, it will perish. If we work upon brass, time will efface it.
If we rear temples, they will crumble to dust. But if we work upon men's immortal
minds, if we imbue them with high principles, with the just fear of God and love of
their fellow men, we engrave on those tablets something which no time can efface,
and which will brighten and brighten to all eternity.
*Daniel Webster*

Form ever follows function.
*Louis H. Sullivan*

## Meanings
The first question is "What do you mean by infrastructure?" Fair enough. There are macro-infrastructures and micro-infrastructures. If you want to take a critical look at your own company, or your own supply chain, that's probably a micro view. If you are considering options in global operations, the macro view might be more useful.

We'll be talking mainly about macro-infrastructures, but the components can be translated to the specifics of your particular situation.

## Where to Begin

For most people, the term "infrastructure" means the elements of physical transportation infrastructure — roads, railways, subway lines and so forth. We would argue that along with these obvious components, the "hardware" of infrastructure also includes some that are not so obvious. Let's take a look at some of the parts:

▪ **Roads.** That's easy, right? But consider the varieties of roadways that are important in supply chain operations, along with descriptions customarily used in North America:

▪ **Motorways,** or what Americans usually call interstate highways, the limited-access, sometimes toll but usually free, multilane, long-distance routes between major population centers.

▪ **Other primary highways,** the free-access roads, generally four-lane, often long-distance (even transcontinental) routes between major and intermediate population centers, including passage through secondary cities and towns.

▪ **Secondary and tertiary roads,** the free-access roads, usually two-lane but sometimes more, paved and maintained, connecting cities and towns of all sizes. Contemporary supply chain transport in North America seldom if ever uses the gravel and dirt roads and lanes found in remote rural locations.

▪ **Other streets and roadways,** the network of city streets, highway access roads, beltways, spurs, and other ancillary components of the total surface-transport system.

▪ **Bridges,** roadways that span water, other roads or rail track (many of which are reported to be in desperate need of upgrade and repair in the United States).

The highway system has long been considered government's responsibility to both build and maintain, despite the legitimacy of our early history of primitive toll roads, bridges, and ferries. Toll roads have held on and expanded, often as part of the interstate highway network.

Lately, a new practice has begun to emerge — privatization. The (toll) Chicago Skyway and the Indiana Toll Road are two examples of early adopters. Some experts see privatization as a key to the continued expansion of road capacity in the United States. Private developers are also increasingly building their own interchanges and access roads on existing motorways to serve both consumer and commercial business developments.

▪ **Rails.** By rail, we mean the track as well as the locomotives and other rolling stock associated with freight carriage along with issues of capacity and maintenance of way. Light rail, commuter, and passenger rail are, in our view, important, but belong to a different type of infrastructure.

The railroad industry, which has long been critical, even jealous, of the public support given to roads, has sometimes in the past suggested that preferential treatment given highways hastened the decline of passenger service and weakened the freight business. Today's market conditions (in particular, the rising demand for long-distance hauls from ports of entry and mining centers) have changed the picture considerably, although not enough to bring back legendary trains like the *Orange Blossom Special* or *The City of New Orleans*.

The major rail operators are sinking billions of dollars — of their own money, of course — into capacity expansion. Not only are they investing in double or even triple tracking for popular routes, but they're also laying down track extensions to reach new sources and markets.

▪ **Inland waterways.** Though water transport plays a much smaller role in the United States than it does in Europe, it still has utility and value in specific applications and industries, e.g., moving iron ore from mines to steel-making centers or getting logs to paper mills. And, lest we forget, vast quantities of agricultural products move down the Mississippi, with other goods moving on the Ohio. Water remains vitally important for transport in Europe and elsewhere in the world, and includes the following options:

▪ **Rivers,** which have influenced the locations of major cities and the flow of trade routes for centuries; e.g., Southeast Asia's Mekong or Europe's Danube.

▪ **Canals,** which are man-made waterways such as Germany's Kiel Kanal and those quaint channels found in the Dutch countryside.

▪ **Lakes,** which have long been used for commercial crossings. Think of Hungary's Balaton, the multinational Bodensee, Russia's Ladoga, Africa's Victoria, and North America's own string of Great Lakes.

On the global scene, a significant amount of cargo from the Far East is now routed through Egypt's Suez Canal for arrival at U.S. East Coast ports in order to avoid congestion and labor problems on the West Coast.

As for the fabled Panama Canal, many of today's ships (the so-called post-Panamax vessels) are too large to fit through the locks of the canal, and Panama is beginning to feel the pinch. In hopes of remaining a viable alternative route for ships bound for the United States, Panama will expand the canal's capacity.

▪ **Ports.** Ports, which are essentially transfer points for both inbound and outbound shipments, offer the facilities needed by ships or aircraft for taking on or discharging cargo. The nation's port infrastructure includes the following:

▪ **Ocean ports,** which are situated on or near harbors and offer facilities for seagoing vessels. Challenges facing these gateways include container handling capability and capacity constraints, vessel size and container-crane capacity limits, issues surrounding access to roads and rails for inland movements, and integration with distribution facilities and shipping centers.

▪ **Airports,** which are essentially tracts of land set aside for aircraft take-offs and landings along with the associated freight storage, perishable goods, and livestock and customs processing facilities. Airports situated in residential areas increasingly must deal with local government and community efforts to restrain flight movements at certain times of day or limit capacity in ways that impede carriers' efforts to improve aircraft utilization.

U.S. seaports, particularly Los Angeles and Long Beach on the West Coast and New York/New Jersey on the East Coast, have struggled in recent years, beset by capacity, congestion, and labor issues. That's prompted some shippers to shift business to less-crowded gateways. Principal beneficiaries of this trend have been the ports of Charleston, Savannah, Brunswick, and Jacksonville, along with Vancouver and other Pacific Northwest operations. The expandability of highway infrastructure (lanes, exits) is a critical factor in limiting or enabling effective port capacity growth.

▪ **Land,** which tends to be overlooked in discussions about transportation infrastructure. The availability and cost of suitable building sites can profoundly affect the economics of supply chain decisions, oftentimes dictating choices of facility footprint size, degree of mechanization, and even supply chain network structures.

Note that our discussion of the various elements of the physical infrastructure assumes that there are adequate fleets to leverage their use — trucks of all varieties and sizes, boats and barges (again of an appropriate mix of size and purpose), and rail cars and power units.

Yes, and ports with the capacity — vessel size and TEU volume — to stay ahead of the wave of incoming products and materials. Fleet availability is not a given in many countries.

## Software to Go With the Hardware?

As crucial as it may be, the physical infrastructure represents just one aspect of the broad supply chain infrastructure. There's also what we like to call "software" — the intellectual infrastructure. The software infrastructure, too, has a number of components. They include the following:

- **Education and research facilities,** which includes not just the colleges, universities, and laboratories that turn out literate and numerate graduates, but also those institutions focused on research and application in logistics and supply chain management. By that, we don't mean institutions with a lone faculty member synthesizing the results of other people's studies; we mean those dedicated to promoting leading-edge theory and practice in the field.

- **The workforce,** an adequate supply of workers who have the skills, motivation, and qualifications needed for jobs in the supply chain execution field. In other words, workers educated in the basics of computation and communication, who are flexible and trainable, and who demonstrate both a strong work ethic and a desire to succeed.

- **Practitioners,** a pool of veteran staff members and managers who have acquired the hands-on knowledge and practical experience and can supervise the efforts of others in supply chain activities.

- **Support resources,** including — dare we say it — consultants, who can help identify and spread the word about best practices and the applicability of techniques and solutions in specific situations.

- **Technology expertise,** including software designers and developers, and material handling system designers. These professionals offer the capability to conceive and generate information and handling solutions, and to advise customers and clients in their application and implementation.

- **Government,** by which we mean legislators attuned to the importance of the supply chain. As sensitive a topic as this may be, the fact remains that a national or local government that gets the picture about supply chain management can be enormously valuable in enabling, incentivizing, and promoting supply chain activities, and in building or shoring up infrastructure components. It helps if that government is honest and committed to free market operations ... and amenable to the free flow of capital.

## What Else?

Beyond that, there's another category we might call "middleware," if that's not stretching the hardware/software analogy too far. In fact, as we see it, there are three vital categories of middleware infrastructure without which the rest simply don't work.

The first is **communications and connectivity,** without which all of the data essential to day-to-day commerce — orders, confirmations and so forth — cannot flow from one party to another. How reliable and extensive is the hard-wired landline system, and how far does it reach? How extensive and reliable are the mobile communications systems? How useful are Internet service providers, and what are the alternatives in accessing them? Are high-speed connections available? What is the state of wireless access? And how free and widespread is access to technology among people as well as among businesses? If these aren't infrastructure questions, we don't know what else to call them.

Another is the **electric power grid,** which is essential to the functioning of society, not just its supply chain. We learned this the hard way a couple of years ago when the Northeastern United States and large chunks of Canada went dark unexpectedly. Just imagine, there are parts of the world that live like that on a regular basis. And consider the impact on supply chain effectiveness when power supplies are erratic, irregular, or just plain unavailable when they are needed. Knowing that the national/regional grid needs to be both powerful and reliable then raises questions about the power-generation systems behind the grid. Are they reliable? Do they have peak generation capacity? Are they prepared for future growth? Are they secure?

Think about Cuba, in which a 100-year-old power plant can't provide enough power to keep the lights on for more than an hour without failing. Consider Istanbul, a 21st century city in which the periodic power outage adds to the quaint charm of the Eurasian experience. Imagine struggling to operate 24/7 in a country that shuts off the power at 10:00 each evening.

Auxiliary power sources are necessities today, and not only in obviously fragile infrastructures. Oh, by the way, simply having water is not enough — there needs to be sufficient volume and pressure to power sprinkler systems.

Finally, there are **standards.** We've been sensitized to the vital role that standards play in making supply chains flow smoothly by recent work with the Standards Engineering Society. Think about it. Products need to have dimensional standards, as well as performance standards and tolerance standards.

Our communications can't work without standards. Electronic Data Interchange (EDI) is rife with standards. Standards are what may make radio-frequency identification (RFID) a winner in the long haul. Bar codes need standards, and the quality of their presentation requires standards.

Now that we're knee-deep in global supply chains, we need to ask how well (or poorly) our prospective trading partners adhere to standards: How their standards might be different from ours — and how we can reconcile them. Which set of standards should be adopted and which must co-exist with translation tables for some time to come — and where we'll have to live with dual standards, and the technology to interpret each.

The people who work daily with these issues — and work them out — are unsung heroes of modern commerce and supply chain management.

## Leveraging Infrastructure

How big a deal is infrastructure quality? Huge. The new members of the European Union have an orders-of-magnitude challenge and a delicate balancing act in front of them as they attempt to do international business, shore up a weak physical infrastructure, and build internal markets simultaneously — all the while starting out 45 years behind the industrialized "Old Europe."

Underdeveloped nations outside the EU have even greater infrastructure challenges. Take Russia, for example. Or better yet, take China. Despite its torrid growth and growing dominance as a manufacturing center, China faces enormous infrastructure challenges. It may never (in the opinion of some expert observers) develop physical capacities comparable to those found in the West.

Meanwhile, locales, and local governments, that get the picture in the realm of supply chain management are promoting themselves competitively. In the United States, Atlanta has established an exemplary program as a formal arm of the Metropolitan Atlanta Chamber of Commerce. It promotes supply chain excellence, attracts new business on the basis of logistics capabilities, and uses critical mass to attract even more academic, consulting, and practitioner-level skills.

In Europe, the Netherlands and Flanders (Belgium) have been active in this area. Both have very active organizations (NFIA, FFIA) devoted to attracting business based on supply chain capabilities and of promoting the success of the enterprises and verticals already there.

Switzerland and Dubai have recently begun to promote themselves as logistics and supply chain hubs as well. The Swiss apparently see themselves as a centroid in a two-dimensional model, downplaying the physical challenges of needing to tunnel through the Alps. For its part, Dubai is investing heavily in development, although the jury will be out on that effort for a while yet.

## Bringing Infrastructure Home

As important as national and local infrastructures may be (and they are), individual companies have supply chain infrastructures, too. Some of the components may be obvious, like plants and capital equipment or distribution centers and fleets (assuming they're owned and not outsourced). But there are others, all of which require planning and attention.

The most important of these may be people — their education, skills and experience. Along with human resources, there is information technology and systems — their functionality and degree of integration in an age of high competitiveness and visibility.

Next comes the structure of the network itself — how and where suppliers are located and linked into physical distribution, and how and where distribution facilities are sited and synchronized with customers, market channels, and corporate service strategies. An often-forgotten ingredient in this recipe is how individual network components link into the overall physical infrastructure and whether that network gives users the flexibility to change their mix of transport modes if needed.

Partnerships and relationships are closely tied to these considerations: How well and for what specific advantage suppliers have been selected, the strengths and qualities of service providers (logistics service providers, lead service providers, etc.), and the nature of communications and joint efforts with selected key customers.

Not least is the internal supply chain organization — in other words, how it's organized, what functions are directly and indirectly included, and how the functions, in fact, work together, plan, and communicate.

Finally, there is the critical question of whether a clear supply chain strategy exists and how it ties to and supports corporate strategies.

Each of these elements is discussed in other chapters. A vital concept to remember is that, like roads and bridges, the components of a corporation's internal infrastructure need regular upgrading and maintenance. The demands placed on them are constantly changing and growing; their capabilities and capacities need to develop accordingly.

## Winding Up

In the world of supply chain management, infrastructure isn't merely a term to throw into the conversation in order to appear erudite. It has real meaning, and vast influence on how — and how well — supply chains work.

In the United States, we've railed (no pun intended) for years about the signs of decay, particularly in bridges. More recently, we've been concerned about cargo throughput capacity, particularly in congested ports. Mike Eskew, the CEO of UPS, has termed the situation "shocking" and has called for an integrated strategy to develop and improve all facets of the physical infrastructure, including how they work together.

But the United States isn't the only nation confronting these issues. As noted earlier, some have observed that infrastructure remains one of China's greatest obstacles to sustainable growth. In fact, it may not be too far fetched to suggest that there is neither enough time nor enough money for China to build a physical infrastructure on a par with Europe or North America — *ever.*

# CUSTOMER SERVICE

The customer is always right.
*R.H. Macy*

How can I be useful, of what service can I be?
There is something inside me, what can it be?
*Vincent van Gogh*

The sole meaning of life is to serve humanity.
*Leo Tolstoy*

You are never giving, nor can you ever give, enough service.
*James R. Cook*

## Beyond the Complaint Window

Everybody's got a customer service story to tell, and often as not, it's something of a horror story. Our view of customer service has been shaped by our experiences in our daily lives, and, typically, we are surrounded by examples of what not to do when it comes to dealing with customers.

But there's more to the customer service story than surly department store clerks or unhelpful help lines. In fact, for businesses that really get what customer service is all about, it can translate into a powerful competitive advantage.

What does customer service mean in the context of supply chain management? The answer is deceptively simple. The supply chain doesn't really begin with sourcing and procurement, as some would have it. It begins with customers — their demands (and those of *their* customers), their profiles, their locations and their buying habits. In fact, it's customer service — the needs and demands of the marketplace — that should dictate where we locate facilities, how we design distribution networks, and what processes and technologies we deploy and employ.

In short, customer service is the reason we are all here.

## Who Are the Customers?

In the context of supply chain operations, our lives are filled with customers. We may, in fact, be dealing with end consumers. Or maybe our customers are other businesses — manufacturers, distributors, retailers, etc. At a minimum, other departments inside our company — and the people in them — are our individual or functional customers. We'll focus on some specific consumer examples, but the concepts and principles apply to customer relationships throughout the supply chain.

## What Is Customer Service?

Fair question. The horror stories about offshore call centers (or retail stores with no apparent sales associates) aside, what is customer service really? If you ask a group of people, they're likely to bring up the following:
- Order intake.
- Sales transactions.
- Complaint/problem resolution.
- Technical support.
- FAQ information.
- Shipping performance/order fulfillment.
- Returns handling.

Only once in our lives (yes, once!) has anyone spontaneously come up with the answer that makes the most sense to us. A guy attending the Supply Chain Short Course at Georgia Tech stood up and simply said, "Everything." And he meant it. Everything.

As for what "everything" includes, at the retail level it would be nothing less than the look, feel, and smell — and location — of a retail operation. How merchandise is displayed, and how much is available. How salespeople greet customers, and how they handle traffic overloads. How they up-sell, how they respond to questions, and how they anticipate needs and next steps.

It would also include the look, feel, and operation of the Web site — whether it's set up for selling, answering FAQs, complaint intake, or information gathering. Is the site easy to navigate? Are the functions straightforward? Is the merchandise presented well, and is the site aesthetically pleasing? Does the copy's tone match the image the company hopes to project?

Going further, "everything" should encompass the product or products themselves and their fitness for use. Do they offer intrinsic quality and aesthetic appeal? Is the packaging or wrapping user and environmentally friendly as well as functional and attractive? Is the manual easy to read and understand?

"Everything" would also include telephone answering menus. Are they clear, well-organized, straightforward, and complete? Are response times reasonable? Are there contingency plans for high-volume periods?

Then there's complaint and problem resolution. Is it easy, quick, and straightforward? How about the staff? Whether they work in sales, service, or technical support, whether they're internal or outsourced, whether they're domestic or offshore, they must meet your standards. Are they knowledgeable and capable? Do they communicate well? Are they reinforcing — or degrading — the company's image in the marketplace?

Keep in mind that "everything" also extends to a host of corporate departments: Accounts Payable, Accounts Receivable, Credit & Collections, IT. Basically, it would include any function that might have contact with a customer or a potential customer. Do all of these departments or functions bring the same attitude and disposition, competence, and capability to transaction handling and problem resolution across the enterprise?

And so on, and so on. Everything that a customer might see, touch, or hear, before, during, and after a transaction is a part of the customer service experience. Call center management barely scratches the surface, doesn't it?

## What Should Customer Service Be About?

What do customers want? It only seems as though they want the sun, the moon, and the stars. In fact, research has shown that they really have only the most basic of expectations:

- **Quick acknowledgment and response.** Whether it's in the store or on the phone, no one wants to wait to be acknowledged, or once acknowledged, to wait for a response (five minutes appears to be the upper limit). Unless they're dealing with a monopoly (such as Amtrak), people will hang up, leave the store, and move the company down on any mental list of alternatives they may be keeping. Many employees still behave as if their companies were monopolies (perhaps many of them used to be) and serve customers accordingly, but make no mistake: The day of reckoning will come — for both those employees and their companies.

- **Human contact.** It may come as unwelcome news to those who are trying to accomplish everything through Web sites and voice-recognition menus. But the fact remains that people like the social experience — and flexibility — of dealing with other people, especially when there is a problem.

- **One-call problem resolution.** Yes, this represents the gold standard for either "fixes" or information, but it's nonetheless achievable. And keep in mind that costs go up — and customer confidence declines — with each successive call.

- **Expeditious solutions.** This doesn't necessarily mean same-day or next-day service, but it does mean a reasonably timely — and consistent — response. You're better off hitting a consistent three-day commitment than promising one day and delivering in two.

- **Choices.** If you can't meet a customer's exact need, at least offer that customer some options. Some examples: "We can deliver half tomorrow and half next Friday, or hold everything for next Friday." Or "We can overnight the item in green this afternoon, or we can get the blue to you in eight business days." Or "We can send a new handle in five days, or offer you a discount of "x" dollars if you can live with the broken one."

- **A positive attitude.** It doesn't take a genius to figure out that a smile in the voice goes a long way toward disarming a potential rioter. (It is very difficult for Web sites and automated menus to have a smile in the voice.)

- **Technical knowledge.** This is more than just knowledge of products and how they work. It also means a familiarity with the inner workings of the company's customer service operations. A representative who leads a customer through the maze of the company's internal resolution process is likely to earn himself or herself a loyal friend.

## The Lean Perspective

In a lean world, which is rapidly becoming the norm or at least the target, customers may have somewhat higher expectations. According to *USA Today*, customers hope — and increasingly, expect — that their suppliers will do the following:

- Solve the problem *completely*.
- *Waste no time* — the customer's or the supplier's.
- Provide *exactly* what is wanted.
- Deliver value *where* it is wanted.
- Supply value *when* it is wanted.
- *Cut* the number of *decisions* needed to solve problems.

## What Leaders Do

In addition to paying attention to what their customers value (above), leaders should make it a point to do the following:

1. Proact. A good example of this was Ford Credit mailing payment "forgiveness" notices to Florida customers following the 2004 hurricanes.

2. Empower employees. Give employees the authority at all levels to fix problems and make errors and omissions right — in person, on the telephone, or online.

3. Focus on overall results. Concentrate too hard on the cost of a single event or solution, and you could miss out on an opportunity to win a valuable customer for life.

4. Treat customer service as an investment, not a cost. A leader must understand the strategy of customer service as a differentiator and source of competitive advantage.

5. Develop and sustain a customer service culture.

6. Translate the "feel-good" into quantifiable results.

7. Build from a set of core values.

Does this pay off in today's dog-eat-dog world? Some studies indicate that customer service leaders enjoy better-than-average stock price performance. Think about some recognized leaders: Infiniti in automobiles, Ritz-Carlton in hospitality, Nordstrom in retail, L.L. Bean in consumer-direct, or Southwest in airlines. Their very names conjure up an image of a quality experience.

Customers at all levels can tell the difference between those who talk the talk and those who walk the walk. You can only fake sincerity for so long, as evidenced by legacy airlines that pull out periodic on-board customer service initiatives that sometimes last as long as 500 miles.

## Downsides and Pitfalls

When a company embarks on a service improvement initiative these days, there's a good chance that it's looking at either automation or offshoring. Though both strategies can succeed spectacularly, both can also prove disastrous.

Take automation, for starters. Well-designed technology *can* leverage the human investment in customer service; conversely, ill-designed Web sites and automated menus can sabotage your efforts and even cost you customers. Before implementing any technology, you've really got to figure out what you want to accomplish. Do you want to cut labor costs? Automate the routine transactions so you can free up the people to handle sensitive and difficult issues? Increase responsiveness and augment other information and service channels? Or, as it so often seems today, do you merely want to provide the appearance of a customer service commitment without investing in the resources needed to make it a reality?

What are we talking about here? Technology that's off target includes Web sites that may seem organized logically to a technology professional, but aren't aligned with customer behavior; sites that are difficult to navigate and can't interpret synonymous language; and sites with rigid search capability. It also includes menus that don't offer the most common options immediately and menus that don't offer an avenue for *all* possible options, including a clear adaptation to human interpretation.

Successful offshoring, too, requires that companies proceed with caution. Yes, there's the seductive promise of cost savings and freedom from the hassles of finding qualified and motivated domestic staff (at any price). But anyone considering an off-shore solution (in whole or in part) to the customer service equation must determine customers' sensitivity to the dynamics of problem solving with service people from other cultures. There is also the ever-present question of language barriers, even when both parties purportedly speak English.

Finally, there is the tragedy of enterprises that are committed to customer service and are willing to spend whatever it takes, but turn out to be tone-deaf when it comes to customer service. In the end, misguided customer service can be worse than bad customer service. To avoid falling into that trap, companies should ask themselves the following questions:

- How much service can you lavish on "C" customers?
- How much does it cost to deliver next day to customers who would be thrilled to get things in two (or more) days?
- What is the point of "delighting" customers who are buying on price alone?
- Who has the courage, and the wisdom, to tell the customer he or she is wrong, and that there's money to be made doing things a different way?
- Why strive to "exceed the customer's expectations" when mastering the basics of service remains a largely lost art?

There's a fortune — several fortunes — being wasted in these efforts that could really be put to better use on targeted customer service.

## From the Experts

*Satisfaction*, by Chris Denove and James D. Power IV, echoes many of our contentions. (You may recognize the J.D. Power name.) Here are some nuggets of wisdom from Denove and Power:

- Customers with swiftly handled problems are more loyal than those with no problems.
- At some point, faster response on the phone is not valued; people will wait, just not endlessly.
- Customer service is a bottom-line proposition.

- The customer service front lines are in the interactions between workers and customers.
- There is a clear link between customer satisfaction and profitability.
- Exceeding expectations matters more than consistently good performance (now, if we could only figure out what the real expectations are ...)

## A Final Note

Time and space do not permit a full discussion of the emergence of self-service as the latest in a string of initiatives to improve customer service (think ATMs, airline kiosks, supermarket self-checkout registers, and fast food order entry/payment stations). If we do it ourselves, there's no one else to blame when things go wrong. Or is there? The technology behind self-service has got to be perfect, crystal clear, and backed up with human help. It can save money, for sure, but the savings are illusory if customers end up being hassled by a machine.

Do take time to consider the importance of satisfying customers in all phases of the supply chain. It's what we are here for, and serving customers in all dimensions of a business relationship can help us to fulfill all of our core reasons for being in business.

# PROCUREMENT

... with all thy getting get understanding.
*Proverbs 4:7*

A study of economics usually reveals that the best time to buy anything is last year.
*Marty Allen*

If you make a habit of buying things you do not need,
you will soon be selling things you do.
*Filipino Proverb*

Buy old masters. They fetch better prices than old mistresses.
*Lord Beaverbrook*

## Background and Definitions

What exactly is the difference between Procurement and Purchasing? Is this just another example of the euphemizing of America? Another manifestation of the disease that causes people to say "utilize" instead of "use?" Or call salespeople vice presidents?

Perhaps it is. If so, we're guilty, too. We all are. Procurement has become the preferred term for purchasing — at least in informal use. But technically speaking, there are differences, and they can be significant.

Purchasing — sorry, procurement — mavens make the point that procurement is the entire process of acquiring goods (and services) from third parties, through the end of a contract or the useful life of a product, whether consumable or an asset — including the initial notion that sparks development and acquisition. The Council of Supply Chain Management Professionals, for one, defines procurement as follows: "The business functions of procurement planning, purchasing, inventory control, traffic, receiving, incoming inspection, and salvage operations."

Maybe that's where the Institute for Supply Management (formerly the National Association of Purchasing Management) got the idea that Supply Management looks a lot like supply chain management. It defines procurement as: "The acquisition, access, positioning, and management of resources that an organization needs ... in the attainment of its strategic objectives."

We could arm-wrestle all night about where procurement leaves off and other functions begin. But that would be beside the point. We can probably agree that sourcing and purchasing are the strategic and transactional elements of procurement. As we see it, sourcing would include spend analysis, purchase strategy, category management, supplier qualification and selection, make-buy, and group buying. Purchasing, then, would be repetitive buying, discrete purchase authorization, effectiveness evaluation, payment systems, and contract management.

Or looking at it a different way, if you subscribe to the Plan-Source-Make-Deliver-Return supply chain perspective, then Sourcing, Supplier Management, Purchasing, and Inbound Material Management would all represent the components of the Source module. With all that in mind, let's get back to the basics — the fundamentals of buying things, no matter what we call the function.

## Getting Started

The supply chain starts with suppliers — at least once one gets past the customer service imperative. The processes of fulfillment — whether it's filling orders or delivering service — begins with the acquisition of the things that move through the supply chain. Therefore, close coordination of the procurement function with the other supply-chain management tasks is an important ingredient in a successful management program.

When it comes to procurement, perhaps the most important rule to keep in mind is to focus on the total cost of acquisition, not just the purchase price. In an integrated supply-chain management program, procurement is one step in improving cash-to-cash cycle time. That is the time elapsed between the outlay of cash to purchase materials and the time when cash is received from the sale of finished products.

## Total Cost of Ownership

Frequently a higher unit price will have a lower total cost. That total cost must include logistics, receiving, and inspection. Costs will be influenced by the speed with which inventory turns, as well as the cost of inbound transportation and administrative expenses.

The process has evolved from purchasing to procurement to strategic sourcing. The oldest of these, purchasing, is simply the function of buying the right quantity at the lowest possible price. Typically, procurement also includes materials management expenses associated with the transaction, so inbound transportation and inventory carrying costs are added to the price. Strategic sourcing, therefore, is the alignment of purchasing activities to support your company's business goals. It is based on the total cost of ownership, including acquisition, use, and maintenance.

## The Impact of Improved Procurement

Improving procurement isn't always as easy as it sounds. The most economical order quantity (EOQ) might strain the capacity of your warehouses. At other times, a bulk commodity purchase might be a sensible way to protect yourself from a looming price increase. In this situation, the master distribution center might be designed for overflow quantities and slow-moving products. Regional distribution centers will handle the fast-moving products.

When the procurement process is improved, the results are a reduction of inventories, better production planning, and greater use of vendor-managed inventory. Under a vendor-managed inventory arrangement, the goods' title passes at the last minute, often allowing the buyer to sell the finished product before it pays for the materials used in that product. Frequently, improved procurement involves strategic alliances with suppliers.

## Trends in Procurement

During the past few decades, the process of procurement has moved from a traditional to a value-managed approach. The traditional approach usually involves adversarial negotiations with many suppliers. Communications are sporadic, and the prime emphasis is on searching for the lowest unit cost.

The value-managed approach, by contrast, features strategic alliances and long-term commitments with most vendors. It includes frequent communication in an effort to better integrate the operation. Where possible, the parties attempt to share risk and reward. Instead of finding the lowest unit cost, the emphasis is on discovering the lowest *total* cost.

Strategic sourcing means buying *better* instead of merely buying for less. Buying better might mean shifting responsibility for quality assurance to the vendor, allowing the buyer to cut out the inspection process. It might also mean a simplified bidding process to reduce the cost of procurement.

Better buying also takes consumption into account — that is, how the product will ultimately be consumed or used. Companies that practice strategic sourcing are likely to put great emphasis on product simplification or standardization, for example. They might also seek out suppliers who are willing to delay final assembly or passage of title to the latest possible moment.

Strategic sourcing requires the sharing of all types of information, including demand forecasts and production plans. It also includes the sharing of best practices. But perhaps the most important element of all is the sharing and coordination of shipment schedules.

## Supplier Conferences

Some procurement people develop a system to provide grades for suppliers. Those who improve productivity and avoid price increases get higher grades than those who do not.

A variety of methods are used to share success stories among vendors. Eastman Kodak developed a program called SOLID — Supplier On Line Idea Database. Creative ideas are solicited from vendors, and a response to every idea is promised within 60 days.

## Sourcing Issues

While progressive procurement people try to reduce the number of vendors they use, they also recognize the dangers of putting too many eggs in one basket. In other words, they recognize that concentrating too much business with a single supplier exposes them to a serious risk of disruption should any of the following occur:

- Your supplier experiences a strike or other labor action.
- You or your vendor experiences a plant disruption, such as a natural disaster or major breakdown.
- There is a management disruption, such as the loss of key people.
- One of the parties files for bankruptcy — whether it's a vendor, a carrier, or even your own company.

Vendor-managed inventory may not be a new practice, but it has attained considerable popularity. The arrival of visibility software has greatly improved the process. Frequently, logistics service providers are retained to facilitate the system. For example, vendors may be asked to position their products in a public warehouse in a strategic location. Title to the product does not pass until the product is withdrawn from the warehouse.

## More Semantics

Now that we've stirred the waters by offering competing views of what constitutes procurement/purchasing, let's look at the difference between Supply Management and Supplier Management. Without making any more waves, we'll postulate that supply management is, at the very least, a strategic component of procurement. Supplier management, however, is a very different story.

Supplier management may have strategic implications stemming from the original strategic decisions themselves. But at its core, it represents strategic tactics elevated to a high level. In the best applications, supplier management is marked by a set of close relationships between a company and the top tier of its suppliers, across its principal products, materials, ingredients, and packaging categories.

These supplier management connections engender multiple teams, often cross-functional, who drive improvements throughout the operating — and planning — relationships. Nothing is sacred; everything from product development to joint marketing is fair game for supply chain improvement. Any and all of these processes are candidates for two-way analysis and problem solving.

The objectives are simple: reduced costs, higher quality, customer benefits — and mutual competitive advantage. This is the level of supplier management that puts teeth into the idea of supply chains competing against other supply chains.

Some consultants promote the concept of Supplier Relationship Management (SRM). Whether this newly coined term gains the acceptance enjoyed by Customer Relationship Management (CRM) remains to be seen. The same holds true of the prospects for SRM software development.

Whether Supplier Relationship Management is accorded its own acronym or not, the point here is that it's the concept that counts, not the name currently in vogue among consultants. Specifically, we're talking about the systematic management of keystone relationships, with specific purposes of cost reduction, process improvement, compliance, and collaboration from the product-development process out. Implementing this approach requires managers to be strategic in their thinking and to use that strategic thinking to leverage technology for their gain.

Unfortunately, few managers excel at such visionary thinking; the remainder are left to try to compensate by paying close attention to the basics. Research shows that about half of survey respondents in billion-dollar plus companies struggle with:

- Inconsistent relationship practices across the organization;
- Effectively holding suppliers accountable for performance;
- Allocating internal resources to supplier management; and
- Misaligned performance measures and reports.

## Why Supply Chain Starts With Suppliers

Every one of your suppliers may have — and probably does have — the capability to help reduce your costs. The procurement department has the responsibility of discovering ways to implement that capability. It includes control of inbound logistics costs as well as vendor-managed inventory and other means of reducing the cash-to-cash cycle.

For years, leaders in supply management have reaped significant benefits by establishing collaborative improvement programs with their key suppliers. They have saved money and improved quality through changes in packaging, production processes, and ordering and replenishment practices.

In essence, procurement is the process of connecting, coordinating, and then monitoring. It is essential to keep looking for new resources, since changing conditions could force a search for a new supplier. At the same time, it is essential to maintain good communication with existing resources. Finally, when it comes to the procurement process, we'd all do well to remember Ronald Reagan's memorable phrase "trust but verify."

# MANUFACTURING INTEGRATION

Quality means doing it right when no one is looking.
*Henry Ford*

A tool is but the extension of a man's hand, and a machine is but a complex tool. He that invents a machine augments the power of man and the well-being of mankind.
*Henry Ward Beecher*

On mechanical slavery, on the slavery of the machine, the future of the world depends.
*Oscar Wilde*

My advice is to look out for engineers —
they begin with sewing machines and end up with the atomic bomb.
*Marcel Pagnol*

## Dependent and Independent Variables

Manufacturing is no longer an independent variable in your world, at least if your world is one in which supply chains are integrated. And if they aren't, you need to think about finding a world that fits better with the 21st century.

The argument for integrating manufacturing with supply chain functions is compelling, whether the manufacturing source is across the street, across the country, or across the ocean. In fact, the need for integration only increases as the supply chain extends its geographic reach.

Whatever the situation, we cannot afford to simply let manufacturing "happen" and deal with the consequences down the road. This is true whether manufacturing is a captive part of the organization, an independent working partner in the supply chain, or a vendor or supplier kept at arm's length.

## Recent History

For the past three decades, manufacturing of all types has been the subject of a constant stream of improvement programs, each with its own acronym. All were designed and promoted as transformations that would elevate manufacturing performance to stratospheric levels. Yet there always seems to be room for one more such program. The list to date includes the following:

- Just-In-Time (JIT).
- Total Quality Management (TQM).
- Kaizen (Continuous Improvement).
- Statistical Process Control (SPC).
- Single Minute Exchange of Die (SMED).
- Efficient Consumer Response (ECR).
- Quick Response (QR).
- Time-Based Manufacturing (TBM).
- Toyota Production System (TPS).
- Six Sigma.

"Kaikaku" has been added to the vocabulary of Kaizen practitioners. While completely legitimate, it is nothing more than a reincarnation of the "breakthrough" approach to operations improvement that was somewhat popular a couple of decades ago.

At the moment the concept *du jour* is "Lean" — lean manufacturing, lean transportation, lean warehousing, lean logistics. You can't go anywhere without reading or hearing about Lean. In the abstract, Lean appears to be the sum of everything that has gone before — a shotgun marriage of Kaizen and Six Sigma, with JIT, TQM, SPC, and SMED in the wedding party.

Technically, Lean (discussed more fully in the Lean Supply Chain Management chapter) rests on foundations of the Eight Wastes and the Five Ss, structured contexts for identifying opportunities and programmatically addressing them. There's been some recent talk about the concept of Lean Six Sigma, which we would hope is more than the latest entry in the Phrase of the Month Club.

We'd like to share a secret. We've peeked inside some Lean programs and have found a remarkable resemblance to what U.S. companies were doing 15 years ago, which in turn wasn't all that different from programs that dated to the '70s.

Does that mean that these efforts have all been frauds? Not at all, although we would point out that there's a distinction between fraudulent programs and fraudulent practitioners.

## Not-So-Recent History

All cynicism aside, what we *do* mean to say is that the concepts behind organized manufacturing improvement have been around for a long time. Today's Lean concepts go back to at least 1926, which saw the publication of Henry Ford's *Today and Tomorrow*, a genuinely visionary book that laid the foundation for contemporary manufacturing systems.

But much of that goes even further back — to the groundbreaking work of Frederick Taylor at the turn of the 20th century and to the pioneering efforts of Frank and Lillian Gilbreth in its first half. That this early work of so-called "efficiency experts" was satirized in film and in management lore does not diminish its importance to modern supply chain management. All this happened well before the Japanese discovered and embraced the ideas of W. Edwards Deming — a development that eventually found the U.S. manufacturing community playing catch-up.

Then there's the famous Hawthorne Effect, so-named because the studies were conducted at Western Electric's Hawthorne Works on Chicago's South Side, which suggests that a simple show of management attention yields noticeable improvement in manufacturing performance. But simple attention alone was not enough back in the 1920s, when the experiments were carried out, and it's even less adequate today when it comes to integrating and coordinating manufacturing activity toward a singular outcome. It takes, despite our cynicism, organized programs with structure and focus to harness all of the elements of production.

More recently, 1993's *Time Based Manufacturing*, by Joe Bockerstette and Dick Shell, gathered together the key concepts in manufacturing improvement, integration, and synchronization. What makes things different today — and makes the likelihood of programmatic success a real possibility — is the richness and robustness of information systems choices. We knew what to do back in the earlier days. But we were frustrated by shortfalls in data analysis capacity, by lack of supply chain visibility, by communications gaps, and by supply chain visions that were still inwardly focused.

## The Keys to the Kingdom

At the heart of things, it's all pretty simple. Today's manufacturing needs to be agile — nimble, flexible, waste-free, and synchronized with ultimate demand. What it takes to make this happen is similarly straightforward and can be summarized in the following four steps:
- Drive up process reliability.
- Build demand-based run strategies.
- Synchronize with demand and respond to demand variation.
- Manage and communicate demand.

Easy? Not really. But it's orders-of-magnitude easier than it would have been 20 years ago. Let's talk about the components of the puzzle and its solution.

## Manufacturing Process Reliability

From JIT to Lean, nearly all of the process-improvement concepts aim at improving asset utilization — human assets, facility assets, and material assets — and at eliminating waste, whether it's waste time, effort, or products and materials.

In manufacturing, process reliability, for instance, has three components: uptime, dependability, and first-run yield. Mastering performance in all three is crucial to achieving reliability.

Reliability is expressed as a composite percentage; e.g., 90% uptime x 90% dependability x 90% first-run yield = 72.9% reliability.

Uptime is the ratio of scheduled operation to the available — 16 hours out of 24, 5 days out of 7, or 50 weeks out of 52. Uptime can be an enormous source of capacity when expansion is under consideration. The downside can be that there are people and equipment stress issues in attempting to utilize unused shifts, days, or weeks. Still, uptime provides an important element in waste elimination. An operation with 95% dependability and 99% first-run yield that only runs two shifts, five days a week has an overall reliability of 44.8% (47.6 x .95 x .99) — not a statistic that will impress the CEO.

Dependability is a measure of actual *versus* scheduled operations, the ratio of the actual hourly run rate to the capable hourly run rate. The factors influencing the ratio include breakdowns, changeovers, time spent waiting for material, and off-speed operations. Dependability is the typical focus area for the application of improvement programs, with so many elements susceptible to correction.

First-run yield is the ratio of good output to input, subtracting waste, spoilage, trimmings, and rework. Sometimes yield is a trivial improvement opportunity; sometimes it is enormous. Occasionally, the cost of correction can exceed the loss of capacity, labor, and material involved, but not usually — and the capacity loss is generally the real target of improvement efforts. Process improvements and corrective actions that boost quality drive up first-run yield.

Run speed is often the dirty little secret in manufacturing that can deliver big-time payoffs. An operation that was designed, engineered, and installed with a nominal rate of, say, 2,400 units per hour can easily deteriorate over time to three-quarters of that rate or less — a massive, hidden capacity loss. Setup reduction, by whatever name, is key to short runs and flexibility.

## Context

So what does all this mean? First, it indicates that the following are the key steps toward manufacturing improvement:

- Chip away at waste product.
- Reduce setup times.
- Restore consistent run-rate capability.
- Optimize facility utilization.
- Take all waste and non-value-added activity out of all processes — direct and ancillary.
- Apply organized problem-solving and analytic tools.
- Display genuine management interest.

It also indicates that the steps should be carried out in a framework of:

- Analysis and understanding.
- Baselining and continuous measurement.
- Problem/opportunity identification and solution design.
- Implementation, evaluation, and refinement.

The complete solution requires many tools and techniques. It may benefit from borrowing from a number of programs — Lean, JIT, or Kaizen — tailoring the overall approach to the organization's specific needs, priorities, and culture.

## Synchronization

Once manufacturing gets its house in order (or at least, is well on its way), the enterprise is positioned to better synchronize production — and inventory — with customer demand. That's easier said than done because:

1) It's not always easy to know demand;
2) Demand can be skewed by unnatural factors that are nonetheless common business practices (e.g., promotions, diversions, minimums, etc.);
3) Multiple supply chain touch points can filter or distort ultimate demand;
4) Events can overlay baseline demand.

From the manufacturing side, given decent knowledge of real demand and good customer communication of events (and mastery of the nuances of flexibility and capacity management), it's possible to develop run strategies to better align manufacturing output with demand patterns. A run strategy might be: "A" items are run every demand cycle, "B" items every few cycles, and "C" items on an even less frequent basis. A cycle is the smallest capable time frame (with daily often being the ideal).

Adjusting the quantities of each item class based on actual consumption tightens the synchronization. Although it will still be necessary to hold some inventories, those inventories will tend to be small quantities and for slower-moving, lower-cost goods. These principles apply in general whether manufacturing takes place in Peoria, Ill.; Pekin, Ill.; or Peking (Beijing), China (though more inventory will be needed if it takes place in China!).

## Demand Communication

Communication — demand communication — is key to making all this happen. It is essential to adjust production based on timely variations in baseline demand, advance notification of events and promotions, seasonality, and event and season tracking, all the while constantly fine-tuning input for optimally balanced output. Collaborative Planning, Forecasting, and Replenishment (CPFR) and Point-Of-Sale (POS) data and information can support the process, but only when leavened with common sense and judgment.

By the way, the top supply chains include suppliers in the synchronization process, communicating demand triggers to them as well.

## Demand Management

It's tough to deal with "normal" (common) cause variations in demand and capability. The out-of-the ordinary cause variations driven by promotional events and special sales deals can stress the best of systems — even with exquisite knowledge. Can we ever force the marketers and salespeople to behave?

Maybe someday, but not today. Given that reality, it behooves us to get the act together in manufacturing. That will allow us to handle the normal day-to-day issues with some grace and style, conserving our energies for the real crises.

# TRANSPORTATION

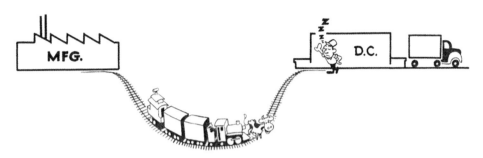

Never mistake motion for action.
*Ernest Hemingway*

A journey is like marriage. The certain way to be wrong is to think you control it.
*John Steinbeck*

Two roads diverged in a wood, and I — I took the one less traveled by,
And that has made all the difference.
*Robert Frost*

If the human race wants to go to Hell in a handbasket,
technology can help it get there by jet.
*Charles M. Allen*

## (Un)common Carriers

Transportation typically represents the largest and costliest link in the logistics chain. In many cases, transportation makes up two-thirds of the total logistics expense.

For nearly a century, American common carriers were regulated under the Interstate Commerce Act. All that changed in the 1970s and '80s, when the federal government deregulated transportation. Yet even today, decades later, there are still many managers who have not completely recovered from the habits of government regulation. Portions of the industry still cling to some of their old monopolistic practices, such as arbitrary pricing and the fortress hubs in the airline business. Of all the modes, motor freight remains the most flexible — perhaps because it's the only one that allows the customer to easily change suppliers or else rent vehicles and do the job himself. This do-it-yourself capability tends to foster healthy competition among the common motor carriers.

## The Transportation Landscape

When it comes to modes of transportation, companies today have a variety of options:
- Pipeline.
- Ocean bulk.
- Rail.

- Barge.
- Ocean container.
- Intermodal (TOFC — Trailer on Flat Car and COFC — Container on Flat Car).
- TL (Truckload).
- LTL (Less-Than-Truckload).
- Air cargo.
- Small package (parcel).

The primary modes for shipping include trucking, rail, air, barge, and ocean freight. None of these are insignificant. Barge traffic, for example, runs about 800 million tons a year in the United States, about half of it petroleum products and coal. Still, trucking remains the top mode, commanding more than 80 percent of total transportation expenditure in the United States, a figure that grows whenever fuel prices rise.

The motor freight industry is highly fragmented and suffers significant challenges in utilization. There are 600,000 licensed interstate common carriers. The top five represent about 5 percent of the total industry capacity. There's lots of room for improvement when it comes to utilization, as trucks run empty 15 to 20 percent of the time. For the average truck driver, dwell time (time spent waiting to load or unload) consumes more than 30 hours each week. Furthermore, drivers who are paid by the mile suffer uncontrolled loss of income when they are caught in traffic or run into border crossing delays. Frustration over unpaid, idle time is one reason that turnover among truck drivers has reached the unprecedented level of 136 percent per year for truckload carriers.

Technology is also changing the trucking business. Cell phones, global positioning systems (GPS), and radio-frequency identification tags (RFID) allow better control of the movement of tractors and trailers than ever before. Taken together, these types of technology allow carriers to offer real-time visibility for every shipment — a feature highly valued by shippers.

## Choosing Among the Modes

All mode options have distinct characteristics in terms of cost, time, reliability, and potential for loss or damage that play into the selection decision. When selecting a carrier mode, shippers consider the trade-offs between service and cost, and between inventory and time. Factors of physical feasibility, service requirements, distance, and product and shipment characteristics all factor into the mode decision. Keep in mind, though, that today's conditions may make yesterday's mode decision seem ill-advised, and tomorrow's conditions may require you to revisit today's choices.

Because of its flexibility, speed, and accessibility, motor freight dominates the landscape on shipments of 500 miles or less, and it remains extremely popular for cross-country movement as well. Air freight usually is reserved for shipments of high-value goods with time-sensitive delivery requirements, as well as for emergency or expedited movement of critical goods. Usage of the other modes typically depends largely on the location of the shipper, but nearly every shipper can use intermodal connections to rail and water transportation. Intermodal transportation involves the transfer of the cargo container from truck to rail car or marine vessel, or from a vessel to rail or truck.

Multimodal transport, by contrast, involves the transfer (and rehandling) of goods among containers, trailers, rail cars, or barges. Examples include containerized goods arriving from Asia that are trans-loaded onto trucks for further distribution.

## Choosing and Using a Motor Carrier

There are a number of printed directories and advertisements that will help a shipper find a carrier. And though shippers commonly rely on personal contacts to find out about a carrier's reputation, it's crucial that they also do their own fact finding. At a minimum, a shipper looking to hire a motor carrier should check into the following:

- Finances — the operating ratio, or profit performance, of the carrier.
- DOT rating — the grade issued by the U.S. Department of Transportation.
- Proof of insurance, especially cargo.
- Service capabilities, including equipment and customer references.

As for trucking equipment, there's a wide variety of choices these days. In addition to the commonly used van body, some highway trailers have open tops to allow crane loading. Other types of equipment are flatbeds and tank bodies. Special bodies include auto carriers and beverage bodies. Within the van body category, there are refrigerated trucks as well as high-cube trailers and vehicles with curtain sides to facilitate rapid loading and unloading.

## Navigating in the Intermodal Storm

The transportation industry faced its greatest crisis in recent history in the autumn and winter of 2004/2005 when ship logjams at Pacific ports caused protracted freight backups. A major contributing factor in that crisis was a surging volume of containers full of Asian imports. The volume of containers entering the United States today is about six times what it was just 10 years ago, and that growth shows no signs of stopping.

To avoid the worst of the congestion (which mainly affected the California ports of Oakland, San Pedro, and Long Beach), some shippers began diverting freight to harbors such as Vancouver, Seattle, Portland, and the relatively new Mexican port of Lázaro Cárdenas. For those wondering about the viability of Lázaro Cárdenas as an alternate West Coast gateway, consider that KCS railroad is running seven-day-a-week service out of it and has successfully beaten back attempts by FerroMex to enter the market, while Hutchison Port Holdings alone is sinking $200 million into a specialized container terminal there.

In extreme cases, shippers have rerouted their Asia-origin shipments from the West Coast to the East Coast or the Gulf Coast. Harbors on the Atlantic Ocean that have benefited from this trend include those in the Charleston-Savannah-Jacksonville corridor, although we should note that these ports have been experiencing strong growth even without these cargo diversions.

The 2004/2005 port crisis was further complicated by another factor: a rail catastrophe. Severe weather in Southern California disabled the roadbed for one of the carriers, and forced two other Western railroads to reduce their train speeds. Every time a railroad is slowed by one mile per hour, that carrier needs an additional 250 locomotives, another 5,000 rail cars, and an additional 180 employees. Even under optimal weather and track conditions, the two primary Western carriers average only 21 mph and 19 mph, respectively.

In the aftermath of that intermodal storm, shippers have begun taking steps to minimize the risks of disruption by developing and executing contingency plans and by closely monitoring carrier performance. While the crisis may have temporarily subsided, these same shippers have not relaxed their vigilance.

## Some Global Issues

In many developing countries, drivers who own their trucks perform the great majority of highway moves. For international shippers, control is difficult and theft is common. Railroads outside the United States, on the other hand, are government-owned and thus are nationalized operations. In Europe, water transportation is used far more widely than in the United States. For the supply chain professional looking at global transportation, the cardinal rule is: *Don't assume that anything will be as it is back home.*

## Private Fleet

Shippers choose the private fleet route for a number of reasons. To begin with, fleets offer improved control of delivery, which may be important for some shippers. The availability of advertising on highway trailers can boost brand awareness. In some delivery operations, such as beverages, the driver also acts a salesman. On the down side, a private fleet is usually less efficient than a common carrier because it must operate with a greater percentage of empty miles.

We should note, too, that private carriage isn't limited to trucking. There are dedicated ship fleets that haul Japanese automobiles. Major auto manufacturers have used dedicated trains, and chemical companies use private barges.

Many common carriers offer dedicated service, which is a compromise. While the vehicle is operated by an independent carrier, that truck is reserved for the use of one customer.

## Parcel

The FedEx model, ridiculed when it was first proposed, revolutionized small-package shipping. With their own fleets of trucks and aircraft, integrated carriers have taken volume away from the U.S. Postal Service, LTL carriers, and courier services.

In the United States, UPS and FedEx are the giants when it comes to integrated carriers. But they have recently been joined by DHL, with its acquisition of Airborne, and with the cash and clout that go along with being a subsidiary of Deutsche Post.

## Quick Notes on Rail

In many respects, the flood of goods from foreign countries, whether arriving at East Coast or West Coast ports, has revived the once-neglected American railroad industry. Shippers are rethinking the economics of rail *versus* TL movement, especially since intermodal rail movement is frequently the only alternative to long-haul truck carriage.

But the surge in freight volumes, which is allowing both railroads and truckers to make decent money for a change, has taxed the capacity of both. In response to the rise in freight demand, the railroads, which operate without the federal infrastructure support enjoyed by the highway system, are investing in new track as fast as they can — to the sum of $8 billion in 2006.

All the major rail carriers are involved — not just the giant east/west lines of BNSF and UP, but also the eastern and north/south lines like Norfolk Southern, CSX, and KCS. They are laying down additional track; in some cases, they're putting track next to existing lines, double tracking as it's called, and, in others, they're even putting two lines of track beside an existing bed, or triple tracking. Will this be enough? We'll see — and we'll also see if continued growth and volume will outstrip this new capacity.

## Challenges and Success Factors

Transportation has come a long way since sailing ships carried cargo around the world. 21st-century technology offers control of transportation that was undreamed of a few years ago. Yet transportation remains relatively expensive, and there is little recent progress in controlling its costs. Trucking scarcity and high fuel prices have aggravated the cost situation. The shortage of truck drivers is critical and getting worse.

Initiatives abound to deal with some of these issues. Take PierPASS, a program intended to relieve congestion at the ports of Los Angeles/Long Beach by shifting activity to off-peak periods. There's also a proposal to widen the Panama Canal to handle large container ships. (That 20-year canal-widening program hinges on the result of a popular referendum.) Meanwhile, the passenger airlines, seeking ways to accommodate the rapid growth in air cargo, are putting more freight in the bellies of multipurpose planes and are even considering the addition of all-cargo aircraft. Are these stopgaps, or are they part of a comprehensive solution set? Time will tell.

Against this backdrop, vast quantities of goods that used to be manufactured in Iowa, or Michigan, or Pennsylvania are now made overseas. When foreign-made products come pouring into U.S. ports, they only add to the demands on the transportation system, clogging intermodal and multimodal transfer points.

In fact, in the nation's history, we have never before faced the level of challenge found in today's transportation network and infrastructure. Ports are jammed and backed up — and vulnerable to labor actions. The Panama Canal can only handle so much traffic — and can only handle vessels of a certain size. We don't have enough long-haul truck drivers to move truck loads, nor do we have spare capacity. Surging freight volumes have led to slowdowns in rail service, with no immediate prospects for improvement. Overall, costs are going up, and service levels are at risk. Fuel is costly, and fuel supplies easily disrupted. Border crossings have become uncertain adventures, and the hoped-for benefits of government programs like C-TPAT (see the chapter on Securing the Supply Chain) haven't kicked in yet.

These challenges represent great opportunities for creative carrier managers, as well as for the discerning shipper. Better management can and should use creative techniques to reduce the frustration of driving a truck and make the job more attractive for new employees. Better planning and execution, enabled by better technology, should drastically reduce the dwell time that is really the result of inefficient warehousing operations.

In a world of driver shortages, escalating fuel costs, changing order profiles, and increasingly differentiated customer demands, cost pressures are enormous. Dynamic management of the transport mode mix, only possible with powerful transportation management software, is one of the few tools left to help take money off the table and put it into a shipper's pocket, where it belongs.

America's most successful airline controls its turnaround time by benchmarking the pit crews at the Indianapolis Motor Speedway. When this kind of thinking is applied to motor freight and railroad operations, there will be dramatic improvement in the efficiency of our overall transportation system. In the meantime, the clock is ticking.

# WAREHOUSING

Thank God, I can sit, and I can stand without the aid of a furniture warehouse.
*Henry David Thoreau*

And one walks past ... the Manhattan Storage Warehouse,
which they'll soon tear down.
*Frank O'Hara*

Tilting up his nose, he inhaled ... emanations blown from warehouse doors.
*Wallace Stevens*

We shape our buildings; thereafter they shape us.
*Winston Churchill*

## Getting Started

Warehousing in any age — especially this one — comes down to only a couple of things: the management of space and the management of time.

These days, it's easy to downplay the role of the warehouse in supply chain operations. With all the sophistication involved in supply chain planning, the intricacy of modern information systems, the complexity of transportation, and the mystery of forecasting, it's tempting to think of warehousing as merely "boxes in and boxes out."

Warehousing has a long and mostly honorable history. One wit has observed that warehousing is the second-oldest profession, with remarkable similarities to the oldest. No matter, some of history's oldest writing, in Genesis, describes the use of warehouses to store up grain against imminent famine. That would make Joseph the first supply chain executive, no doubt.

It hasn't been that long since prominent thinkers were predicting the demise of the warehouse. Yet we're using more warehouse space than ever before, and there's no slowdown in sight. We're seeing more pallets in and pieces out of the warehouse. The requirements for perfect order fulfillment and seamless cross docking have made the warehouse a vital cog in supply chain operations. And the value-added services being supplied in today's warehouses would dazzle an old-timer.

Whether we call them warehouses or distribution centers, they are indisputably still with us and they're playing an increasingly crucial role in meeting customer expectations. That said, when it comes to warehousing, the basics are still the basics.

## More Background

As transportation speeds, capacities, and varieties have increased over the past two centuries, transport has also become progressively more expensive. Population growth and expansion of the living area, along with the emergence of dispersed material sources and manufacture, have increased stresses on the means of getting goods from points of origin to points of consumption. Warehousing was, and still is, used to manage freight costs in this environment. It is also used, in concert with advances in delivery capabilities, to improve customer service.

The design and redesign of distribution networks (discussed further in the chapter on Facility Location and Network Design) is part of the supply chain professional's constant effort to balance the components of the cost/service equation. Within the warehouse, though, we should focus on space and time.

## Challenges in Space Management

Where's the right balance? In general, too much space is preferable to having too little. But too much space can lead to bad habits, when planning and discipline are not seen as necessary to success … or survival.

Although skimping on space poses a serious threat to any warehousing operation, it's often the solution favored by top management. That's because management often clings to the misguided belief that "there's always room for one more." But when warehouse capacity has been reached, material gets placed in aisles, in staging areas, on docks, and in locations designed for other products. Accuracy breaks down, efficiency suffers, and performance plummets — ultimately dragging customer service down.

The temptation to overfill a facility is particularly great when the focus is on warehousing (storage) *versus* distribution (movement). The "storage" mentality is driven by cubic foot (ft3) utilization, filling the building to its maximum capacity. Today's reality is that ft3 utilization is only one part of the cost/service equation, and that effective movement — in and out — typically trumps the added cost of space needed to do so.

A rule of thumb in a distribution center is that available ft3 (or cubic meters) must be calculated with aisle, staging, and other non-storage space subtracted from total building capacity. Then the facility is "full," from a practical standpoint, when it reaches 80 to 85 percent of available storage capacity — and that presumes that the available space has been configured correctly for storage mode mix (floor stack, pallet rack, flow rack, etc.). Some figure in this general range will be cited by almost every warehousing consultant, academic, and experienced manager. Whether it is absolutely correct or not, and whether or not it can be "proven," this recognition certainly illustrates how our collective thinking has changed as the role of warehousing has shifted from pure storage to a focus on movement and speed.

One key to effective space use lies in effective space planning. That necessitates repeated analysis of products and flows for dynamic layout of the facility and its storage (and order selection) modes. It's a little like painting San Francisco's Golden Gate Bridge — when you've finished, it's time to start over. Still, without practical layouts, exquisite understanding of slotting, and discipline in putaway and replenishment, operations can unravel pretty quickly. When that happens, cost and service unravel as well.

Finally, all warehouse activity needs to be tied together with solid systems (see the chapter on Information Systems for Supply Chain Management), beginning with a warehouse management system (WMS) that fits your product, your market, and your way of doing business.

## Problems in Managing Time

Today, time demands drive what we do in warehousing — order fulfillment time, pick lines per hour, dock-to-stock time, and same-day/next-day delivery requirements. To some extent, we can approach time imperatives through better technology application and through process redesign. But often managing time in the warehouse is really about managing people (see the chapter called Human Resources — You Win With People).

Time study as an engineering discipline was developed late in the 19th century, and flourished in the first half of the 20th. Sometimes misunderstood and misapplied, it fell into disrepute in the popular idiom. Charlie Chaplin's *Modern Times* in 1936, following the *auteur's* Socialist bent, focused on The Tramp, struggling with, and losing to, the pace of the assembly line. The theme reappeared a couple of decades later in television's "I Love Lucy," which saw Lucy and Ethel come to grief on a chocolate candy packing line.

The notion of evil speed-ups prevailed some 50 to 75 years ago, surfacing again in *Pajama Game's* Adler and Ross song, *"Racing With The Clock."* In the modern supply chain world, that outmoded idea is as dead as Madame Butterfly at the end of Act III.

Conducting time and motion studies can prove challenging in warehouses because people tend to be in constant motion throughout the facility. Still, it's important for warehouse management to know how long each job will take. Supervisors need to know so they can assign crews and assess performance. Managers need to know so they can meet their budgets. Third-party service providers need to know so they can establish fees for services provided.

Despite advances in time standards development, a more enlightened industrial engineering community, and the advent of information systems that can integrate performance management reporting, most warehouse operators still don't have a clue about their efficiency. In fact, only a minority of warehouse operators follow really good measurement and related time-based management practices.

Today, time-based management no longer creates the kind of labor hostility it might have sparked in the past. Fewer workers today will react negatively to time study, standard-setting, and performance reporting. Workers tend to come around as they gain familiarity with the underlying processes. That bodes well for those organizations that want to get more precise — and serious — about managing time.

Some still look upon productivity and quality as two sides of the same coin. Certainly, quality cannot be sacrificed in favor of quantity. But the two are not necessarily trade-offs, in the same way that high customer service and low inventories are not necessarily incompatible. That said, productivity measures *must* consider quality, and *vice versa*.

In summary, when there is a conflict between the space and time components of the equation, time wins. Space should be used as needed to meet the time requirements. Put another way, speed is more important than storage density. And if you're forced to sacrifice speed in some aspect of the operation, do so in putaway and maintain a quick pace when it comes to pick/pack and order fulfillment.

## Defining and Measuring Quality

This subject deserves a separate discussion. Until that time, let us propose that active, rigorous metrics (see the chapter titled Metrics in the SCM World) are hallmarks of acceptable warehousing. The possibilities are almost endless, including fill rate, shipping accuracy, shrinkage, and damage as a percentage of total movement.

Exceptional warehouses tend to have exceptionally relevant metrics — and to obtain exceptional performance against metrics targets.

In the department of non-metrics, great housekeeping affords the surest indicator of overall performance quality. Indeed, poor housekeeping is the first tip-off of quality shortcomings in a warehousing operation.

## Connectivity

When all else is said and done, the warehouse is not an island. It supports (or should support) the overall corporate mission. The way a warehouse is managed will reflect goals and priorities, whether they are growth, superior service, cost reduction, or increased volumes. The warehouse manager will be judged by how well he or she aligns the organization, the associates, and their performance with corporate objectives. Not only is the warehouse, or distribution center, intimately connected with corporate performance, it is the link between production and customers — a dynamic player in creating supply chain success.

## Management Programs

Warehouses have not been untouched by the floodtide of improvement programs and other "magic bullet" solutions that have overrun businesses of all sorts over the past few years. For some, the effort may have been worth it.

While the details of these initiatives might not fit into the context of a "fundamentals" discussion, their existence and possible efficacy should be noted. *Material Handling Management* magazine conducts a recurring study that contrasts the involvement of leading warehouse operators (self-designated world-class, or nearly so) with that of operators making little or no progress toward improvement.

Without exception, the leaders were more involved than the followers in contemporary management practices, including:

- Continuous improvement (81% vs. 42%).
- Benchmarking (48% vs. 22%).
- Lean (42% vs. 18%).
- ISO and other certification (36% vs. 12%).
- Six Sigma (25% vs. 3%).

Conclusive proof positive? Maybe not, but difficult to ignore despite the skepticism with which we so often greet highly hyped program initiatives.

Whether you subscribe to advanced program participation and its benefits, or whether you prefer to keep on keeping on, there are a handful of questions to consider when thinking about the basics of your warehouse operation. They are:

- Are you aligned with the corporate mission? How well?
- How do you stack up with other warehouses in the company? In the community?
- How are you performing compared with your competition? With best-in-class in any industry?
- Are this year's results better or worse than last year's? How do they stack up against results from the last five years?

Then, once you've answered the questions, think about what you're going to do about what you've learned.

# MATERIALS HANDLING

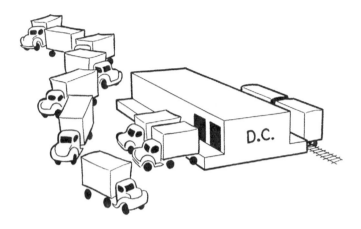

Elbow grease is the best polish.
*English Proverb*

To curb the machine and limit art to handicraft is a denial of opportunity.
*Lewis Mumford*

As machines get to be more and more like men,
men will come to be more like machines.
*Joseph Wood Krutch*

Work expands so as to fill the time available for its completion.
*C. Northcote Parkinson*


## Now Then, Where Were We?

As we have often observed, most recently in the Warehousing chapter, warehousing is little more than the effective management of time and space. Effective time and space management will drive good cost management.

One would think that the materials handling tools used in facilities would be designed to conserve both time and space as well. But there are inevitably trade-offs to be made. When warehouse space is at a premium, for example, enormous creativity is applied to using the least amount possible. When time is the principal driver (see the chapter on Speed) and space is relatively inexpensive, it will be the other way around.

When both people costs and real estate costs are high, the time/space economic calculation tends to fly out the window, as highly complex and extraordinarily compact technology solutions are introduced to minimize footprints. This has happened in the crowded cities of the Far East and in much of Europe (often aided by government regulation), even when full employment is not constraining labor availability.

Along with conserving time and space, materials handling technology also must work well with people. That means ergonomic considerations will also exert a strong influence on its design. Ergonomics is defined as the science of organizing human effort in a way that minimizes opportunities for personal injury and undue physical stress. (See the chapter on Health, Safety, and Ergonomics.)

## Categories of Equipment

There are materials handling equipment applications outside of distribution center operations, such as special-purpose rail cars, purpose-designed trucks, off-road haulers, pipelines, etc. But we will focus on the types of materials handling equipment more commonly found within the four walls of the warehouse and in the yard outside the building. This materials handling equipment is broadly divided into three major sub-sets:

- Static equipment.
- Mobile equipment.
- Tools to pick and transport orders.

## Static Equipment

Static equipment consists primarily of items without wheels. It's usually storage equipment in the form of metal rack. While some varieties are movable, none are really mobile. There are eight different types of basic storage rack:

- Single-deep, also known as selective pallet rack.
- Double-deep pallet rack.
- Self-stacking pallet rack.
- Drive-in rack.
- Drive-through rack.
- Gravity flow rack.
- Pushback pallet rack.
- Mobile rack.

TYPICAL RACK SECTION & STORAGE TECHNIQUE

PALLET RACK STORAGE

DRIVE-IN AND DRIVE-THRU RACK SYSTEMS

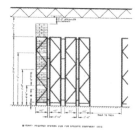

DOUBLE-DEEP RACK STORAGE

STACKING PALLETS

Single-deep is the most commonly used type of pallet rack, but it is also the design that takes up the most space. Double-deep requires a lift truck with an extending device that allows pallets to be placed two deep. This type of racking is efficient in any warehouse that normally has at least two pallets of every item. Self-stacking pallet rack is a venerable technology that allows a very flexible layout and high-bay storage for products such as tires that have no packaging and no stacking strength. It is also used for some applications in the rug and apparel industries.

Drive-in and drive-through rack are essentially the same thing, except that the former allows entry from just one side of the installation, and the latter allows entry from either side. Gravity flow rack uses a skate conveyor to allow product to move downhill from the top of the storage lane to the aisle. Pushback pallet rack allows the lift-truck operator to store several pallets in a protected row by pushing the older stock uphill.

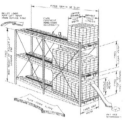

PALLET LOAD FLOW THROUGH RACKS

Mobile rack is racking on wheels, which allows the elimination of unneeded aisles. The racks can be rolled in either sideways direction, creating a single aisle, to permit access to any pallet location in the system. Mobile rack can be effective in cases of very limited demand for a large number of SKUs, but is both costly and inefficient for high-volume distribution. Lighter-duty applications of mobile rack concepts are popular for holding files of medical records in doctors' and dentists' offices, and for retaining archived files in public accounting operations.

Some storage systems are designed to hold units rather than pallets. These include shelving and cantilever rack. The shelving may be something quite similar to that found in any library. Cantilever rack resembles a metal Christmas tree, and its arms are designed to hold long products such as pipe, lumber, vinyl or aluminum siding, or any other item that is too awkwardly shaped to be transported on pallets.

The oldest and perhaps most vital piece of static equipment is the pallet itself. This wood platform was virtually invented to accommodate the forklift truck, which could only be useful if it was accompanied by a large number of storage platforms. These platforms, or pallets, had no standards for size or construction method until the '60s, when General Foods demanded a degree of substantive uniformity in size and design of pallets so they could be exchanged and interchanged without having to reconfigure pallet loads. The passage of time has substantially degraded the quality specifications that were built into the General Foods pallet, but its size of 48 x 40 inches (1.2 x 1 m for those in the metric world) has become a widely accepted standard. Nevertheless, some companies and industries, notably telecommunications, continue to go their own way in defining "standard" pallets in other sizes.

BASIC PALLET SIZE

## Mobile Equipment

Mobile equipment is just that. It can go from location to location within a facility (and sometimes outdoors, as well). Its principal purpose is to move goods from one location to another, to transfer products from one "status" to another (e.g., reserve storage to active pick slots), in a manner that reduces reliance on brute-force human labor and saves time in handling, processing, or movement.

Manually powered handling vehicles are the oldest devices, and they are still widely used. They include two-wheeled hand trucks, four-wheeled platform trucks, and hydraulic pallet movers.

The "Model T" of materials handling is the counterbalanced forklift truck. It is the most widely used and probably the oldest motorized materials handling vehicle.

*Note: The Model T Ford was the first American automobile built on assembly line principles, and affordable to the mass market. It was manufactured with little change for 20 years in the early 20th century.*

As the technology evolved, forks were augmented with a variety of other attachments, such as clamp devices to hold cartons or paper rolls, push-pull attachments designed to handle fiberboard pallets that are called slip-sheets, and multi-pallet forks designed to haul several unit loads at a time. Other special-purpose variations have been developed for specific industries, notably home appliances (often called "white goods").

TYPICAL COUNTERBALANCE TRUCK

While the earliest lift trucks were powered by internal combustion gasoline engines, later models were developed to handle other fuel sources, including propane, diesel, and compressed natural gas (CNG). Battery-powered electric vehicles became a popular replacement for internal combustion, and hybrid gas/electric power was developed for lift trucks long before it was seen in automobiles.

As the need to conserve space became widely accepted, lift-truck manufacturers began to produce vehicles that were designed to run in very narrow aisles. The most extreme example is the turret truck, which has a device that turns the fork carriage without turning the remainder of the vehicle. These trucks can operate in an aisle just a few inches wider than the truck itself.

## Order Picking and Transport Tools

In most distribution facilities, selection of orders is the most costly activity. When it comes to materials handling equipment used to reduce the labor involved in order picking, conveyors and sorters are the most effective, but they can also be very expensive. Most con-

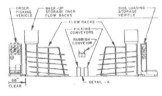

ORDER PICKING AREA
(NARROW AISLE STORAGE/CASE PICKING)

veying systems are a combination of mobile and static equipment. The frame is static, but there are rollers or wheels within the frame. The moving parts may be either motor or gravity powered. Gravity flow racks come in two types — one that moves single cases, and one that moves full pallets. Other materials handling options for order selection include pick-to-light, a combination of case gravity flow rack and signal lights that allow the order selector to complete the job by simply following a trail of illuminated signals and picking the number of pieces indicated by the signal. Motorized conveyors are often a key part of a pick-to-light solution.

Other tools used for order selection include radio-frequency (RF) bar-code scanners (advanced technology 10 years ago, but a commonplace today), voice-recognition (VR) systems, and radio-frequency identification (RFID).

When it comes to order picking, warehouse managers have to decide whether to move the order picker to the part or bring the part to the order picker. Carousels and automatic storage-and-retrieval systems (AS/RS) are designed to take the product to the picker. In manufacturing applications, AS/RS equipment may take the part to the point of use.

Carousels can prove quite effective in improving performance when there are sufficient numbers of items of appropriate size and weight with relatively modest demand profiles. Even so, they may still be less than optimal if the application requires fewer than two or three units. AS/RS technology enjoyed a tax-incentive-fueled boom in the United States some years ago, but it fell out of favor as the Just-In-Time wave swept through industry and the tax incentives were eliminated. These systems have remained popular and useful in high-cost real estate locales, notably Japan, Singapore, Hong Kong, and industrialized Europe. At the moment, they are beginning to make a bit of a comeback in selected applications in the United States.

The automatic guided vehicle (AGV) offers an effective way to accomplish horizontal travel at a manageable cost. These electric vehicles are usually designed to carry a single unit load, but are occasionally used as tractors for trains of up to four wheeled carts. Originally, they were guided by wires embedded in the warehouse floor. Today, most are guided by laser beams. In either case, and particularly the latter, it is relatively easy to change the travel path as layouts are altered. Because of their relative flexibility, AGVs have replaced older horizontal movement devices, obviously including towlines but also traditional conveyors.

Comprehensive systems for conveying and sorting are musts for large distribution centers supporting high-volume order fulfillment. They can involve thousands of feet, if not miles, of motorized conveyor, induction stations, recirculation lanes, and reader/scanners, and require sophisticated control systems for reliable operation.

These systems combine elements of static tools with moving components. They are used for transporting selected goods to packing and shipping stations or for moving packed materials to selected points for staging and shipment. They may also take in products from delivery points — either rail or truck dock doors — for movement to palletizing and/or putaway staging. Some intake conveyor is mobile and extendable, and can be incorporated into systems that reach multiple doors and extend into a trailer as cases are unloaded.

Integrated materials handling system design, installation, and maintenance employ untold numbers of engineers, designers, integrators, manufacturers, and consultants. Powerful and impressive as these systems can be, they can also be too sophisticated and rigid. The pace of change in the supply chain world requires operational flexibility — *pronto.*

Overseeing materials handling systems is the job of special software known as the materials handling control system. Today's control systems are increasingly sophisticated, and they let DC managers make changes on the fly. The hardware behind the software is increasingly flexible. It provides more variable speed drives, more intelligent accumulation options, and more attention to recovery from back-ups and downtime than its predecessors.

As for sortation systems, these too come in a variety of types. Principal varieties include pop-up sorters, push diverters, sliding shoe sorters, and tilt-tray sorters. Innovations continue to come to market in this arena. Spiral and other vertical conveyors, for example, can replace elevators in multi-floor facilities and save floor space compared with linear conveyor solutions.

The induction of items into sortation systems — and their movement through the systems — relies on accurate carton identification. The range of identification technologies includes manual, photo eye, fixed-beam laser scan, RF tag, scan, omni-directional scan, and optical systems.

These elements are typically found in large, high-volume operations at the top end of the scale, and will not be discussed in detail. However, every practitioner at the fundamental level needs to know that they exist. As costs fall and demands rise, technology has a way of working its way down the chain.

## The Unfulfilled Promise of RFID

No warehouse technology in the past half-century has generated more hype than radio-frequency identification (RFID). RFID tags, which consist of a microchip and an antenna for transmitting data inscribed on the chip, can be applied to products, product packaging, or product documentation as a way to mark and identify goods. RFID tags come in both an active (send and receive) and a passive (send only) variety. Leaders in almost every industry segment are working to develop practical and cost-effective RFID applications.

Although it's clear that the technology has great promise, it has some limitations as well, notably involving liquids and metals (which tend to interfere with radio signals). Unfortunately, it also remains quite expensive. Because of the cost challenge, it is difficult to justify an RFID investment in most current environments. Experts agree that RFID remains an emerging technology.

The great hope within the supply chain community is that as chip production ramps up, prices will be driven down. In fact, it is beginning now, but the timing is highly uncertain. Remember that bar codes, which today appear on items as inexpensive as a pack of chewing gum, took two generations to become ubiquitous. Their early application in railroads was far from successful. Although retailers later embraced them, bar codes initially met with suspicion and were associated with process breakdowns in the retail arena as well.

Today, the most logical application of the technology is to use RFID tags to identify rental cars, furs, designer apparel, airline passenger luggage, and other similarly valuable assets. RFID tags also have great potential for identifying unit loads of less-costly goods. There are other burgeoning applications, including car keys, ski lift tickets, and toll highway passes. We believe that it will be some time before RFID tags are applied to every box of breakfast cereal or tube of toothpaste. The cost of this application remains prohibitive for everyday, unit-level commerce.

## The Magic of Voice Recognition

Voice recognition is a technology that allows warehouse workers to achieve better accuracy while at the same time increasing work speed. With a voice system, the worker wears a headset that allows him or her to receive task instructions. Because his or her hands and eyes remain free, the worker is able to move from one task to the next without paper, pencil, or scanning gun. By simply listening to instructions and speaking back into the microphone to confirm that the work that has been done, the order picker completes tasks faster and more easily than before. Most users are reporting a payback of 12 to 18 months for this technology, with a savings based upon improved productivity and reduction of errors. Unlike RF applications, which often *add* steps to the location/selection process, VR *removes* steps and facilitates parallel processing of movement and communication.

Not only does this technology work, but it is also cost-effective — today. The recognition systems themselves are very flexible, recognizing various languages and acclimating to individual voices. Voice recognition in supply chain operations is the culmination of technology development that had its beginnings over 40 years ago, with computers as big as boxcars. Other successful applications of voice technology include telephone reservation, sales, and customer service systems.

## The Requirements Definition

As is the case with other investments in supply chain operations, the evaluation of alternatives and the acquisition of solutions demand a thorough analysis and a rational business case. The days when technology was installed based on hype and the knowledge that the facility down the road had one are long gone, or should be.

Before determining the best approach to improving the task of order picking and the application of mechanization and control systems, we suggest that supply chain professionals ask themselves these eight questions:

1. How many stock-keeping units are maintained? What is the distribution of demand among them?

2. How many lines per order?

3. What is the average order size — pieces and cube? And weight?

4. Are there multimodal distributions of order profiles that need design recognition?

5. Is batch picking practical? What are the pick-wave options?

6. How frequently are orders picked within a shift, or within a day?

7. How critical is order cycle time? What are the mission-critical time cut-offs?

8. How are today's customer, product, and order profiles — and service requirements — likely to change over the next five years?

## Warehouse Technology — Tools or Toys?

The noted materials handling expert Jim Apple has eloquently pointed out that, with the progress of time, many of yesterday's warehouse tools have become today's toys. Two examples are the floor-mounted towline and most high-rise AS/RS systems. The towlines were hard to maintain and impossible to modify without substantial expense. They have since either been abandoned, or, as noted above, replaced by laser-guided vehicles.

TYPICAL TOWLINE SWITCH OPERATION

Although AS/RS systems conserve space, they frequently require substantial sacrifice in materials handling time. This "lights out" warehousing technology is not only expensive, it is also highly resistant to change, and even less hospitable to flexible operational demands. These, too, have often been either abandoned or replaced, or may still be in use at a lower level of effectiveness than originally contemplated.

The difference between tools and toys is typically complexity and payback. Too many technologies combined in one system may result in something that is overly complex. In such cases, the right technology may well be a low-tech solution.

As we have moved from hand-powered materials handling devices to the most sophisticated equipment for conveying and sorting, the evolution has 'most always been based on the need to reduce the human effort involved in order selection and shipping, as well as in receiving and stocking goods. Some forms of mechanization work better than others, and it is inevitable that new techniques will replace those that are used today. It is equally likely that some will be tools, and others will be — or become — toys.

# VALUE-ADDED SERVICES

Price is what you pay. Value is what you get.
*Warren Buffett*

It is not hard to make decisions when you know what your values are.
*Roy Disney*

Quality ... is what the customer ... is willing to pay for.
*Peter F. Drucker*

... the time will come when people will recognize that [my paintings]
are worth more than the value of the paints used ...
*Vincent van Gogh*

## Commoditization, Specialization, and Reality

In the world of logistics service providers, the concept of value-added services has developed a mystical aura. Like virtue and motherhood, they've become a magic touchstone for both the customer and the provider. But let's take a dispassionate approach and try to understand just what the idea really means.

Years ago, Affiliated Warehouse Companies, a sales representative for public warehouses, developed a motto: "These firms do more than ship and store." Value-added services are the "more." Providers face the danger that buyers will see the core services they offer as commodity purchases. Just as most consumers buy gasoline, milk, or paper based on price rather than brand-name or quality features, some buyers of logistics services feel that price is more important than any other factor in provider selection and retention.

It is the terror of being commoditized — perhaps commoditized into extinction — that makes service providers look for and cling to value-added services as the life preserver that will keep them afloat on the stormy seas of price competition.

## What Are They?
Value-added services are a miracle adhesive. When properly designed and applied, they cement the relationship between the user and the logistics service provider. They convert that service from a commodity into a specialty. Furthermore, the best of these services are not easily copied or transferred to another source.

Value-added services are all about problem resolution. The provider gains an edge by developing a proactive service that solves a problem for the customer.

The defining characteristics of higher-level value-added services are twofold: 1) they're scarce and 2) they're complex. Precisely because of that scarcity and complexity, they are not easily duplicated by competitors.

You might not think that value-added services are particularly scarce, based on the attention that they get in the trade press. But there are really two factors at work here. First, as with so many notions in our business, there is often more talk than action around the concept of value-added services. Second, as some services become popular and more widely offered, they lose their cachet and eventually cease to be thought of as "value-added." If everybody's doing it, it's not special any more, is it?

## The Customer's Viewpoint
For the buyer, a value-added service might be anything that improves productivity and therefore increases sales and profits. A service that attracts more customers adds value. A service that reduces errors and other hassles certainly adds value. Anything that improves morale within any link in the supply chain will add value for the customer.

## The Change Management Challenge
In some cases, implementation of a new service represents a potentially disruptive change, particularly for the provider. How well that organizational change is managed will likely determine the success of the new value-add's implementation. In addition, the ability to easily adapt to change may have a significant impact on the overall competitiveness of the service provider.

## Examples of Value-Added Services
One of the most frequently discussed value-added services is packaging. Relatively few transportation and warehousing providers are able to also offer packaging services. But for the shipper, there can be a significant advantage in shipping product in bulk liquid or dry bulk form and having the final package filled at a distribution center that's close to the marketplace. Sometimes the packaging service is simply labeling or branding, converting a can or bottle from "plain vanilla" to a private-label product. In other cases, packaging is simply the assembly and shrink-wrapping of multiple consumer packages to provide a "club pack" for the discount retailer.

Another value-added service is marking or recording. A chain retailer may have the retail prices for each item applied at the distribution center rather than at the point of manufacture. When serial number control is important, recording of serial numbers may be performed by the service provider. Similarly, weights — particularly catch weights on variable-weight products such as hams — may be recorded as the product is shipped.

In some cases, the value-added service includes light manufacturing, testing, assembly, or kitting. A few also involve sequencing, in which products or components are arranged in the expected order of use. Still others might entail arranging products and packaging for store-ready display.

A furniture manufacturer might distribute tables or beds in a knocked-down (KD) form, with final assembly performed just before the product is delivered. A maker of computers may have final assembly or testing performed in a warehouse just before the product is shipped. In some cases, the manufacturing service may convert an item from one SKU to a different one. In other cases, the service provider offers home delivery, field installation, or removal.

When the service provider offers customer fulfillment, a variety of value-added services are performed. There are three typical fulfillment services: first, the distribution center may operate a call center or receive electronically transmitted orders directly from customers, and the center may be asked to provide information directly to those customers. Second, the distribution center may provide a pick-and-pack service that converts bulk merchandise into a consumer shipping carton. Third, the fulfillment operator may process credit card transactions.

Transportation management represents one of the oldest value-added services provided by operations whose primary service is warehousing. Sometimes the service provider is asked to select the carriers and to monitor carrier performance. This may be done through transportation management software. Frequently, service providers are asked to audit or pay freight bills (or both). Some warehouse companies offer freight consolidation and deconsolidation services designed to save transportation dollars for their customers. Others use transportation capabilities to offer Just In Time (JIT) delivery. The combination of two shipments — known as merge in transit — is another value-add. Many providers offer pool distribution or cross docking as well.

Special storage features are always considered a value-added service in warehousing, and these include temperature-controlled storage, storage in security vaults, customs-bonded storage, and hazardous material control.

Many providers offer information systems that provide reports on productivity and quality. Information services might include Internet supply chain visibility or electronic data interchange (EDI). Some providers offer consulting, including transportation network optimization, along with process re-engineering. There is an obvious risk of conflict of interest when such services are offered by a vendor (as discussed in the chapter on the role of consultants in supply chain management).

Sometimes, quality management features, such as International Standards Organization (ISO) certification, are offered as value-added services.

A few service providers offer inventory management as well as inventory control. In managing inventory, they will identify slow-moving items and suggest liquidation and simplification of the inventory, in addition to executing replenishment and cycle counting functions.

As value-added services go, the ultimate service is for a logistics service provider to take on the role of lead provider, procuring and controlling subcontractors that offer additional services. Such services might include customs brokerage, duty-drawback management, and arranging for cargo insurance — or even the basics of transportation and/or DC operations in geographies in which the lead provider does not have a presence.

## The Commodity Trap — Signs and Signals, Omens and Portents

In essence, the serious logistics service provider expects to add value with every supply chain function that is performed. These providers will — and should — walk away from the prospective customer who is a commodity buyer. Cardinal Logistics CEO Vin McLoughlin posits that the progressive service provider will usually decline to bid when *any* of the following conditions are present:

1. More than five logistics service firms are on the bidder's list.

2. One or more of the bidders is a small local firm with a telephone and three trucks.

3. Bid proposals are limited to filling in the blanks on an RFP form sent by e-mail.

4. Bidders are not permitted to inspect the existing operation or meet individually with operations people.

5. The buyer has no interest in learning about your technology.

6. There is no process map, and the buyer will not permit you to create one.

7. One of the steps is an online auction.

8. The procurement process has been entirely turned over to a consultant (unless the consultant has a reputation for integrity and can incorporate value concepts into the process, and direct contact with the buyer is not precluded).

## The Eye of the Beholder

Remember, no service is a value-add unless the customer thinks it is. When that service is neither scarce nor complex, the buyer no longer perceives it as something that adds value. With the passage of time, special services that were once considered exotic have come to be taken for granted. There was a time when warehouse companies advertised fireproof storage, and later the progressive ones offered computerized inventory reporting. Promoting either of these as value-added services would be laughable in today's environment. Ultimately, it is safe to predict that some of today's highly prized services will be not only common tomorrow, but in the words of David Dickinson, "cheap as chips."

## Taking the Long View

Actually, we might take the position that there's nothing terribly special about value-added services. Functionally, there's nothing new here. Packaging has always been done somewhere by someone, for example. Price marking has always been done, maybe at the store, maybe at the DC, and now by a third-party logistics service provider (3PL). What we're seeing now is part of the continuing evolution of supply chain structures for all the usual reasons: cost, speed, quality, flexibility — many of the essential attributes of supply chain performance that are always in continuous improvement mode.

This evolution explains how it became normal for trucking companies to provide warehousing services, and for warehouses to provide transport services, and for broad-based

3PLs to do kitting and assembly in the customer's facility, rather than in their own.

In the short term, these value-adding steps can be competitive differentiators. Eventually, however, it will become apparent that they are simply repositioning *where* in the supply chain certain tasks are accomplished and will come to be accepted as routine.

Make no mistake, today's breakthrough is tomorrow's commonplace. The leaders will be looking at tomorrow's breakthrough — the next functional repositioning within the greater supply chain.

# REVERSE LOGISTICS

The deeds of a man's hands will return to him.
*Proverbs 12:14*

You can't go home again.
*Thomas Wolfe*

Life's a voyage that is homeward bound.
*Herman Melville*

A consumer is a shopper who is sore about something.
*Harold Coffin*

## Introduction

Finally, Reverse Logistics is getting some of the attention that it deserves as an important component of supply chain management. Though many might be surprised to hear it, Reverse Logistics wasn't invented yesterday. There are people who have excelled at planning and managing reverse flows for decades. Nevertheless, we're grateful for the current level of academic and practitioner interest in the subject.

Going back in time, many distribution centers contained a returns processing function. You could spot it right away because all the people there were moving with the speed and purpose of extras in George Romero's *Night of the Living Dead*. Typically, they were handling returns and, typically, they weren't happy about it. Neither was management.

Today's world is — or had better be — different. That's because an army of "Rs" drive the flow of items coming back to the distribution center. Returns, of course, but also Repairs and Refurbishment, Recycling, Recovery, and Recalls! And don't forget Reuse.

In fact, there's so much going on in the field that it's not always easy to keep up with it all. The prominent academic experts are Dr. James R. Stock at the University of South Florida and Dr. Dale S. Rogers at the University of Nevada. Dr. Rogers also chairs the Reverse Logistics Executive Council (RLEC), a collaboration of manufacturers, retailers, and academics, which can be reached through www.rlec.com. Another information resource is the Reverse Logistics Association, which is more of a trade group (www.reverselogisticstrends.com).

Despite all the current attention, reverse logistics (RL) still carries the stigma of a necessary evil. And all too often, it's treated as an afterthought.

## Definitions

For decades, reverse logistics had no formal definition. It meant whatever an organization wanted it to mean. Dr. Rogers in *Going Backwards*, the seminal text in the field, helped us to get our arms around a real definition. Dr. Rogers describes reverse logistics as: "The process of planning, implementing, and controlling the efficient, cost-effective flow of raw materials, in-process inventory, finished goods, and related information from the point of consumption to the point of origin for the purpose of recapturing value or proper disposal."

Of course, with the explosion in offshore production, it's often no longer practical to aim to return each item to its point of origin. But that's probably not where processing and disposition ought to be attempted, anyway.

## Many Happy Returns

Actually, most enterprises aren't happy about returns. Unfortunately, they're a fact of modern business life. We think about them in terms of taking a garish tie back to a department store after Christmas, or sending a size 8 garment that doesn't fit a size 12 body back to the catalog retailer. But the problem of returns is more complex than that.

Everybody's got returns, it seems. Beyond the obvious of clothing, there are electronics, books and magazines, greeting cards, processed foods, auto parts, and anything sold at The Home Depot. And the return rates can be staggering — 10 to 12 percent is common, and 30 percent is not rare. Can you guess the business with 100 percent returns? (It's tuxedo rental.)

## Repair and Refurbishment

A big part of reverse logistics is dedicated to making the pain go away in the retail and wholesale sector. If that's all there were, the problem would be big enough. But there's more to it than that. There's also the problem of the many things that are returned for reasons other than because "the customer is always right."

Things are often returned because they don't work. Or don't work any longer. Or because they've worn out. If they're repairable, there's an entire *demimonde* of industries that will make them whole (or nearly so) again and ready for resale. That's particularly true of electronics, auto parts, and technology components — a diverse universe ranging in value from a few dollars to over $100,000 per unit.

These items often aren't really broken or defective. They simply require repackaging to be ready for resale. (Note: Always make sure the unit is plugged in before calling Customer Service.) The disposition of repaired and refurbished items takes many paths — resale at retail outlets, resale through alternate channels, and reinstallation in different operating configurations.

## Recovery

A major aspect of reverse logistics involves turning products into their component parts and materials, for reapplication into other products or reintroduction into production processes. It might involve disassembly for component reuse. It might involve stripping wires and recycling their plastic sheathing. It might involve transforming telephone cable into granulated copper of a purity rivaling mined and refined product. It might involve isolating components and melting them down into basic elements, for reuse in other processes.

Recovery can also entail removing obsolete technology from service, for diversion into any number of alternate channels after being replaced. As in Repair and Refurbishment, the units can range in value from the trivial to six figures.

## Recycling

Recycling should not be confused with Recovery, even though many processes and dispositions may be similar. Growing federal, state, and local government pressures are driving Recycling. There are also public relations issues with Recycling, as well as cost and environmental impacts.

Europe has led the United States in comprehensive environmental laws, but you can bet that they're going to show up here, and sooner rather than later. European Union directives such as those on Waste Electrical and Electronic Equipment (WEEE) and Restriction of Hazardous Substances (RoHS) are making corporations responsible for end-of-lifecycle product disposition.

## Recalls

This is a topic that deserves comprehensive coverage elsewhere. For now, let's recognize that more industries, companies, and products than ever before have become vulnerable to recall actions. Anyone who remotely suspects that they might have to face the recall question someday should have a recall plan in place. And any recall plan should be tested periodically, just as we have fire drills when there's no fire.

## Challenges in RL Supply Chains

Unfortunately, Reverse Logistics is a more complicated matter than just running an item through the outbound supply chain in reverse. Issues unique to Reverse Logistics include:
- Little warning of RL arrivals.
- Quantities of one vs. outbound truckloads.
- Slippery inventory management.
- Destinations other than manufacturing source.
- Complexity of disposition decisions.
- Need for scarce IT support.
- Decisions involving where to do the physical handling.
- Complexity/diversity of RL activities.

Plus, network design is tricky for Reverse Logistics. It takes careful planning to determine where to accumulate, where to process, and where to redistribute. Intake requires some planning as well. Few companies beyond Sears have enough presence and penetration to accomplish self-intake. The new combinations of FedEx/Kinko's, UPS/Mail Boxes Etc., and DHL/OfficeMax, however, are making effective intake possible for the major parcel carriers when it comes to dealing with the population as a whole. One wonders if intake may finally provide a genuine value-adding role for the U.S. Postal Service.

## Disposition Options

"Back to the factory" is not only unpopular, it's often not even close to feasible. Today's RL processes include sophisticated analyses to plan and manage channels for disposition. In addition to the recovery and recycling options, returned and refurbished goods have options of:

- Liquidation.
- Sale in offshore/secondary markets.
- Sale at auction.
- Sale in outlet stores.
- Sale in employee/company stores.
- Sent back to the DC shelf for resale.
- Donation to charities, with further options in schools, churches, shelters, food banks, and third-world countries.

But there will be questions related to products, such as:

- Age.
- Quality.
- Style/season.
- Sensory attributes.
- Liability.
- Repackaging requirements.
- Need to "de-kit" pre-assembled product configurations.

And saturation in one channel may force diversion into an alternate.

## Scope of Reverse Logistics Activities

It's not just a matter of getting stuff back. There are a host of related things that might be done — either internally or by a third-party specialist:

1. Inquiries fielded by a help desk/call center.
2. Recycling/full disposal.
3. Collection/sorting/testing.
4. Returns authorization management.
5. Transportation and distribution.
6. Fulfillment and kitting.
7. Warehousing/storage.
8. Spare parts management.
9. Depot repair.
10. Asset management.
11. Replacement management.
12. Warranty management/service contracts.
13. Remanufacture/refurbishment.
14. Redistribution/resale.
15. End-of-life (EOL) manufacturing and EOL management.
16. IT management.

… and more, as time goes on and capabilities expand.

## How Can All This Be Mastered?

The reality is that few companies are good at reverse logistics — it's just not a core competency. And maybe it shouldn't be. With all the newfound interest in the importance of RL processes and a recognition of the underlying complexities involved, a burgeoning industry of RL specialists has sprung up. The specialist field, which was pioneered by GENCO some four decades ago, continues to grow today. It's hard to say how many service providers currently populate the RL field, but 50 seems a safe bet.

## A Few Secrets of Success

Despite the challenges, reverse logistics processes are working well for those who've invested in learning how to make them work. The keys to success include:

- Dedicated (separate) management and organization.
- Independent processing/storage facilities.
- Strong IT support.
- Quality, timely data.
- Good process design and staff training.
- Strategic context (often overlooked, but vital).
- Solid dollars-and-cents business case.

With these, you've got a better than fighting chance; without them you could fall short of the potential for reverse logistics in your organization.

# FACILITY LOCATION AND NETWORK DESIGN

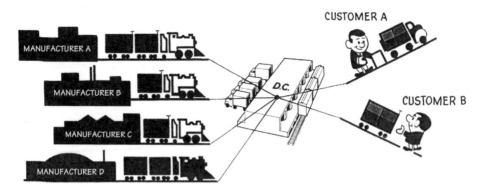

Oh, what a tangled web we weave ...
*William Shakespeare*

No man acquires property without acquiring with it a little arithmetic also.
*Ralph Waldo Emerson*

The shortest distance between two points is under construction.
*Noelie Altito*

A moment's insight is sometimes worth a life's experience.
*Oliver Wendell Holmes*

## Is Now the Time to Talk About This?

When it comes to facility location and network design, not all projects are created equal. If all you're concerned about is which side of the tracks to put the warehouse on, that's as close to a slam dunk as things get these days. If you've been charged with deploying facilities in a complex supply chain, especially a global operation, that's a different story.

Is a topic of this intrinsic complexity really something we need to discuss among the Fundamentals of Supply Chain Management? As they say in Fargo (or at least in the film), "You betcha!" Here are a few situations that might plunge you into a distribution network design and redesign project:

- Your company acquires another company or another company acquires yours.
- A line of business is picked up or dropped.
- Your company decides to expand into new geographic markets.
- Your company finds that it's running out of space.
- Company management decides to centralize or decentralize operations.
- Labor, environmental, or community pressures prompt the company to consider a move.
- The company makes radical changes to its sourcing policies and begins importing goods from places like Central America, the Far East, Eastern Europe, or Africa.

60

If none of those sounds like a reasonable prospect, read no further — you're not in the game. If any of them seems likely, press on.

As you begin to consider the question of facility location, there are really two components to the decision. One is the obvious "where." The other is the "why." Distribution network structure is fundamental to the ultimate strategic commitment to customer service levels. From that determination, distribution locations, facility missions, and inventory deployment details are derived. Without that strategic pole star, there's not much point to playing with network ideas.

Time was, alert and aggressive companies would take a hard look at their network structure every five years or so. The pace of globalization now makes that an every-two-year requirement.

## The Devil Enters the Room

Of course, once the magic word "network" has been invoked, there's a tendency to get overexcited about the subject of network modeling. Truth is, once you get beyond a couple of locations, modeling can be enormously helpful for number crunching and quick assessments of alternatives.

There is a tendency at this point for techno-geeks and executives alike to get all caught up in the esoterica of modeling. That's unfortunate, because there's so much more to the location question than modeling packages are equipped to handle. These issues include:

- Strategic issues of "right" solutions for markets and channels.
- Sizing and operating-cost factors for facilities in addition to location.
- Potential changes in sourcing locations and related sensitivity and confidentiality.
- Considerations in operations-outsourcing potential.
- The right level and right locations for value-adding services.
- "Clean sheet of paper" thinking about automation potential and its economic feasibility.
- The possibility and probability of blended, mix-and-match solutions delivering optimum outcomes.
- Solid, realistic total-cost analysis, implementation planning, and business case development.

## Notes on Modeling

There are many choices of modeling packages available to companies, consultants, and modeling specialists. But passions can run high about which package works best.

Some of the most mature products were developed by respected academics from prestigious institutions. They are each and all justifiably proprietary about the sophisticated analysis and thinking that went into the absolutely unique algorithms that distinguish their individual products. (You've got a good chance of starting a fight that would make a biker bar proud if you can get them in a room together to discuss the relative merits of the various offerings.) Yet they all deliver remarkably similar results.

Some practitioners and users swear by one product or another, despite the evidence of adequacy among many of the alternatives. We chalk this up to, primarily, comfort and familiarity (in much the same way Americans define themselves as Ford people or Chevy people, with the occasional Dodge aficionado thrown in for variety).

Among the stand-alone packages, CAPS Logistics' Supply Chain Designer has been around forever. Although this software application has undergone considerable change in corporate ownership over the past several years, it remains much in demand. LogicTools, a newer provider that takes a different approach to data intake and graphics presentation, is also enjoying considerable popularity right now. Neither of these examples should be taken as an endorsement. There are several other excellent products on the market today, with more coming online all the time.

In the end, *which* modeling software package you choose is far less important than *how* you use it. The model is merely a tool, ultimately sensitive to the quality of questions posed to it, the reliability of data employed in the solution, and the business context of the exercise.

In fact, the modeling tool only begins to answer the critical questions in the overall assessment; other tools and analyses are needed to get at things like facility size, inventory requirements, storage modes, and staffing and labor costs.

The real keys to successful network modeling lie in:
- Asking the right questions.
- Using the right data.
- Aggregating data to the right level.
- Validating the right assumptions.
- Understanding modeling's limitations.
- Having enough data and auxiliary tools to evaluate the complete solution.

Is there a place in here for simulation? Maybe, but that's a topic for another day. Certainly simulation at a facility level can be practical and useful. However, there would have to have a lot at stake to justify the effort of a networkwide simulation.

## Modeling's Dark Side

Powerful as these modeling tools may be, there are some things to keep in mind regarding their use. One is that there is often a big difference between an optimal solution and a practical one — and models can't make that distinction. They'll change a solution for a $1 cost advantage. Another is that, often, a majority of savings or benefits come from a subset of the modeled solution. That's because models don't know how to fragment their solutions to find the "bang for the buck" payback. Further, models can't contemplate the cost or time for implementation in devising a solution. In short, they can't edit or interpret their work, which places a considerable burden on the user.

In addition, models are often tough to build, are quite difficult to verify, and consume data as if an information famine were imminent. Some newer products are somewhat more user- and-data-friendly, but modeling is not an exercise for the faint of heart or the resource-constrained.

That said, modeling tools are indispensable in solving complex network and facility location questions. Just remember they're only tools, not oracles. They can't answer questions that you can't ask. They can't solve problems that you can't define. And they can't think out of the box.

## Going From Macro to Micro

Inevitably, a facility location project turns out to be a multistep process. After you've determined that a given city is an ideal site for a facility, for example, you then have to identify the exact locale in town and the specific site.

There are other factors that influence location decisions as well. One is the Von Thunen theory, which suggests that high-value items, such as gemstones, can be shipped relatively economically from almost anywhere in the world. The inverse is that low-value commodities, such as salt, need to be shipped from quite near the point of consumption.

Another factor that might influence the choice of a distribution site is the potential for postponement operations. That's because the best location for finished-product shipment may not be the best location for postponement execution.

## Going After Specific Sites

Specific site selection is best accomplished with an organized process. It's not enough — and may be deadly in the long run — to focus on price as the sole factor in the decision. Begin with a Requirements Definition, which both lists and prioritizes the factors that are important in a new facility or construction site. Examples include:
- Access to specific transportation modes, such as rail sidings or water transport.
- A union-free labor environment.
- Potential for tax abatements.
- Access to airport or helipad.
- The ability to expand by "x" percent.

Don't forget some other important factors such as community attitudes. In fact, there's little in business life more fearsome than the NIMBY (Not In My Back Yard) lobby. Financing alternatives, too, can radically affect build-or-buy decisions.

Be sure to have requirements defined *before* the specific search begins. Making them up based on what you're seeing is self-delusion of a dangerous kind. Your shortcut could turn into the Beatles' "long and winding road."

## Looking Outside

Site and facility selection is one activity in which taking all the outside advice offered is probably a good thing. You can save time and leverage the experience of many advisers. On top of that, you can preserve your anonymity, a very good thing in a run-up to negotiations. Some sources of help:
- Real estate brokers or a developer's consulting division.
- Warehouse sales representatives.
- Carrier (especially rail) representatives.
- Utility (gas and electric) development departments.
- Chambers of Commerce; state and local development agencies.
- Consultants.

## Finally

When you're ready to make the final pick, be sure to check multiple sources for information and opinions. Aggressively look for hidden trouble, such as floods, seismic activity, soil problems, and access difficulties.

In short, be organized, be creative, and document, document, document.

# LOGISTICS OUTSOURCING

The ideal manager is a man who knows exactly what he can't do himself,
and gets the right people for those things.
*Phillip Rosenthal*

… Benedict Arnold CEOs …
*John Forbes Kerry*

… outsourcing is just a new way of doing … trade …
*N. Gregory Mankiw*

Amateurs hope. Professionals work.
*Garson Kanin*

## Is There Any Limit?

Outsourcing has been a hot topic in American business for the past several years. Unlike offshoring, outsourcing does not mean a net domestic job loss, although different people might wind up doing the old job. Although we're here to talk about logistics and supply chain impacts, the facts are that almost any corporate activity can be outsourced, including:

- Manufacturing.
- Design.
- Information Technology.
- Accounting.
- Tax processing.
- Medical diagnostics.
- Customer service.
- Tech support.
- Inventory management.
- Repair and refurbishment.

- Reverse logistics.
- Maintenance.
- Procurement.
- Supply chain operations.

In the abstract, outsourcing is just another procurement exercise, subject to the same basic rules and recommendations as everything else. But supply chain outsourcing is actually a bit more significant. Supply chains are our lifelines, the channels through which our products reach our customers.

Providers of outsourced logistics services are prominent in our profession. Further, despite the visibility and good reputations of these logistics providers, estimates are that 25 to 50 percent of outsourcing deals fail (or at least fail to meet expectations).

Given the consequences, the decision to outsource or not is a major one for any company. Whether they realize it or not, companies are making a "bet the business" decision whenever they embark on a supply chain outsourcing initiative.

## Who Are the Players in the Game?

First, what is the game? We've used the term "3PL" to refer to third-party logistics service companies for a long time. Now, however, the term "4PL" has come into vogue. One consultant has attempted to introduce 5PL, but that didn't fly. A friend in the U.K. tried to tell us that he was heading up a 4 1/2PL (that company, by the way, is no longer in business).

We prefer two terms promoted by Cliff Lynch: logistics service provider (LSP) and lead logistics provider (LLP).

The distinctions between and among providers are changing. We used to talk about those who had their origins in transportation and those who began life as public warehouses — and it was easy to tell which were which. That was before globalization.

Today the marketplace is very fluid, with almost daily changes. We used to categorize players as global non-U.S. operators, global operators with U.S. acquisitions, major national (U.S.) operators, super-regional U.S. companies, and local or regional specialists.

Now, after waves of domestic and international acquisitions, the LSP world is moving toward a bi-modal model. Ultimately, the marketplace will consist of a few large multinational/global players at one end, and several niche specialty (by function or geography) companies at the other.

As the major leaguers assemble portfolios of skills and establish a presence across the globe, their objective becomes clearer. They want to plan, manage, and control execution of supply chain activities from manufacturing and extraction sources to customer delivery.

Not convinced? Take a closer look at what's behind a lot of the current mergers and buy-outs. When a freight forwarder buys a warehousing company; when a trucker (Schneider) buys a port services operator *and* an international airfreight operation; when a transportation and warehousing giant buys a port services and transloading specialist; when a former regional warehouser not only manages transportation but provides global freight forwarding — well, the handwriting is on the wall, in whatever language it's written.

## Contract or Transactional Services?

Until the 1980s, nearly all warehousing services were performed under 30-day contracts, and most transport service was common carriage. But in the '80s, contract warehousing spread like the West Nile virus, encouraged by Wall Street analysts who saw contract ware-housing as a better financial bet than public warehousing. They ignored the reality that nearly all contracts have, and have always had, performance clauses that allow users to ter-minate at will.

Furthermore, a long-term contract does not suit the needs of a user who has big season-al surges and seeks the flexibility inherent in using public warehousing or common car-riage. If you needed lodging for a couple of nights, you would not lease an apartment — you would go to a hotel. Public warehouses and common carriers were the equivalent of hotels for merchandise.

As the LSP world has evolved, and as the scope and range of services provided have grown, the service providers' roots (whether in warehousing or in transport operations) seem to matter less and less. But there are still vestiges of transactional pricing in some LSP charges. Indeed, many contemporary contracts require a lot of high-priced legal and consulting expertise to structure arrangements for flexible space consumption.

## How Big Is Too Big?

Some research suggests that LSP mergers are not delivering the cost and synergy benefits that the providers have trumpeted. There appears to be a glaring mismatch between the logistics companies' reports (which claim that 80 to 90 percent of their customers have had a positive experience) and the reports from the customers themselves (which indicate that 20 to 30 percent are satisfied with the arrangement). More striking still is the gap between the percentage of companies that claim to offer fully integrated supply chain services (94 percent) and the percentage of customers who say their providers truly offer that capabil-ity (7 percent).

As LSPs merge and acquire one another, a dichotomy inevitably develops: When an LSP is big enough to truly execute a customer's supply chain management from origin to consumption , is it then too big to be efficient and effective? In other words, at some point, does the elephant grow too big to dance? We don't know the answer.

But we do know that nimbleness counts, and that price counts even more in the real world. Further, there is probably a balance between the values of scale and local relationships when considering how to construct outsourced solutions of some complexity. As Meredith Willson's characters in *he Music Man* remind us, "You've got to know the territory!"

## Scope of LSP Services

What will the new generation of 3PLs do? As an industry, they've come a long way from simply providing warehousing space or operating the old private fleet. Here's a sampler of what today's LSPs are offering — routinely.

- Warehousing.
- Transportation.
- Inventory management.
- Repair and refurbishment.
- Reverse logistics management.
- Transportation management.
- Freight bill payment.
- Freight audits.

- Procurement.
- Sourcing management and integration.
- Order management.
- Light manufacturing.
- Assembly.
- Kitting.
- End-of-life product management.
- Returns processing.
- Value-added services (tagging, store-ready prep, display prep, etc.).
- RF and bar-code labeling.
- Freight forwarding.
- Customs brokerage.
- Cross docking.
- Network optimization.
- Project management.
- Port services.
- Transloading.

The new scope of services, along with continually growing capabilities, changes the traditional analysis of when to consider using LSP services and how to use them.

## Why Consider Using (Outsourcing to) an LSP?

There are loads of really good reasons to evaluate what an LSP can do for a company. They include:

1. High internal costs.
2. The decision to enter new geographic markets.
3. New sources of products and materials.
4. The need to off-load difficult (cube, weight, demand pattern) products.
5. The addition of new roles, e.g., order fulfillment, value-added services.
6. The need for operational and staffing flexibility.
7. A need for overflow capacity — space and people.
8. The desire to preserve capital for core business activities.
9. A shift to variable external costs from fixed internal costs.
10. The lack of internal resources or skills for changing requirements.
11. A strategic decision to shed non-core business processes.

The list goes on, but experience indicates that there may be more reasons to contemplate the possibility than there were 10 years ago. The supply chain world is changing, and it's become more demanding — and it requires more skills — than ever before. LSP successes in activities beyond transport and warehousing continue to demonstrate the feasibility of that type of solution.

## Cautions

But all is not roses. There are ample opportunities for disappointment, even failure. The major misconceptions center on two points. First, contrary to popular opinion, LSP outsourcing is unlikely to save the customer money in the short term, especially when business processes don't change and communications are less than complete. Second, the transition to the LSP is unlikely to be seamless, particularly for customers. The keys to overcoming these issues are to avoid becoming fixated on short-term cost savings, and to choose an LSP that's able to recover quickly when things don't go according to plan. The myths and misconception list is lengthy, but these are the critical ones.

## Current Events

There has been debate over the future of LSPs for years, along with speculation as to if and how LSP penetration of the U.S. market might change. The results are becoming a little more clear.

After five years of stagnation, the last four years have seen a leap in LSP usage to 80 percent of survey respondents in a Georgia Tech study. While impressive on the surface, we think the real growth — and the future potential — lies in users' partaking more fully of the constantly growing menu of services that LSPs offer. Many of those respondents in the 80 percent group were using LSPs in highly limited ways.

On the technology front, LSPs have, in our experience, long recognized the importance of investment in technology support. But the Georgia Tech study showed widespread dissatisfaction with LSP technology services within the user community. That seems to indicate that LSPs have failed to deliver process innovation as part of their solutions to users who clearly seek creativity and best practices from their outsourcing providers.

Part of this disconnect could result from the still-too-common practice among users of squeezing the absolute lowest prices out of their LSPs. How much creativity — or leading-edge technology support — can they really expect to get for free?

## The Offshoring/Outsourcing Riddle

When manufacturing is outsourced — usually to another country — it's a different game entirely. Despite all the media attention to the issue, a recent survey showed that less than 5 percent of companies had outsourced all, or nearly all, of their operations. Only another 5 percent had done more than 75 percent, and only another 6 percent were at the 50 percent mark.

However, when companies take a thoughtful and balanced approached to offshored outsourcing, they realize that the manufacturing and logistics outsourcing issues are often intertwined. A few years ago, manufacturing was often blindly offshored, based on perceived savings in labor costs. We've learned the hard way that there's more to outsourcing than labor cost. Furthermore, we are now painfully aware that moving one part of the supply chain without paying attention to the logistics component can be a dreadful error.

While we have tended to think first about low labor costs in offshoring activity, the fact is that material costs were cited as the prime driver as often (actually fractionally more) as labor costs in a major survey of offshoring/outsourcing corporations. And logistics costs were cited about two-thirds as often as materials or labor costs.

The locales involved are not surprising:

1. China — 70 percent.
2. India — 48 percent.
3. Asia — 47 percent.
4. Eastern Europe — 36 percent.
5. Latin America — 22 percent.

6. Mexico — 20 percent.

Still, offshoring carries obstacles and risks. The obstacles are usually infrastructure, complexity, immaturity, trade regulations, culture, and government regulation. The risks involve quality, delivery, security, efficiency, and politics.

## How Should the LSP Question Be Approached?

The short answer is, not casually. In fact, not with anything less than eyes wide open. And certainly not with unrealistic expectations. Here's a sequence of activities that can get an LSP relationship off on the right foot.

- **Rough-cut the likely scope.** This is a time to brainstorm and be free-thinking in your approach.
- **Test probability.** Apply sanity checks to the first effort.
- **Size up the potentials.** Do the best you can to get your arms around the possible benefits.
- **Select the top handful.** Narrow your list to a small number (5–9) of providers most likely to meet your immediate (and next five-year) scope of need. Get advice to find the right fit of players (don't forget to look at where the business is going).
- **Identify, prioritize, and weight critical factors.** Decide early on what the show-stopper and nice-to-have issues are — and do so systematically.
- **Prepare, send, and evaluate Requests for Information (RFIs).**
- **Short-list the top three.**
- **Proceed with the RFP process.**

Short-changing this assessment can derail the process for a long time. Once you've reached this point, continue forward with an organized approach, as it represents the key to achieving LSP outsourcing objectives. Steps in this process include:

- **Baselining.** Nail down where your performance and costs really are.
- **Risk assessment.** Define what can go wrong, what's at stake, and what can be done to reduce the odds of failure — bravely and honestly.
- **Benchmarking.** Quantifying the level of performance achieved by the industry leaders will help set the bar for your future accomplishments.
- **Draw up the RFP.** Set out the specifics of what the service candidates are expected to achieve — and to commit to.
- **Contracting for value.** Negotiate and set hard targets for cost and performance that include incentives and penalties.
- **Selection.** Pick your new partner — and keep the next best in reserve in case things don't come to consummation.
- **Implementation.** Get all the pieces in place and turn on the switch.

## Success Factors

In addition to the approach outlined above, the customer has a number of other responsibilities when it comes to creating a successful 3PL/LSP partnership. Among others, it must:

- Provide great data.
- Get to know the people.
- Give candidates enough time to prepare quality responses.

- Hide nothing.
- Write clear, simple, contracts.
- Establish flexible, changeable performance targets.
- Know real costs — on both sides.
- Get over misconceptions, early.
- Build the problem resolution process in advance.
- Integrate broad working involvement — the "bowtie" relationship.

With these steps, success is more than a possibility — it is likely.

*Author's Note:*

*Useful information about outsourcing and logistics service providers may be found at www.cflynch.com and www.3plogistics.com.*

# LEAN SUPPLY CHAIN MANAGEMENT

Do not remove a fly from your friend's forehead with a hatchet.
*Chinese Proverb*

Waste is worse than loss. The time is coming when every person who lays claim to ability will keep the question of waste before him constantly. The scope of thrift is limitless.
*Thomas A. Edison*

Waste neither time nor money, but make the best use of both.
Without industry and frugality, nothing will do, and with them everything.
*Benjamin Franklin*

Love of bustle is not industry.
*Seneca*

## Not Kids' Stuff

Consider the children's rhyme, "Jack Sprat could eat no fat; his wife could eat no lean." In Jasper Fforde's update on the classics, *The Big Over Easy*, the trim Mr. Sprat has a new wife. The previous one, who could not tolerate lean, didn't make the cut.

## Introduction

We've made passing reference to "Lean" in discussing the integration of manufacturing into supply chain operations. Further, we've taken the position that there's not much new regarding the Lean concept, whose foundation elements date back to the principles outlined by Henry Ford in 1926's *Today and Tomorrow*.

More recently, the concept of Lean has re-entered supply chain and logistics terminology. Craig Hall's LeanLogistics Inc. concentrates on improved transportation efficiency and asset utilization. Lean warehousing has now been extensively written up, notably in *Lean Warehousing* (2006, Kenneth B. Ackerman).

We are convinced that the principles of Lean can — and should — be applied throughout the supply chain. Implemented with focus and purpose, they have the potential to elevate and transform performance in sustainable ways.

However, if the approach is tried inconsistently or if it's implemented without a sense of direction or objective, then the Lean supply chain initiative could prove to be disappointing. Success requires a comprehensive program, organized and prioritized with high levels of communications and buy-in as well as the *imprimatur* of management commitment. Now, that's the ticket.

But what is Lean? And how can its impact be felt throughout the supply chain? We'll skip manufacturing, which has been exhaustively documented. (Besides, manufacturing integration has been discussed in its own chapter, earlier in this book.)

Without digging through each element of the supply chain, let's begin by recognizing that customer service can create and meet customer expectations for performance with a Lean approach (discussed in the chapter on Customer Service). The rest of the pieces should fall into place after that.

## The Lean Foundation

Lean begins with the creation of a lean-thinking organization and a refusal to deal with programs that restrict their focus to specific functional tasks. It is, to some extent, a catalyst for making everyone in supply chain planning and operations recognize that they are part of one entity, that they belong to a single organization with common goals and a unifying approach to meeting them — Lean.

Lean, like *kaizen*, homes in on waste, which in Japanese is called *muda*. Such an ugly word, *muda*, makes clear that waste is so filthy and vile that it deserves all-out effort toward its eradication.

The eight wastes identified by Taiichi Ohno (Toyota) can be summarized as follows:
- Overproduction.
- Waiting.
- Unnecessary movement of products.
- Over-processing.
- Ineffective inventory control.
- Unnecessary movement of people.
- Defective parts.
- Unused creativity.

## Context for the Eight Wastes

Initially developed from a manufacturing perspective, some of the eight wastes are universal. Others have clear counterparts in a number of supply chain modules. For example, "unused creativity," which is failing to capitalize on the ingenuity of both workers and managers, is a near-criminal waste in any function, whether sourcing, procurement, or physical distribution.

"Defective parts" translates to errors of all kinds throughout the chain from picking errors to ordering incorrect quantities. It also includes shipping by the wrong carriers or the wrong mode. Errors consume resources — time, people, and materials — to no useful end. Even worse, additional resources are usually needed to correct or overcome the original error.

"Waiting" relates to time. In the factory or in the warehouse, resources (people, machines, forklifts, trucks) might be idle while waiting for tools, products, or materials to arrive or to be taken away. In other arenas, time cycles, such as replenishment and order fulfillment, might be longer than optimal, requiring unnecessary inventory to compensate or additional effort to expedite. In transportation, waiting (dwell time) for long-haul trucks and drivers can approach the magnitude of a "normal" work week all by itself. Waiting constitutes an abuse of people, time, and physical assets.

"Overproduction" has counterparts in over-ordering at both the macro- and micro-levels in supply chain operations. Either way, an oversupply of product, often simultaneously at different points in the supply chain, represents a horrible waste. Money, physical assets, time, people, and material have all been consumed for something that is not needed. When excess stock continues to consume space and money, it becomes vulnerable to becoming damaged or obsolete. Meanwhile, resources consumed for storage might have been diverted from ordering, making, storing, or moving genuinely needed items, thus requiring even more resources to make or acquire the right stuff and ultimately resulting in stock-outs or lost sales or both. It's a slippery slope, indeed.

"Over-processing" can take place in any activity. Quality inspections, redundant approvals, and order reviews at the conclusion of pick/pack are some examples. It negates the value contribution of the original activity by adding unnecessary time and effort to the process. It is a costly way to overcome a lack of sound training or a failure to design quality and accuracy into processes.

Another form of over-processing is the failure to rationalize the supply base, and concentrate on a few top-tier suppliers. Yet another is the failure to rationalize and align the carrier base. Both result in inefficient duplication of resources, decisions, and communications.

Like "overproduction," the "unnecessary movement of products" can occur at both the macro- and micro-levels — within a warehouse, within a factory, or with too many steps and too many stops through a supply chain's distribution network. Movement from suppliers, through master DCs to regional DCs for further deployment to customers (or into customers' physical distribution networks) can be deadly from the standpoints of cost and time — and the consumption of critical resources. Too much labor in handling, too much cost-inefficient transport, too much space taken up, too many opportunities for error, too many chances for damage — and shrink.

"Unnecessary movement of people" certainly applies to both manufacturing and physical distribution. In warehousing an enormous percentage of peoples' time is devoted to movement such as picking, putaway, and replenishment. If a facility is not well laid out with easy access and short pick paths for "A" items, the unnecessary movement and associated time can reach staggering levels, sucking up human and material handling resources. If the expected goods are not in the correct location, the movement to get them has been wasted. Even more time and effort will be spent in finding them. If the designated putaway location is already full, more waste has occurred.

"Ineffective inventory control" creates more waste at several levels. Based on bad inventory data, too much may be manufactured or purchased. In turn, that generates inventory waste and diverts precious capital funds into the creation and maintenance of waste. A scarcity of items purchased or manufactured results in stock-outs or lost orders. An abundance of material, on the other hand, results in the assignment of valuable space to hold unnecessary stock. Having too little means time spent in trying to find the items and frequently generates expedited purchasing and transportation — more waste.

Forms of these wastes are all over the supply chain. Examples include misplaced sourcing, a fragmented supply base, inefficient ordering processes, tolerance for less-than-optimum incoming products and materials, failure to match storage modes to product order and movement profiles, unbalanced distribution network structures, service-deficient carriers or transportation modes, empty backhauls, inefficient load creation, inaccurate forecasting, siloed planning, misapplied technology, ineffective and uncoordinated information systems — and the list goes on.

*Muda* — all of it *muda*.

## The Role of the Five Ss

The key to addressing the problems of wasted time, cost, capital, space, assets, and intellectual potential lies in establishing a culture of Lean thinking. This requires attention to the Five Ss. They are:

- **Sortation** — separating needed tools and materials from the unneeded, and removing the unneeded.
- **Straightening** — arranging items in easiest-to-use order.
- **Shining** — cleanup; good housekeeping.
- **Standardization** — systems and procedures to accomplish and monitor the first three Ss.
- **Sustaining** — maintaining and continuously improving the operation.

It is admittedly easier to think about these in the contexts of manufacturing and warehousing. But when you extend the idea of sortation and straightening to include the development of good processes and procedures for functions throughout the supply chain — planning as well as execution from procurement through delivery — their universal application becomes more clear.

Good housekeeping applies across the board — to facilities, to rolling stock, to offices. It also applies to systems, to files, to data bases — every aspect of physical and information infrastructure.

Standardization, then, refers to the institutionalization of the processes and policies developed for Lean operations — domestically and (when feasible) globally. Sustaining means that the Lean workplace never quits getting leaner. Lean must become a way of life throughout the organization. Making Lean simply the latest in a long line of programs is a sure way to limit its impact and, ultimately, to doom the initiative. Making Lean anything less than an organization-wide effort will have similar consequences.

With those definitions and notions in hand, we must note that Lean is not an exclusionary program — the one and only true path to excellence. It welcomes tools and techniques from other sources to enhance analysis, problem solving, and implementation — Six Sigma, Statistical Process Control (SPC), and the like.

## The End Game

What's the ultimate objective? Achieving perfection means no waste and no errors. It means absolutely accurate records and perfect orders, all the time. It means seamless unit flow through the chain, not just through one function. It also means "Pull" flow based on real end-user demand, in the smallest feasible quantities. Finally, it means total visibility, continuous flow, and the integration of information and financial flows with physical movement. In sum, it means minimal moves, minimal touches, minimal interruption, minimal cycle times, and minimal inventory.

Is perfection achievable? Not exactly. But Lean can bring an organization significantly closer to it. It can help a company continue to move nearer and nearer toward the grail, year after year. One day, not all that far off, a Lean organization might awaken to discover that its performance looks like perfection to those who have yet to embark on the Lean journey.

## In Conclusion

Persuaded yet? Remember the former Mrs. Sprat.

*Author's Note:*

*More information is available in Lean Warehousing, a book available at www.warehousing-forum.com*

# THE IMPORTANCE OF PACKAGING

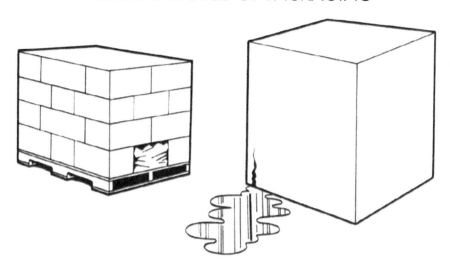

The most perfect technique is that which is not noticed at all.
*Pablo Casals*

Everything that deceives may be said to enchant.
*Plato*

Hood an ass with reverend purple ... and he shall pass for a cathedral doctor.
*Ben Jonson*

A fair exterior is a silent recommendation.
*Pubilius Syrus*

## Thinking Outside the Box

Unfortunately, the subject of packaging is seldom raised in discussions of supply chain management. Yet packaging is one of the many elements of SCM that has to be got right for successful day-to-day supply chain operations. Like other elements of supply chain, it took a long time for packaging to receive the academic attention that it merited. One early leader in the field was Michigan State's School of Packaging, where Dr. Diana Twede has succeeded Paul Peoples as a resident guru.

## Packaging, Really?

Those who think that packaging doesn't matter are the same ones who think that distribution center operation is no more complicated than "boxes in and boxes out." Of course, packaging enthusiasts can get a little carried away with the world-saving attributes of their arcane specialties. But the truth is that we wouldn't have much of a supply chain if it weren't for packaging.

## What Does Packaging Do?

Packaging plays so many diverse roles it's hard to know where to begin. Among other things, packaging accomplishes the following:

- Encloses products, large and small.
- Contains selling quantities, from one to many.
- Identifies contents, via text, bar codes, and radio frequency labels.
- Advertises and promotes suppliers and products.
- Arrays contents within a larger package.
- Aligns and stabilizes irregular shaped items.
- Enables efficient handling at numerous quantity breaks, e.g., unit, case, pallet.
- Insulates contents against heat or cold.
- Protects products from moisture; conversely, permits moisture to escape.
- Maintains storage medium integrity, whether liquid or gas.
- Deters degradation of a product's sensory attributes.
- Bars contaminants from entry or contact with product.
- Diminishes risks of damage from movement or vibration.
- Protects items from physical (handling) damage.
- Supports efficient space utilization — pallet, warehouse, transportation.
- Stabilizes product accumulation in all modes.
- Enables safe, efficient movement and handling.
- Promotes re-use and recycling.
- Communicates contents, status, and events (RFID).

There are no doubt others, but you're getting the idea. Packaging is much, much more than "the box it came in." Similarly, the science of packaging involves far more than how to orient the corrugated for efficient mill runs.

## Some Specialty Areas

There are separate and distinct packaging techniques and attributes in different industries. Food packaging is a world unto itself. The same is true for packaging in electronics and technology. Frozen food has a unique set of concerns, as does the beverage segment.

Take a product like wine. It has seen a series of packaging revolutions from synthetics to replace natural cork stoppers and screw-top closures that preserve intrinsic characteristics of the product. From a logistics standpoint, the wine "box," which is made possible by special spouts and closures that prohibit the entry of air during pouring, radically alter the shipment characteristics of consumer-level units.

In fact, aseptic packaging has the power to transform the food industry (particularly when coupled with irradiation techniques). But it has not been able to really break through the very high wall of consumer resistance. This technology, which "locks out" external air, light, and moisture, has largely been confined to beverage and dairy applications.

## Shifting Into Reverse

Relatively recent packaging developments are having a tremendous effect on reverse logistics. Not so long ago, packaging was recyclable, returnable, and reusable. Then materials and manufacturing became compellingly inexpensive and we turned to what we thought was disposable packaging.

The elements of the equation keep changing, though, and practices that were once socially acceptable and economically attractive are less so today. Although usage of returnable totes, bins, and boxes has gone up, the plastics used in making those containers has become more expensive due to a recent run-up in petroleum prices. The logistics implications of these alternatives to disposable and recyclable corrugated boxes include both the routing and handling for the reverse trip, but also the cube implications of the nesting and collapsible options.

In the department of questionable value-added services, these options can also involve cleaning requirements for reasons of contamination and life extension. Their increased use has spawned a sub-genre of consulting devoted exclusively to returnable packaging, another dubious advance.

Other returnable packaging includes corrugated, plastic corrugated, bulk bags, and molded foam.

## Back to School

Michigan State's Hugh Lockhart has developed a comprehensive approach to the analysis of packaging, "The Packaging Matrix," that links the full range of packaging functions (not simply those related to supply chain operations) with the environments in which packaging comes into play. The functional groupings of protection, utility, and communication are matched with human, biospheric, and physical environments.

Although packaging can be enormously powerful in marketing and promotion, eight of the matrix's nine cells relate in some fashion to supply chain operations or physical handling, at either the consumer or the commercial level.

In the physical realm, elements of protection include cushioning, external shipping containers, corner posts, air bags, filler materials, and compression strength for stacking. Other utility components include stretch wrap. shrink wrap, self-heating and self-cooling packages, freezer-to-oven capability, ergonomically sized containers, and handles for carrying (either external or integral). Packaging also takes several communications elements into account. Examples include signage for warning and handling (e.g., "This side up"), RFID, pictorials, accelerometers, and temperature and stacking limitations.

Biospheric elements protect products (and those who handle them) and permit extended shelf life times in the supply chain. They encompass amber colors, UV absorbers, oxygen barriers/absorbers, films, other barriers, wet strength external packaging, controlled atmospheres, edible films, time and temperature indicators, and pictorials.

In the human environment, protection functions are exemplified by tamper-evident features, child-resistant closures, and designs that don't demand scissors or knives to open. Utility functions include making the package resealable and reclosable. They also include easy-to-open designs, pre-measured units, special pharmaceutical packaging, ergonomic shapes, talking packages, and the like.

## Where Packaging Plays — and Pays

As you may have gathered, we consider packaging to be integral to supply chain management as well as to the product's success. Packaging may be considered part of the product itself, contributing to product performance, which includes shelf life and ease of use. Packaging certainly remains vital to protecting products from manufacture through the distribution channel and into the hands of ultimate users, either consumers or businesses. Anyone who has tried to extricate a music CD from its packaging will appreciate the point about "ease of use." If you've ever opened an outer carton only to discover damaged products inside, then you understand the critical role of packaging in physical protection.

In the physical environment of the supply chain, packaging plays a critical role in ensuring safe transfer and movement. Here, effective handling is paramount so package weight is important. Handles can help promote safe movement for weighty cartons. For oversized items, such as big-screen television sets, they are indispensable.

Compared to wooden pallets, plastic pallets, with their lighter weight, lack of splinters, resistance to breakage, and downright lack of appeal to rodents, can improve physical utility. In an age of global trade, the inherent resistance of plastic pallets to insect infestation is extremely attractive because it limits the need for chemical treatments.

Stretch wrap is a special film for wrapping and packaging a load of mixed products onto a pallet. It offers a valuable tool for handling pallet loads. Stretched-wrapped pallets reduce the likelihood of product damage and enhance safe handling throughout the supply chain.

## Waiter, There's a Fly in My Soup …

Globalization has added another twist to packaging. Importers must comply with an international treaty — the IPPC — to stop the spread of pests. The most notorious pest is the Asian long-horned beetle, a ravenous killer of hardwood trees. Next comes the emerald ash borer, another émigré from Asia.

To stop the spread of such pests, the IPPC has developed a rule, ISPM 15, that requires that pallets be chemically fumigated, heat treated, or made from alternative material.

## The Challenge of Putting Packaging in its Place

Despite its importance, packaging continues to maintain a low profile in supply chain management. No one notices it or pays it much attention, until packaging fails in one of its manifold missions. Very few think in advance about the power of packaging throughout supply chain planning and operations.

In extended global supply chains, however, packaging grows in importance. There's more handling, often involving less-sophisticated people and equipment. Oceanic container transport involves different stresses than over-the-road trucking might. Standards might be different — and variable — in diverse sourcing locations.

National regulations and consumer sensitivities are certainly different. It's our challenge to define packaging requirements throughout the supply chain if we expect to preserve the safety and quality levels we've been taking for granted for all these years.

# ON-DEMAND SUPPLY CHAINS

Nothing is too small to know, and nothing is too big to attempt.
*William Van Horne*

It's pretty hard to be efficient without being obnoxious.
*Kin Hubbard*

Do what you can, with what you have, where you are.
*Theodore Roosevelt*

Good is not good, when better is expected.
*Thomas Fuller*

## In the Beginning

On-demand supply chain management— it's an intriguing concept, but what does it mean? Is it about physical supply chain management to support businesses providing on-demand service to their customers? Or is it about the information systems supporting these processes?

Or is on-demand an invented term designed to superficially differentiate usage-based supply chain management information systems in the marketplace?

Both are possibilities.

## Confusion Reigns

There are two principal schools claiming the on-demand domain, and they offer radically different views of what it means. One school, led by IBM, stakes out its territory in the realm of supply chain operations and the development of on-demand businesses. The other school of thought includes a number of vendors that are promoting "on-demand" supply chain management software. GSX, Mitrix, and Kinaxis are among the early providers, although more vendors are emerging all the time. So-called on-demand software is typically accessed through the Internet. Unlike traditional software, where a user buys a license for the application, providers of on-demand software charge their customers user fees for access to their wares.

## A Software Perspective

The research organization Aberdeen Group covers the software industry and has reported positive developments in the use of what it calls software-as-a-service (SaaS). Aberdeen contends that early adopters of on-demand supply chain software are also early beneficiaries of cost savings, faster implementations, and quicker return on investment (ROI).

Aberbeen's research indicates that on-demand is catching on with customers, too. The company reports that more than half the respondents to its recent surveys have indicated that they're considering on-demand applications for at least a part of their total supply chain management software applications. In addition, it says that companies can be up and running with on-demand software in as little as three months, which is considerably faster than the traditional software implementation. They also realize an ROI in less than a year and obtain a significantly lower total cost of ownership.

Current on-demand solutions are not expected to replace traditional applications. But they do appear to be finding favor with small and mid-sized businesses by bringing them into a milieu in which only larger companies could previously afford to play.

As for functionality, Aberdeen Group reports that on-demand vendors offer the following functions: forecasting, customer inventory management, supply chain visibility, and transportation management in customer-facing and supplier-facing applications.

## Provider Positioning

Not surprisingly, the software developers appear to have a somewhat more grand view of their landscape. Each seems to define on-demand supply chain management to fit the limitations of its own particular product set. It takes a close reading of the developers' materials to work through the extravagant language and ferret out what the software *really* does.

For example, one well-known firm promotes its product as "revolutionary" and a "first-ever," that offers "critical functionality." At its core, the software facilitates the creation of on-line trading communities and allows information to be exchanged. Among other functions, it offers modules designed to manage forecasting, logistics, replenishment planning, sales order entry and fulfillment, warehousing, inventory, and more. Does the vendor truly offer everything a company needs to manage its supply chain? You may be the judge of that. Is this a useful product for certain companies in specific circumstances? No question that it is.

Another software and services provider focuses its on-demand supply chain management solutions on a role in business-to-business (B2B) cross-enterprise process coordination and simplification. Apparently aimed at a somewhat larger company, its products typically support demand planning with joint forecast models as well as product development with customer behavior analysis, and marketing and sales with joint promotions planning.

The vendor's trading grid approach links a company with both suppliers and customers, and provides complete flexibility in what software features and functions are used. Many standard e-commerce transactions are supported (e.g., payments, orders, advance ship notices) and the on-demand supply chain capabilities enhance the core offering. Our impression is that the software does not claim to do everything, but that a savvy user can use the data provided to improve plans and decisions throughout the supply chain.

A third provider takes another tack, concentrating on support for supply chain agility in the manufacturing arena. The high spots include real-time visibility into systems throughout the supply chain; alert and event management capability; change-impact analysis; what-if analysis; and collaborative scorecarding. The vendor is clearly positioning this product for decision support in a rapid-response world.

Because each software vendor is pushing its own agenda, we do not have uniformity in definitions of on-demand supply chain management.

## Big Blue Speaks

If IBM were just another small consultancy, it would be easy to dismiss its position and concentrate on the software vendor's take on on-demand supply chain management. But it's not. With an army of thousands upon thousands of consultants and an advertising budget large enough to keep several Third-World nations in rice and beans for the foreseeable future, IBM cannot be ignored.

IBM has been promoting its concept of on-demand business for some time now. Even if it is merely marketing hyperbole, its message is powerful: IBM contends that the process of energizing the supply chain is *the* key to enabling the on-demand business and transforming the base model for sustainable, competitive advantage.

When IBM canvassed CEOs, its survey showed responsiveness to be the number two top issue, after growth. Eighty percent of the respondents rated their companies as "less than capable" in responding to changing conditions and supply chain events. That assessment is interesting in light of the attention given the subject recently (see the chapter on Supply Chain Resilience).

IBM has focused on responsiveness and the on-demand concept after recognizing the impacts of major business trends, including:

- Increasingly demanding customers.
- Shrinking product life cycles, with innovation and speed-to-market the make-or-break factors.
- Supply chain complexity, including globalization.
- Physically extended supply chains, involving more players.
- Prevalence of e-business techniques and transactions.
- Unrelenting pressure for cost cutting.

Its vision for on-demand supply chains embraces four key capabilities:

- 1. Dynamic and fast response to events and changing conditions.
- 2. Open architecture systems infrastructure with real-time visibility throughout the supply chain.
- 3. Adaptability to seize market opportunities quickly.
- 4. Variable cost sensitivity, moving up or down, based on revenue.

A fifth element may be the development of sense-and-respond capability to monitor and manage exceptions, as well as to respond to demand shifts.

Other features of the on-demand supply chain include: on-line and real-time order configuration, updates, and status; scalable infrastructure for technology, organization, and processes in the distribution network; dynamic product and service bundling; and tight integration with supply chain partners in the areas of technology, communications, information, and planning.

Of course, IBM's process for determining the position of a company relative to its on-demand status and the steps necessary for improvement is designed to generate any number of consulting projects. That is to be expected.

In its view, the on-demand supply chain and the on-demand business are the next steps in the evolution of enterprises, taking the flexible and collaborative business to another level of technology-enabled integration. They make the strong case that, ultimately, on-demand is not an option, but a necessity.

## How We See It

On-demand supply chain management is here to stay, no matter how it's defined or what it's called. On the software side, we expect to see the continuing development of better and better tools for broader markets. We can only hope that the people selling them haven't recently escaped from a used car lot.

As for IBM, the consulting firm espouses solid concepts about the direction that our supply chain world needs to travel. Even though they are being used to provide gainful occupation for all those consultants, it doesn't negate the value of what they're saying.

Whether all of us will include on-demand supply chain management in our professional vocabularies remains to be seen. We're reasonably sure that we'll be using the concepts and the tools in the future in some form or another.

# SUPPLY CHAIN FINANCE AND ACCOUNTING

Everything was numbered and weighed, and all the weight was recorded at that time.
*Ezra 8:34*

The pen is mightier than the sword, but no match for the accountant.
*Jonathan Glancey*

It is time that financial types developed a greater tolerance for imprecision,
because that's the way the world is.
*John C. Burton*

The best way to destroy the capitalist system is to debauch the currency.
*John Maynard Keynes*

## Green Eyeshades and Balance Sheets

We've elsewhere spoken to the need to couch what we do in supply chain management in the language of the executive suite, paying particular attention to the chief financial officer. For example, what are the financial ramifications of supply chain performance? Which levers of corporate achievement can we pull? What needles of company performance can we move on the dials?

Two leading thinkers on these topics are Dr. Stephen Timme of FinListics Solutions and Dr. Terrance Pohlen of the University of North Texas. Timme writes, teaches, and trains extensively in the arena of increasing shareholder value through supply chain management. Pohlen researches, publishes, and speaks on cost and cost accounting issues in supply chain management.

There are numerous techniques available to measure financial performance and the contributors to it. The least useful are the traditional ones — cost accounting, performance to budget, etc. In their place, we're going to delve into management accounting, rather than accounting as a function or cost accounting, or the transactional aspects of "keeping the books." Management accounting concerns organizational financial performance — converting data (quantitative financial data) into information, and information into intelligence that can be acted upon for the corporate good.

Contemporary alternatives such as Activity-Based Costing (ABC), the Balanced Scorecard (BSC), and Economic Value Added (EVA) provide different perspectives on financial performance. Integrating them provides a powerful view of overall performance. In fact, research continually shows that EVA leaders are shareholder value leaders. As we said at the start of this book, driving shareholder value should be an ultimate objective of supply chain management.

## Wait a Minute — What's Wrong With Traditional Accounting?
Well, a lot, to be blunt. In brief, traditional accounting takes approaches to reporting that can obscure, rather than reveal, what operating managers and executives really need to know to strategize and run the business.

Generally Accepted Accounting Principles (GAAP) provide a framework intended to result in fair and honest presentations of results. In fact, the accountant's job is to be as clever and creative as possible in GAAP application and interpretation, with the objective of presenting income statements and balance sheets that put a company in the best possible light even if that light distorts underlying reality. That exercise can ignore the ultimate test of performance — from a shareholder perspective — of whether the company has more or less value than it did in the prior period.

In our opinion, within the details of the income statement, traditional accounting tends to take shortcuts for ease of reporting and transactional processing. Accordingly, allocations are often used to simply — and simplistically — spread large cost elements over and among a multitude of transactions, products, and processes. Costing systems may ignore process realities in favor of techniques that have tax benefits or ease-of-reporting advantages, e.g., LIFO, FIFO, and variations of average-actual and standard cost bases.

## Activity-Based Costing (ABC)
When examining the cost side of things, ABC can transform the quality of data and information underlying key operational and strategic decision-making by changing the way costs are presented. To be honest, it is detailed, and it takes a fair amount of work to implement. But when done well, ABC can make for what Dr. Phil calls "a changing day in your life."

Among other things, activity-based costing:
- Can more accurately show how changes in service affect cost — and profitability.
- Can link indirect costs and resources with specific customers and supply flows.
- Can bring focus to high-cost activities and processes.
- Can provide more complete and more accurate visibility to costs and trade-offs.

How do you go about setting up and using ABC? Although detailed, demanding, and time-consuming, ABC does not need the services of rocket scientists to be useful and successful. The objective of the exercise is to understand which customers and products are more profitable — and why. To understand cost drivers, you shine a strong light on where cost reduction and value creation need to take place. When you learn *why* costs go up or down, you are able to communicate ABC information throughout the organization consistently.

In summary, activity-based costing provides a methodology to *accurately* associate both direct and indirect costs with those elements that consume an organization's resources — activities, customers, products, and individual supply chain flows. It translates and transforms traditional reactive cost reporting into proactive actionable information.

The process begins with a two-stage approach to assigning costs. First, resource costs are assigned to activities, and those activity costs are assigned to products and customers. Not only does the activity cost show *all* the resources, it also identifies resources needed or not needed when activity volumes change.

The level of costing detail must be carefully considered. It generally falls into the range of plus-or-minus 30 in finding the right balance of comprehensiveness and detail. In all cases, costs are assigned on a per-activity basis — per shipment, per unit, etc.

Finally, cost objects are defined for all customers, channels, products, and so forth. This results in a bill of activities, resembling a manufacturing bill of materials, which incorporates all relevant activities and their costs.

## Economic Value Added (EVA)

Like most of what we're discussing, Economic Value Added (EVA) is considerably simpler than brain surgery. But it offers a powerful tool in corporate performance analysis. EVA, a proprietary term coined by the research, analysis, and consulting firm Stern Stewart & Co., advances the proposition that nothing we do is important unless it helps create value. EVA is one of a family of Value Based Management systems, and is premised on the notion that only surplus value — after the cost of capital is considered — is real for shareholders. The following equation defines EVA: Net Operating Profit After Taxes (NOPAT) minus the Cost of Capital times Total Asset value.

Total Assets are the sum of Current Assets plus Fixed Assets. Current Assets are inventory, cash, and the like. Fixed Assets consist of plant, equipment, and similar items. Simple so far.

NOPAT is simply Net Profit minus Taxes, and Net Profit is merely Gross Margin, less Total Expenses. Gross Margin is Sales minus Cost of Goods Sold. No mysteries, yet.

Supply chain management, however, can profoundly affect several elements of the EVA calculation, beginning with Asset Productivity. For example, getting more out of existing plant and equipment assets improves productivity. Inversely, reducing space and equipment improves asset productivity. Managing inventories to the right levels of investment and the right levels of performance can boost turns, service levels, and customer satisfaction.

We can drive out costs — waste — and manage costs to the optimum when reduction is not in the cards (see the chapter on Supply Chain Cost Reduction). We can affect sales and market share — top-line performance — through superb operational execution in fulfillment and customer service.

Our work in reducing cycle times, improving flexibility, and reducing all forms of waste affects many elements of the EVA equation. We can show these impacts in a DuPont financial analysis model.

This sample DuPont model illustration demonstrates how individual elements — if changed or improved — can affect levels of corporate performance, such as ROI and ROA.

In short, supply chain management professionals in manufacturing, procurement, physical distribution, planning, and information systems can move the EVA needle like nobody else can. Increasingly, the EVA needle is the most important one of all.

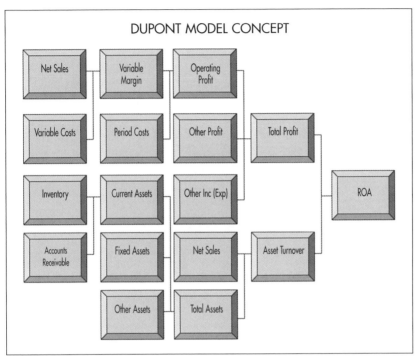

## Balanced Scorecard (BSC)

Some good early work in defining and describing the balanced scorecard was produced by David Norton and Robert Kaplan in the early '90s. They outlined the four interlinked BSC perspectives as follows:

- The internal business perspective — what must we excel at?
- The customer perspective — how do customers see us?
- The financial perspective — how do we look to shareholders?
- The innovation and learning perspective — can we continue to improve and create value?

The balanced scorecard approach links the cause and effect elements of the four perspectives, with innovation and learning driving improved operational performance. That performance, in turn, supports improved positioning with customers. That, in turn, ultimately translates to increased shareholder value based on a stronger top line, well-managed costs, a better bottom line, and increased asset utilization.

There are variations on the balanced scorecard theme in which diverse performance metrics — output, quality, human resources — are displayed. That's a good thing in general, but it's not as useful as connecting all the links. When you can demonstrate how training drives pick accuracy, and increased pick accuracy supports greater customer satisfac-

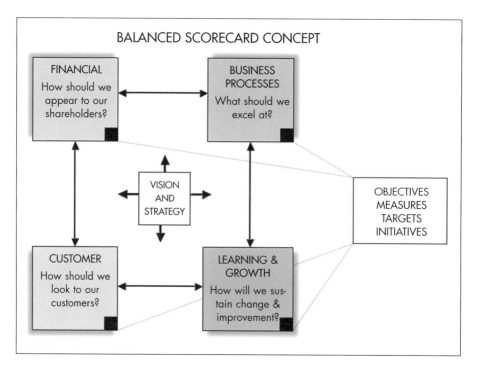

BALANCED SCORECARD CONCEPT

FINANCIAL — How should we appear to our shareholders?

BUSINESS PROCESSES — What should we excel at?

VISION AND STRATEGY

OBJECTIVES MEASURES TARGETS INITIATIVES

CUSTOMER — How should we look to our customers?

LEARNING & GROWTH — How will we sustain change & improvement?

tion, and that, in turn, leads to higher sales, margins, and ultimately, share value, that story becomes compelling. It's also a story that C-level executives want and need to hear.

A word of caution. It's possible to create a diverse scorecard that may be called "balanced," but that does not show the real drivers and their impact on how the supply chain succeeds or fails.

## All Together, Now

How powerful is this notion of tying ABC, EVA, and BSC together? Well, imagine managing from reported BSC results, and managing toward BSC objectives. Consider what it would be like if the financial perspective focused on economic value added — real, after-tax growth in the company's underlying economic value — and its positive impact on share value. Think what it would be like if you added to that the ability to know the costs and profits associated with major activities, core products, and key customers. You get the picture.

Does this combination and integration define Utopia? Of course not. Is it practical and real? You bet. Is it easy? Not at all. Is it worth the effort? Just look at the companies doing it. They're the leaders in cash-to-cash cycle performance. They're the leaders in shareholder value gains. They are outperforming their industries, and they have been in the top tier of supply chains, irrespective of industry. Think Dell and Apple. Think Best Buy and Wal-Mart. Think Toyota, Procter & Gamble, and Johnson & Johnson. Think Tesco.

Are they all doing everything perfectly in terms of ABC/BSC/EVA integration and execution? Probably not, but they're clearly focused on knowing costs, building value, and general supply chain excellence.

# INVENTORY MANAGEMENT

Prediction is very difficult, especially about the future.
*Niels Bohr*

Everything in excess is opposed to nature.
*Hippocrates*

Excess on occasion is exhilarating.
It prevents moderation from acquiring the deadening effect of a habit.
*W. Somerset Maugham*

Gentlemen prefer bonds.
*Andrew Mellon*

## Clearing the Air

Inventory! Where to begin? When it comes to customer service, there's never enough. When management takes a look, there's always too much. What's the deal?

We'll skip over much of the arcane terminology and mind-numbing explanations of how to calculate Safety Stock and Reorder Points. There are whole books devoted to discussions of ROP, EOQ, MAD, and FIFO as well as our favorite acronyms, FISH (First In, Still Here) and LID (Last In, Disappeared).

The core rules of thumb are as follows:

- 1. The order quantity, for most products and organizations, is simply expected consumption over the period of the order replenishment cycle. Then you add to that the impacts of known events, such as promotions, deals, holidays, or weather — also known as "special cause variation."

- 2. The reorder point is reached when the working stock on hand is equal to expected consumption over the replenishment cycle.

- 3. Every inventory replenishment cycle has a "risk period" equal to its length; i.e., if the period's demand all occurs on the first day, there may be no inventory left to fill any orders that might trickle in on other days.

- 4. Safety stock is intended to provide protection for variability in supply performance and demand patterns (also known as "common cause variation").

▪ 5. Safety stock quantities are in addition to the working stock. They are not included in reorder calculations.

▪ 6. Special cause variation should not be included when calculating safety stock requirements.

## Risk, Punishment, and Reward

Most everyone in the supply chain world faces the Hobson's choice of keeping a lot of inventory on hand to hide problems or lowering the inventory in order to expose and fix the problems. Each choice brings risk, cost, and the prospect of punishment. What are some of the problems? Here are a few:

▪ Rummy prognostications (a British euphemism for lousy forecasts).
▪ Incomplete, inaccurate, and delayed communications when things go awry.
▪ Inventory inaccuracy.
▪ Inexplicably long lead times.
▪ Customer demand spikes or collapses.
▪ Unreliable vendors and suppliers.
▪ Manufacturing breakdowns.

Is any of this sounding familiar? It should. These are what people who haven't come to grips with permanent fixes in the inventory management arena face regularly.

We don't want to make light of a serious condition. Research by Dr. Walter Zinn and others at The Ohio State University has shown a remarkable resistance of inventory levels to the improvements wrought by improved supply chain management. In the era of globalization, 10,000-mile supply chains, monsoons, and port congestion, inventories *must* rise even in the best of circumstances.

After lengthy analysis, we've concluded that there are two approaches to the persistent and growing inventory problem. One emulates the 12-step recovery programs used to combat addictions (yes, inventory can be addictive) and puts together a 12-step program for good inventory health.

The other approach recognizes that, all other factors aside, good inventory managers tend to do a handful or two of positive things that set them, and their inventories, apart from the mediocre. Stealing shamelessly from Dr. Stephen Covey, we've assembled the Seven Habits of Highly Effective Inventory Managers.

Both the seven habits and the 12 steps can make a powerful difference in whether you manage inventories or inventories manage you.

## The 12-Step Program to Good Inventory Health

Like all such programs, this one requires lots of hard work and persistence as well as strength and stamina. Here are thumbnails of the 12 steps:

▪ **1. Use Pareto analysis.** It's difficult to have too much analysis, and most everything is subject to the 80/20 rule and ABC analysis. Remember that As account for 80 percent, Bs 15 percent, Cs 5 percent, and Ds 0 percent. 80 percent of what? Almost anything — sales,

*Note for the curious: Wilfredo Pareto was an Italian economist, sociologist, and writer whose research on the distribution of wealth was adapted by Joseph Juran, an early pioneer in the American quality movement, and applied to operational as well as economic analysis, becoming known as the "80/20 rule" in the process.*

inventory, cube movement, SKU counts. You'll quickly see the imbalances between and among sales, inventory, space, etc. You'll also find "C" customers buying "C" SKUs — a lucrative target all by itself. As to Ds, solving the mystery of how SKUs with no sales can consume inventory has a big payoff.

- **2. Reduce replenishment lead (cycle) times.** Suppliers sometimes welcome a collaborative effort to make them more efficient and find ways to take time out of their supply chains. Don't forget that some of the time might be on your end, too.

- **3. Restructure order cycles and quantities.** Sounds like a no-brainer. Just order half as much twice as often. Unless the advantage is eaten up by increased transportation costs. Then you'll need to get creative. Aggregating all of a supplier's SKUs into one shipment can help on the transportation side. Of course, it's not as easy as it sounds, but it's not as hard as the doubters would have you believe, either.

- **4. Improve forecasting.** The dreaded "F" word is coming back into vogue and usefulness. Almost made obsolete in the Just-In-Time world, forecasting takes on new relevance in a world of extended supply chains.

- **5. Eliminate obsolete stock.** Sounds easy, we know. But it often requires enormous strength to overcome objections from either the Sales or Finance departments. If you can't get rid of it, at least move it off the premises.

- **6. Centralize inventories.** Particularly for high-cube and low-unit-volume items, or for those with a genuinely lower service level requirement. Consider having a master distribution center approach for selected items and product families.

- **7. Customize service levels.** More heresy, but not every customer deserves top-of-the-line service. And certainly not on all products.

- **8. Manage SKU counts.** Making blanket reductions in SKU counts isn't a practical approach, but intelligent and disciplined product and product family life cycle management can lessen SKU proliferation.

- **9. Reduce demand variability.** Get real about intrinsic underlying demand. Next, quantify how much apparent demand is artificial — created by deals and specials, etc. Then work with Sales and Marketing on smoothing the curves.

- **10. Reduce supply variability.** Attack this with all you've got. A consistent four-week replenishment cycle is preferable to one that averages three, but ranges from two to seven. Shine a bright light on suppliers, how they perform, and how they can be motivated.

- **11. Control inventory accuracy.** You wouldn't think this would still be an issue in the 21st century, but it is. It's all about good processes, good discipline, good technology, and good problem-solving methods. Cycle counting helps.

- **12. Get metrics right.** Disconnected, siloed measurements will bring an organization to its knees, contributing to high inventories. Comprehensive and unified metrics need to be part of your way of life. Think total supply chain cost, perfect orders, and customer satisfaction.

These 12 actions are powerful, all by themselves. But there is another set of activities that can augment these and magnify their impacts on inventory performance. We've summarized them as a collection of seven practices, as outlined below.

## The Seven Habits of Highly Effective Inventory Managers

Some managers seem to do a good job with inventories, day in and day out. Nothing is really effortless, but these folks don't seem to sweat inventory problems as much, or as often, as some of the rest of us. OK, what do these people do that makes them better than average? Looking at improving inventory performance from another angle, we see real advantages from:

- **1. SKU-level inventory management.** Inventory is not a singular entity. It can be managed, even analyzed, in the aggregate. The battle is won by being smart about line items — quantities, dollars, demand, the whole works.
- **2. Supplier-level planning/ordering.** A potential gold mine with willing supplier partners, when short-cycle orders for reduced quantities can be aggregated for effective transportation.
- **3. Aggressive product life cycle management.** The market tells us when a product or line's time is up. We just can't afford to be blind to the signals.
- **4. Continuous analysis.** Analysis can't be the program of the month. It's got to be a way of life, with everyone trained in techniques and problem-solving.
- **5. Application of proven tools to problem-solving.** Use tools instead of guesses, data instead of opinions. If it was good enough for W. Edwards Deming, it's good enough for us.
- **6. Intimate key supplier relationships.** The quality of relationships with principal suppliers provides a key to unlocking the potential for closer integration, reduced cycle times, improved quality, and greater reliability and dependability.
- **7. Manufacturing integration.** This is a little like an in-house version of intimate supplier relationships, but is frequently a tougher sell.

All these are easier to say than to do. Communication provides the glue that holds it all together — for suppliers, customers, and internal departments — to give a clear picture of stock levels, order status, transportation issues, quality, and performance!

## Wait, There's More!

Those highly effective inventory managers have another trick up their sleeves. It is exquisite knowledge of their costs — all the costs associated with acquiring, holding, and disposing of inventory. Call it the 8th Habit, if you will. They recognize that inventory held for between three and four years has cost as much to hold as it did to create in the first place.

They have another Habit — a habit of expressing costs in language that the boss can understand. They aren't afraid to use graphics to tell a cost story in place of columns of figures. Or to use DuPont models to show how inventory can impact corporate performance.

## In Closing

Never forget these key points:

- Inventory is a liability, not an asset, no matter what the accountants say.
- Inventory can't be managed — reduced, eliminated, whatever — in a vacuum.
- Building inventory is a delusional way to "improve" manufacturing efficiency.
- "You can't sell it if it's not on the wagon" hasn't been true since the sales force really did sell off the back of a wagon.
- Most important of all, inventory is the result of doing things right — or doing them wrong.

# GLOBALIZATION'S IMPACT ON SUPPLY CHAINS

The Internet levels the playing field, and lets companies reach
into the farthest corners of the planet for partners and customers.
*Eric Chabrow*

Like all great travelers, I have seen more than I remember,
and remember more than I have seen.
*Benjamin Disraeli*

The world is a book, and those who do not travel, read only a page.
*St. Augustine*

The new electronic interdependence re-creates the world in the image of a global village.
*Marshall McLuhan*

## Introduction

Let's deal with some misconceptions right up front. To hear some people and organizations talk, you'd think that offshoring had just been invented, and that European supply
chains are right after iPods as the next big thing.

But globalization is not something that's coming, something we need to get ready for.
It's here. In fact, globalization has been a reality of supply chain life for several years, even
decades for some companies.

So, if you're not involved in a global supply chain now, you are behind. Or maybe you
don't fully understand how far your supply chain really reaches.

In any case, the phenomenon of globalization affects many dimensions of supply chain
planning and operations. Let's talk about a few ...

## Sourcing and Procurement

When it comes to offshore sourcing, China is the nation that immediately comes to mind. But offshoring is not only about China. There are countries all over the world that offer low-cost, well-educated, and highly motivated workforces as well as the technological support needed to produce at a world-class level. The choices for offshoring operations are diverse — from Asia to the Pacific islands, to Central and South America, and, finally, to Africa.

It has become a major sourcing challenge to balance sources with markets. It requires making trade-offs between cost, quality, and reliability. It also requires assessing the risk of sharing designs and technology with partners who might not have the same reverence for intellectual property that we do.

Finally, sourcing and procurement decisions have a profound impact on the time consequence of extended geographic supply chains.

## Inventory Management

Overall inventory levels in a global supply chain must inevitably rise. The time involved demands greater working stocks than in any traditional inventory planning calculation. Time uncertainties because of weather and port congestion drive added safety stocks to accommodate variation in delivery from suppliers.

The inventory quantities involved can be enormous — multiples of what we've been accustomed to with domestic sourcing. On top of that, there are limits to how much we can rely on such techniques as postponement to offset the inventory effects of time and uncertainty.

## Distribution Facility Location

The creation of time- and cost-effective distribution networks has been made significantly more complex by globalization. Not only have sources been rearranged around the world, but markets have also tended toward global diversity.

What was once a set of simple national or regional manufacturing and distribution nodes and spokes has become a complex network of integrated source and destination solutions. When choosing facility locations, companies need to look at the whole network rather than just individual or independent components.

An Excel spreadsheet and some mapping software won't do the network design and facility location job in a world of globalized supply chains. Major league network modeling tools are required in addition to cleansed data.

## Logistics Service Provider Outsourcing

Similarly, globalized supply chains change the game when it comes to selecting logistics service providers (LSPs). Given the complexities inherent in international trade, it's no longer practical to use one LSP for distribution center operations and another for transportation once the supply chain begins to stretch around the world. This is a job for a single LSP that offers global reach, consistency in execution, technology support, and information visibility.

Furthermore, the LSP needs to be capable in planning and managing — and sometimes operating — the global supply chain from sourcing through delivery to customers. It needs to be capable of working across oceans through continents over borders, handling both container loads and fulfillment of "eaches" — all in the most appropriate mode and all with the perfect order mentality.

It's a far cry from the old days of public warehouses and private fleets.

## Transportation

Over the past decade, the world of transportation has seen plenty of structural change, independent of the impacts of globalization. That change is driving volume increases, certainly in air and ocean, but also in truckload movement from ports to points of distribution. Globalization isn't changing anything intrinsic within trucking, rail, air cargo, or ocean operations. It is, however, driving more points of integration among the modes in pursuit of comprehensive solutions.

Today a company or its LSP(s) must know more about all modes and understand how they can best fit together. In the global supply chain, there's every chance that most, if not all, modes will be involved to one degree or another, especially when both ends of the supply chain are considered.

Goods manufactured offshore must get from the factory to a port by truck, rail, or even air. If it's a seaport, they will move by ocean carrier back to the United States. Of course, there will have been decisions about how to load the containers, taking into account downstream distribution preparation. If it's an airport, the goods will move by air carrier, either on a planned or an expedited basis.

Once the goods arrive in the United States, there are more choices to be made. For example, you have to decide whether to use rail or truck to move the containers to their destination, whether it's a DC, a retail store, or some other location.

It was easier to deal with these questions when they were periodic events. Today, the movements across oceans or borders are expected to operate as synchronized components of corporate supply chains.

## Other

The integration of manufacturing into a quick-response cohesive supply chain makes up a much tougher challenge when the supply chain is thousands of miles long, crisscrosses back upon itself, and has an order fulfillment cycle time measured in weeks instead of hours or days. Just-In-Time needs serious redefinition in the global supply chain model.

Warehousing, especially receiving, is heavily impacted by the global supply chain. Unloading containers is often different from handling other media. Order and, therefore, received quantities tend to be greater than with replenishment from domestic sources. A resulting inventory increase can stress physical capacities, requiring a new level of planning as well as flexible access to storage and operating space.

If reverse logistics flows require that returned goods be sent back to a point of overseas manufacture, the timelines get longer than they would be if domestic manufacturers were involved, and the planning and execution of the necessary logistics becomes more complicated.

Information systems in the globalized supply chain place greater demands for synchronization and interface across the chain, and the requirement for visibility throughout the chain becomes both intense and vital.

## OK, What About China?

China's growth has been staggering to date, and it's projected to continue unabated. Supply chain problems with sourcing from China have so far been covered over with rice paper. Armstrong & Associates' *China Logistics Report 2004* (as reported in *Global Logistics and Supply Chain Strategies)* points out 10 challenges the Chinese must solve for long-term supply chain logistics success. They include:

- Lousy physical infrastructure, including transport and warehouses.
- Over-regulation at multiple levels.
- Bureaucracy that imposes Communist Party contacts at many levels, and its reluctance to let Western profits leave the country.
- Deficient training, and disinterest in better ways of doing things.
- Lack of technology infrastructure, both computing and communications.
- Underdeveloped domestic logistics industry and commodity mentality.
- High transportation costs that are a hidden offset to low labor costs.
- Substandard warehousing and storage, made worse by poor training and management.
- Unbalanced internal and external trade flows resulting in lopsided container and transport location and utilization.
- Domestic trade barriers, adding time and cost to internal movement, including from manufacturing to port locations.

Until these are fixed, there are real limitations to the offshoring solution in China. It's time for U.S. companies to look beyond the rosy reports, and be realistic about the total cost of doing business there.

Here's something to keep in mind. For all the hoopla over China, the Number One exporter in the world is ... Germany — by a margin of 40 percent, according to France's *Le Monde*. The Number One importer, the United States, is also the Number Two exporter, so not all the jobs have left the country. Admittedly, China is moving fast. In fact, it has already passed Japan for the Number Three spot. In short, not everything has gone to China, or is going there, as may be witnessed by the emerging search for alternatives to China in Asian sourcing.

## Considerations in Offshoring

If you are getting close to moving selected operations offshore, there are a few key components for planning and decision-making. First and foremost, be certain that offshoring is really the right answer. Being less-than-stellar in performance may not be a good enough reason. Internal improvement or the application of technology really ought to be evaluated as solutions before leaping into the offshoring abyss. The statement "everyone else is doing it" may be as bad a reason for a company as it is for a teenager. Critically, it is vital to understand that offshoring won't fix bad processes and may even make them worse.

Next, a company must select a structural model — whether to set up a subsidiary, captive operation, or to outsource as part of the offshore move. That decision must take into account quality concerns as well as intellectual property issues. By the way, some companies are pursuing hybrid solutions that are an amalgamation of captive and outsourced operations.

Getting the remainder of the organization to support the offshored solution is mandatory for success, even more so than in the case of simple outsourcing. Associates and mid-managers can either kill or cure an offshoring adventure.

Be prepared for the need to invest more time than you might imagine in getting operations started — and in keeping them going. Throwing processes over the transom doesn't work when operations are next door, and that approach misses the mark by a greater margin when the new nerve center is thousands of miles away. The need for time and effort doesn't go away once things are up and running. Ongoing training is important, even vital, and quality control never goes away as an issue.

Also recognize that the offshore operator must be treated as an equal. This is a major factor in a good start-up and in a long-term success. To get the best effort and the best thinking from offshore partners, treat them as — surprise! — partners. Even if the service is seen as mundane in some quarters, avoid making the relationship an arms-length commodity purchase.

Finally, one alternative to consider is "near-shoring." This creates Tier One or Tier Two supply networks in reasonably low labor cost areas that are not as far off as Asia. This tactic is being used in Europe and in North America.

### And in the European Union . . .

Much has been made of the prospects generated by the expansion of the European Union (EU) from 15 to 25 member nations and plans to add a few more over the span of several years. The reality is that supply chain design and development has gone on somewhat independently of the artificial boundaries of the union.

Manufacturing has already migrated to where it needs to be for wage and market demand. Russia, Ukraine, and the rest will continue their economic evolution, whether the EU beckons or not.

One interesting benefit of opening borders, though, has been the potential to move skilled professions and labor from high-unemployment member countries to welcoming locales with expanding economies and indigenous labor constraints. This explains the Polish truck drivers and distribution center employees relieving the shortages in the Netherlands, the legendary number of Polish plumbers in London, and the Polish assembly line workers in a newly prosperous Ireland.

### End Thought

Despite all this offshoring and global movement, customers' expectations for service remain the same. In a globalized supply chain, we've got to execute a significantly more complicated dance just to stay even with the game. Welcome to the world we are already in.

Don't forget to review the source material in Tom Friedman's *The Lexus and the Olive Tree* and *The World Is Flat.*

# SUPPLY CHAIN COST REDUCTION

Problems cannot be solved at the same level of awareness that created them.
*Albert Einstein*

A person who can't pay, gets another person who can't pay, to guarantee that he can pay.
*Charles Dickens*

Willful waste brings woeful want.
*Thomas Fuller*

There is nothing so useless as doing efficiently that which shouldn't be done at all.
*Peter F. Drucker*

## Once Upon a Time ...

Way back when, before we began to drown in high-concept management fads, cost reduction was a straightforward and constant management objective. No one was hesitant or bashful about admitting it. Almost all of the major consultancies, and many of the minor ones, provided cost reduction services to clients. Some outfits did nothing but cut costs, and they created legends around themselves and their founders. Names like Alexander Proudfoot and George S. May in the United States, and Berenschot in Benelux come to mind.

To be honest, the term "cost reduction" got a little tarnished as the years passed. Some individuals and firms may have lost sight of the bigger picture, pulling out all stops to achieve short-term and unsustainable results. The legendary "Chainsaw" Al Dunlap took what had come to be seen as a dark art to either new highs or lows, depending on one's perspective — well before there were reports of cooking the books.

Many of us in the business at the time sought balance and context in pursuing cost reduction in organized and systematic ways, recognizing two cardinal principles:

- *You can't save your way to success, and*
- *You can't spend your way to survival.*

## More Recently ...

In the supply chain business, and all business in fact, we have not lacked for programs and initiatives intended to streamline supply chains, simplify operations, and generally change the world. They've all pretty much promised to:

- Reduce cycle times.
- Improve service.
- Delight customers.
- Close the gap with leaders.
- Leapfrog the competition.
- Create new paradigms.
- Lower costs.
- Wring inventory out of the system.

We'll forget the part about seamless integration for a moment.

Remember ECR (Efficient Consumer Response) in the grocery industry? A few years ago, it promised to take $30 billion out of the supply chain. Don't know about you, but we're still waiting for the price of victuals to come down.

It's not just ECR, of course. There have been plenty of other acronym-heavy programs touted as the path to business salvation. They include VMI (Vendor Managed Inventory), QR (Quick Response), CPFR (Collaborative Planning, Forecasting, and Replenishment), and CRM (Customer Relationship Management). One of the hottest at the moment is PLM, which stands for Product Lifecycle Management. Nor can we forget the old ones: JIT (Just-in-Time), TQM (Total Quality Management), and SPC (Statistical Process Control). Their ideas live on in many "newer" solutions — including the ubiquitous "Lean."

## What Happens to These Great Ideas/Concepts/Programs?

It's not that they don't work or that they don't pay off. It's that they don't pay off often enough — and with a big enough payoff — for enough of the companies that try them. Implementation programs unravel. The results never materialize. And that scenario gets repeated over and over again, year after year. And so, the search goes on for the magic bullet that will slay the demons that are keeping us from reaching our full performance potential.

Unquestionably, there are many factors behind this parade of disappointments. I'll submit that one is that we, too, often lose focus on accountability for the hoped-for operational results.

It's not enough to merely hope — or even to believe — that inventories will shrink, or headcount diminish, or unit costs drop, or transportation costs fall, or service performance escalate, or customer satisfaction rise, or lost sales decline, or space utilization rise.

In parallel with program implementation and all the attendant project and risk management, you've got to devote equivalent effort and intensity to key outcome metrics and reporting. You must pay serious attention to:

- Reporting formats and frequencies.
- Target audiences and perspectives.
- Data and information sources and integrity.
- Relevance to and dependencies on the new program.
- Organizational importance, independent of the new program.

But the purpose here is not to bash the things that haven't perhaps gone quite right in the past. The real messages are:

▪ Practical and real cost reductions are embedded in the idealism of the newest programs. You've just got to organize and concentrate on going after them — relentlessly.

▪ Cost reduction opportunities typically abound within today's operations. You don't have to wait for the latest management program (with its companion acronym), or the newest software offering, or the big budget allocation needed to fund either one. You need to go get them.

## What Can We Do About Cost Reduction Now?

Plenty. There are actually opportunities for cost reduction in a number of areas throughout the supply chain.

If you can go at the challenge in the right way, it's very often possible to use the earlier, easier savings to fund the deeper, longer-term efforts that bring the greatest savings with the most sustainable impacts.

In general, each category of prospective cost reduction or savings opportunities contains both short-term and long-term potential. A thorough assessment can help sort through, sequence, and prioritize them, setting up an operational punch list to deliver a really big payday.

## Where's the Money?

The opportunities will vary from organization to organization. The hunt for cost reductions is, therefore, more of a process than a methodology — a journey of discovery that's likely to include a few false starts and wrong turns before the eventual destination is reached. Some focus areas for investigation include the following:

▪ 1. Inventory.
▪ 2. Transportation.
▪ 3. Facility layout and design.
▪ 4. Materials handling systems.
▪ 5. Labor.
▪ 6. Facility network rationalization.
▪ 7. Sourcing and procurement.
▪ 8. Manufacturing integration.
▪ 9. Employee retention.

Now let's examine each of these areas a little more closely.

## Inventory

Everybody picks on inventories. They're an obvious target because they're visible. But almost the worst thing you can do is to arbitrarily cut them. It is reasonable, though, to decide to completely rethink how they are built and maintained. It's also fair to challenge the math behind them, to re-engineer replenishment, to really understand customer demand, to look at deployment alternatives, and to mercilessly clean out the trash. The pain of the write-offs goes away after a while.

The literature is full of success stories about inventory-reduction programs that have brought seven-, eight-, and nine-figure savings, freed up capital, and driven greater return on assets (ROA) — all without degrading service. The notion that inventory and service levels are always in conflict is more true in theory than in actuality, especially when all the other options are explored.

All inventories are worth a close look: raw materials, work-in-process, finished goods, supplies, and consumables. The impacts can be enormous — a smaller asset base for improved return on investment; capital expenditures redeployed into productive assets and activities, or cash conservation during tough times.

With inventories going through the roof because of offshoring, the need for careful management and close attention is now greater than ever.

## Transportation

There's more to cost-effective transportation management than beating the lowest rates out of your carriers. Sometimes, higher nominal cost with greater flexibility and reliability proves a better way to go.

But when the fundamental transportation structure and mix have not been assessed in years, a total rethinking of carriers, modes, and alternatives can pay big dividends. After all, it's easy to fall into the habit of using overnight parcel service to make up time when things are going wrong upstream in the supply chain.

Private fleets should be examined as well. Savings can result from boosting productivity and equipment utilization. You may also find new opportunities to earn revenues from backhauls.

Inbound transportation is another area that often hides enormous opportunities. When vendors and suppliers specify carriers, when freight is "free" on over-minimum orders, or when price quotes include freight, inbound freight cost becomes a black hole. If you can get your suppliers to shed some light on those numbers, you may uncover some excellent prospects for cost reduction.

Case after case has been documented of the savings and other benefits of outsourcing to a 3PL for transportation management and transportation execution. Obvious candidates for outsourcing include operations whose fleet is sized for peak volumes, or whose drivers are a fixed-size crew of full-time employees, enjoying the same wage and benefit packages as highly compensated technical employees. But outsourcing is not always the answer.

The challenge is greater than ever today, with cost and capacity stresses in all modes, and unholy pressures from management to do more with less. When rising fuel prices are added to the equation, it's time to step back and reassess everything about the modes and processes used for freight movement.

## Facility Layout/Design

Most distribution centers are designed intelligently for the day they open for business. Things change over the years, though. Common changes include products handled (weight, cube, packaging, diversity, special requirements), customer order profiles (lines per, unit vs. case quantities), customer demands (labeling, pallet building, wrapping, value-added services), for example.

Every few years, it's worth taking a fresh look at the operation. That means re-examining layout, slotting, putaway processes, "hot" SKU pick and replenishment, cross-docking, and mechanization, and looking for alternatives that can give new life to a facility. Benefits include improved productivity, greater throughput, and improved space utilization. It's not uncommon to be able to avoid facility expansion — even replacement — by re-engineering the existing one.

The secret to success in this arena lies in integrating solution elements. It means understanding the delicate inter-relationship among the solution components. A manager has to understand the required inventory levels to meet service imperatives, material sources and arrival patterns, materials handling systems' capabilities and capacities, layout design driven by demand patterns, and information and system support needs. Finally, it means a full understanding of the nuts and bolts of work flows, processes, and timing.

## Materials Handling Systems

Time and change are not usually kind to mechanized systems.

Tweaking and fine-tuning can restore and even improve what the system was supposed to deliver in the first place. Removing bottlenecks, finding shortcuts, and elevating both performance and reliability can have profound impacts on both service levels and operating costs. Payback typically requires the most modest of investments.

Continuing shifts in SKU attributes, order profiles, and customer demand ought to be forcing periodic retrofits, anyway. If they haven't, the savings opportunity could be even greater.

Remember fixing 75 percent of the problem at 25 percent of the cost, and delivering 90 percent of the benefit is what makes corporate heroes.

## Labor

Facility design and materials handling improvements should obviously drive lower labor costs. But they require companion management initiatives to plan, track, and report if they are to succeed.

With or without the other labor-saving advances, workforce management can provide both cost and performance opportunities. Approaches need to include the application of process redesign, performance standards development, clear work and task assignment, flexible workforce planning and scheduling, hands-on floor supervision, and visible performance reporting. Ideally, these approaches should be part of an environment of high-performance continuous improvement.

Resist the temptation to announce arbitrary staffing cuts of "x" percent. Many organizations will find a way to scrape along with "x" percent less until the survivors hit the wall or warehouse volumes increase.

It's far better to establish unit cost and performance targets than to decree flat dollar amounts. It's also generally better to not over-engineer performance standards, and do not try to measure individuals. Logistics operations — particularly in warehousing — really represent team efforts.

Setting targets and managing workforce productivity are best done in the context of comprehensive process, workflow, IT, and cultural improvements.

## Facility Network Rationalization

The location, size, and mission of your DCs can make the difference between failure and success in dimensions of overall cost and service levels. Even companies that have built networks with elaborate modeling and simulation tools redesign the network every five years or so.

In looking to manage total transportation costs, it is vital to take the location and sources of supply into account. In evaluating service imperatives and options, it is critical to understand the differing requirements of specific market channels and of specific customers.

Understand that the network needs to include facilities with different missions. The facilities themselves may contain material and merchandise with different qualities. A single network solution doesn't work for every company.

Give some thought as to whether it makes sense to centralize "C" and "D" items. Perhaps high-weight, high-cube items should come out of central facilities. Master DCs might contain the entire network's safety stocks. High-volume, high-cube SKUs could be shipped direct from suppliers.

Having the correct network builds the ultimate foundation for:

- Managing transportation costs.
- Planning inventory investment.
- Containing facility and operations costs.

It also enables the delivery of the consistently high-quality service that customers need and demand.

Rationalization can be a code word for reducing the number of physical facilities in the network. A different structure or geographic network arrangement might be more suitable for meeting service needs.

Should you decide to rationalize, keep in mind that network modeling is primarily driven by transportation cost and service time considerations. A companion set of analysis tools is required to get the facility sizing, staffing, and inventory level questions answered adequately. By the way, transition costs are another issue entirely.

## Sourcing and Procurement

Supply side savings of the supply chain are no longer a matter of browbeating suppliers into dropping their prices.

The keys are in setting up process improvement and cost reduction teams in partnership with key suppliers — and in finding suppliers who want to play in this brand-new ball game. There's little limit to what can be accomplished with this approach.

Everything in the relationship is fair game. That includes packaging, ingredients, processes, physical handling, and product development. You should consider everything that can raise your quality, improve your manufacturing reliability, and enhance your relationship with *your* customers.

## Manufacturing Integration

Sometimes this facet falls under the Sourcing and Procurement umbrella. And sometimes it stands alone as you deal with internal manufacturing. In either case, driving up manufacturing reliability will lower costs and make downstream handling and distribution easier — and less expensive.

Synchronizing run strategies with demand at the customer level reduces stress and cost in distribution operations.

## Employee Retention

What does this have to do with cost reduction? Plenty.

Let's say you have an employee base of 1,000 and turnover amounts to 15 percent a year. That means you've got to source, hire, and train 150 new people a year. How much does that cost? $50,000 each? That would be $7.5 million a year. If it's only $10,000, it's still in the millions.

How long is the learning curve for the new worker to achieve proficiency? Six months? What is the productivity loss during the learning curve? How about the lost productivity of those around — and helping out — the new people?

By the way, can you even measure the cost of errors and customer service failures — even lost sales — related to the new staff? How many of the new hires don't make the cut and require a second replacement for the original departure?

This is, in total, a multi-million dollar opportunity in many, many companies, and it's worth calculating what the real cost is in your company. The total will almost certainly astonish you.

What to do? First, invest whatever it takes to find the right people in the first place. Second, create a winning culture in which leaders lead and listen, while contributors are recognized and rewarded. Third, weed out the poor performers early; this will send the right message to the "keepers." Fourth, be wage competitive. Yes, that does mean being the highest-paying organization in the area; it's just not worth losing good people for pennies "saved" in wages. Fifth, set turnover (voluntary, management decision, and circumstantial) objectives, and track actual turnover regularly. Analyze turnover reasons critically and honestly and execute programmatic solutions for them. Sixth and finally, when you reach your target objectives, set new ones, and go after them.

You don't have to be a big company to derive benefit in this area. If it's only a $4 million problem for you and you can cut turnover in half, that's $2 million to the bottom line. That can mean $2 million less to reduce through other ways.

## Summing up

Outsourcing would seem to be a natural stand-alone topic for inclusion in a summary of cost reduction opportunities, and it's usually worth considering third-party alternatives. But truth is, the economic advantage might not be as great as suspected when you're managing labor and inventory well in an effectively laid-out facility, with appropriate and up-to-snuff mechanization, and with your arms around transportation — in the context of the right network structure.

That doesn't mean that outsourcing isn't the right thing to do. But a third party's ability to do more with less ultimately relies on its ability to manage the cost elements outlined above.

How much might any of these efforts be worth? It's hard to say without knowing the individual situation. Years of experience suggest, though, that double-digit improvements in productivity, in throughput, in transportation cost, in labor cost, and in inventory investment are well within the realm of probability.

In conclusion, we have no shortage of places to look for cost reduction opportunities. But the savings don't necessarily come easily or automatically. The key to ultimate, sustainable success in this arena remains trying to keep cost reduction in the bigger picture of where a company needs to be competitively and strategically. Consider cost reduction initiatives as part of an integrated whole, and not simply as single-focus projects. There's nothing incompatible between intelligent cost reduction and a long-term, holistic view.

While we're waiting for the next big thing to capture our imaginations, and our bosses' checkbooks, maybe it's time to take another look at the nuts and bolts of supply chain cost reduction. It's worth considering how we can leverage straightforward and focused cost reduction efforts to make a difference in our operations — and on the bottom line.

# SECURING THE SUPPLY CHAIN

Put all your eggs in one basket — and watch that basket.
*Samuel Langhorne Clemens*

Better be despised for too anxious apprehensions, than ruined by too confident security.
*Edmund Burke*

Only in growth, reform, and change, paradoxically enough, is true security to be found.
*Anne Morrow Lindbergh*

What men want is not knowledge, but certainty.
*Bertrand Russell*

## The Day That Changed our World

We thought we had a fairly clear idea of what supply chain security was all about until Sept. 11, 2001. But on that day, we awoke to the realization that terrorists would not hesitate to exploit our transportation system to spread death and destruction. Suddenly the supply chain security challenge had taken on a whole new dimension.

Today, we remain somewhere between concerned and terrified about the prospect of lethal devices' being introduced into the supply chain — devices whose presumed targets are not the people, products, and distribution assets in that network, but rather, entire populations. We worry about the limited number of incoming containers that can feasibly be inspected. We look upon trucks as prospective ground-based missiles or delivery mechanisms for agents of mass destruction. We've poured extraordinary effort into developing technology solutions to detect tampering or to "see" into unopened containers and packages.

It's nearly impossible to attend a professional conference today without hearing about the latest security initiatives from Customs and Border Protection (CBP). Or about the challenges of safeguarding our borders without choking off trade. But as we debate how best to "harden" the nation's transportation system, we sometimes forget there's more to supply chain security than how to foil terrorists. There are plenty of challenges for us right here at home protecting our DCs, the people who work in them, and the products they house.

## The Basics of Securing the Supply Chain

In supply chain management, security involves three factors in priority sequence: protecting people, protecting property, and protecting product while controlling theft and mysterious disappearance.

## Protecting People

Everybody wants to improve workplace safety. Injuries and accidents are expensive, whether they happen on or off the job. Federal studies indicate that it is not the newly hired worker who's most likely to be hurt on the job. Those with five or more years of experience are more liable to be injured than those with less. Experience causes carelessness, which in turn leads to accidents. Surprisingly, fatigue is not the prime factor in accidents. More than half occur during the first four hours on the job. The most dangerous work in a warehouse is the unloading and loading of freight vehicles.

Ergonomics is the study of work methods that minimize the chance of on-the-job injuries. In warehousing, companies can improve ergonomics by avoiding conditions that cause an awkward or strained posture in the manual handling of merchandise. To reduce the risk of injury, carefully plan out the arrangement of stock in the warehouse. Those items that move fastest should always be stored in the "Golden Zone," the space between the average worker's belt and shoulder height (and as close as possible to pack locations/belts). Too often, they wind up in the "Twilight Zone," as time and change work their magic. Training and job review are essential. Every order picker should be taught the best way to select orders without undue fatigue or wasted motion. Here are a few ways to control the risk of manual handling injuries:

- Redesign the job.
- Train workers in better ergonomic techniques.
- Improve the employee selection process by hiring healthy people with healthy life styles.
- Change the layout so the average worker can get the job done more safely.

Rotating jobs every few hours has some advantages. When workers do different tasks, you reduce the possibility that repetitive motion will cause injuries. Job rotation also allows cross training and development of new skills. Finally, it reduces the possibility of job boredom.

## Substance Abuse in the Workplace

Though people are often reluctant to address it, another widespread problem in the workplace is employee substance abuse. In a typical workplace, at least 10 percent of the employees are likely to have some kind of problem with drugs or alcohol, or both. In a tight labor market, up to 50 percent of the people who are looking for work may have such problems, so it is vitally important for managers to be proactive in dealing with substance abuse in the workplace.

When considering discipline for substance abuse, it is well to recognize that there are three levels of violations that differ markedly in their impact. The first level would be the employee who reports to work while still under the influence of substances consumed during leisure time. That worker poses a safety threat to fellow workers.

The second level is the more serious offender who comes to work in possession of mood-altering substances. Possession suggests consumption on the job.

Most serious of all, the third level, involves the worker who brings substances to the workplace for the purpose of selling them to others on the crew. That offender may or may not be personally consuming the substances, but your workplace is being used as a market. This third-level offender deserves the strongest discipline.

Much has been written about the symptoms. But keep in mind that any single symptom of substance abuse might also be caused by something else. It is impossible for a layman to conclude that substance abuse is present. Unless the act of consumption is also observed, there is always reasonable doubt.

The most difficult challenge in handling abuse is intervention when an employee exhibits suspicious signs. A proven answer is to use the services of the company physician. The supervisor has the right to question the health of any employee who seems to be impaired while on the job. That includes the right to insist that the employee immediately visit the company doctor for a checkup to find out what is wrong. When this is done, the employer has an obligation to pay for the time spent during this process, and it is essential to control transportation to and from the doctor's office. Any physician can tell whether the symptoms are caused by substance abuse. If the employee refuses the medical visit, dismissal for insubordination is the available remedy.

Any prevention program should be based on the assumption that the goal is safety and health, not spying or discipline. Four steps are necessary for successful implementation of a substance abuse prevention program:

- Publication of a policy.
- A screening program for all new hires.
- Training and retraining of supervisors and managers to deal with intervention.
- A rehabilitation program.

The ramifications of substance abuse may be felt in damage to people, property, and product. It can be manifested in the world of information systems as well.

Here's a current reality. Methamphetamine manufacture and use has become epidemic and is by no means confined to biker bars and trailer parks. It has spread to the warehouse as well. Although a crystal meth habit impairs health, judgment, capability, and honesty rapidly, it also is not something a user can mask easily for long. Then things can go to pieces quickly.

## Protecting the Property

Though we tend to associate casualty losses with natural disasters such as fires, windstorms, floods, and earthquakes, it's also true that man-made disasters can cripple operations. In fact, nothing will paralyze a business as completely as a total power failure. Therefore, a growing number of operations are equipped with emergency generators that provide sufficient power to maintain computer operations and at least partial illumination in the buildings.

These major losses may cause business interruptions as well as loss of facilities and merchandise. One of the best ways to control casualty loss risks is to buy both insurance and loss prevention advice. The more progressive insurance companies have ongoing research and development programs that focus on loss prevention, as well as inspection services to measure their clients' ability to control the risk.

Cargo damage is usually caused by mishandling of the product. Damage to stored merchandise, however, is usually caused by one of these natural factors:

- Biological changes (e.g., spoilage).
- Chemical reactions.
- Cross-contamination.
- Improper temperature control.
- Age.

There are also possibilities for product tampering. The most notorious example to date was the Tylenol scare of the '80s.

## Theft and Mysterious Disappearance

While any product that moves through the supply chain can be stolen, thieves are more likely to target products that are either valuable or marketable, or both. Most cargo handlers apply selected standards, establishing more secure areas for those items that represent the greatest risk.

There are two kinds of warehouse thefts. Pilferage, also called *mysterious disappearance*, often involves small amounts of material that are stolen over a long time. Mass theft generally involves hijacking of a truck or break-in at a warehouse. Some locales in North America are more susceptible to the loss of an entire truck than others, and theft has become endemic in certain elements of global supply chains.

Typically, pilferage is the result of collusion, usually between a warehouse employee and a truck driver. This is the most difficult type of theft to control since no one has yet devised a 100-percent failsafe electronic or paper tracking system. Obviously, the best way to reduce the risk of theft is to be certain that every worker is honest.

Some psychological testing services claim that their products will expose the willingness to steal. Another deterrent to collusion theft is random detailed checking of outbound loads. A third method is the undercover investigation. Undercover services are provided by detective agencies as well as some specialist consultants. The investigator is hired as an ordinary employee and does everything possible to blend into the crew. This is a delicate and dangerous occupation that requires complete confidentiality.

Some companies install an employee "hot line" and encourage workers to use it to anonymously report suspicions of theft or other illegal activity in the workplace. Though critics of this approach argue that employees are unlikely to turn in their co-workers, advocates insist that if workers are persuaded that security is essential to the company's survival, they will expose dishonesty and criminal behavior.

## When Hacking Is Not a Cough, but a Crime

The Information Age has given rise to a new and potentially catastrophic security risk: the threat that your vital data and information will be compromised. Mission-critical information about customers, suppliers, accounts, products, and employees can be accessed by skilled and tenacious hackers. Both preventive countermeasures and reactive forensic computer specialists are vital weapons against this spreading threat.

The consequences of compromised information systems can easily be as serious as any physical security breach. Unfortunately, the tools for electronic breaking and entering are available to international terrorist communities, as well as to domestic criminals and "harmless," but warped, mischief makers.

## The Never-Ending Story

In the wake of 9/11, the federal government and Congress have been pushing for ever-stricter security measures. For example, the Department of Homeland Security's Transportation Security Administration (TSA) has proposed use of the Transportation Worker Identification Credential (TWIC). Under this program, a worker would have to show his or her TWIC card to gain entrance to secure areas associated with the maritime, air, rail, trucking, and mass transit sectors. Somewhere between 11 million and 15 million workers could be affected by TWIC.

The government has long been concerned about the security of containers, which can potentially be used to smuggle humans as well as dangerous substances. The use of special seals to secure containers has been proposed. Some have suggested the seals could be combined with RFID as a way to furnish information about the container and its origin, owner, and contents.

Customs is also looking to make revisions to the Customs-Trade Partnership Against Terrorism (C-TPAT), a program that promises members quicker border crossings in exchange for adopting security programs and procedures. That agency may also tighten air cargo security rules, unchanged since 1999, as well as stiffen import controls.

Meanwhile, the European Commission has finally got 'round to developing legislation for the land-based supply chain, featuring an emphasis on "known" cargo, shippers, and transporters. The long-awaited move has generated an expected mix of enthusiasm and guarded optimism.

## How Much Is Enough?

Admittedly, it's a scary world out there, and it's getting scarier. We have more and more security issues to worry about all the time. Tightening security — physical, electronic, personal — runs counter to our natural inclinations to openness and accessibility, which means we must put a lot of thought into how to proceed. When we make conscious decisions in favor of relaxed security, we need to understand the consequences. And when we commit to increased security, we need to understand the relevance and likelihood of the threat we're guarding against.

# STRATEGIES AND SUPPLY CHAINS

I WANTED JIM TO GET AN OVERALL VIEW OF WHAT GOES ON AROUND HERE.

The past does not equal the future.
*Anthony Robbins*

It's not what you put in, but what you leave out that counts.
*Andrew Wyeth*

Life is either a daring adventure or nothing.
*Helen Keller*

Business is a combination of war and sport.
*Andre Maurois*

## Introduction

We tend to get so wrapped up in the execution of supply chain activities that it's easy to forget about the strategic part of the equation. We're living and dying on a day-to-day basis, trying desperately to manage escalating costs while making customers happy with higher order fill rates and reliable deliveries. But if we believe the pundits, supply chain management is supposed to be strategic — a differentiator that can set us apart from our competitors in the marketplace.

Is that just a lot of hot air? Not at all. Well, not completely, anyway. The fact is, you do need a strategy. But there's a huge caveat here. SCM visions, strategies, and transformations are of limited use and less value if they aren't plugged into the corporate strategy. Having one without the other can yield consequences ranging from costly to fatal.

## Supply Chain Strategic Visions

There's no question that thinking about what *might* be — that is, envisioning the supply chain of the future — can be a compelling exercise. Consider the case of the telecommunications giant that labored with a distribution network of three primary DCs, nine regional warehouses, dozens of dispersed technology component storage centers, and several hundred end distribution points. Supply sources were many and varied with lots of potential overlap.

It was a fascinating exercise to reach a strategic vision that contemplated a network of one primary DC, no regional warehouses, a highly compressed number of technology centers, and 25,000 end distribution points for the moment — and with the potential for adding 30,000 additional distribution points for new products and markets in the longer term. All this with more concentrated and stronger supplier relationships, and the ability to bypass traditional storage and handling "touches" for selected lines.

But the exercise would have little point without the context of a corporate strategy. The company needed to set the objectives for marketplace position, customer relationships and service levels, and cost performance that the redesigned supply chain would enable and support.

## Foundations of Corporate Strategy

Defining the corporate strategy begins with an understanding of what business you are in as well as what business you *want* to be in, in the future. In thinking about supply chain structures and strategic design, it's vital to know that there are differences — at the corporate level and in supply chain management — among companies that manufacture and distribute complex, customized products; high-value, fast-moving, short-life products; medium-value, long-life, seasonal products; and low-value, high-density products.

There may be further complications (or simplifications) if a company operates in a complex replenishment environment, such as the case of an organization that delivers services that are dependent on the arrival and integration of products and materials.

Then you might consider the special challenges of designing cost- and time-efficient strategies for the distribution of a wide array of items. For instance, the strategy might have to take into account significant variation in size, cost, application, and movement patterns — from screwdrivers to $100k circuit boards.

Sometimes, the options are not obvious, and the strategies are far from traditional. Europe's Ryanair is three times as profitable as Southwest. Ryanair makes enormous profits from everything *but* ticket sales, and expects half its passengers to be flying for *free* by the year 2010. It is, instead, looking to baggage fees, beverage and meal charges, and prospects for on-board wagering to more than offset "lost" ticket revenue. It is an absolute master at pricing the desirable flights and times sky-high, while featuring the itineraries to lesser locations at dreadful times in the range of one to 10 euros.

## The Chicken or the Egg

Which comes first, the corporate strategy or the supply chain strategy? The easy, and generally correct, answer is the corporate strategy. Yet the president of a large specialty distributor recently told us that he is spending all of his time in operations. The reason — he can't begin to get specific about the details of corporate strategy until he can rely on his supply chain infrastructure to perform, grow, and adapt as the business evolves.

## Position in Life Is Everything

Recognizing fundamental differences in the core business is just the beginning, however. A company's supply chain strategy will also be largely determined by the company's position in the supply chain.

A retailer's comprehensive strategy is not going to look anything like a supplier's. A manufacturer will — actually *must* — design a different path to the future than a distributor will. The LSP (Logistics Service Provider) will necessarily have a different take from any of the above, but it needs to face up to strategic issues just as much as they do.

Another enormous consideration in the development of a supply chain strategy is the company's relative strength in the supply chain. Irrespective of its position in the supply chain, the company that is the dominant force in that chain is the one most likely to design a more comprehensive solution — nearer to the ideal of "end-to-end" — and help its trading partners fit into the grand scheme of things. That dominant force can be a retailer, and often is these days. It can also be a manufacturer as often was the case a decade and more ago.

The weaker, or more incidental, player can't hope to drive the end-to-end strategic design — and shouldn't even try. All the brilliance in the world can't overcome the reality that the rules are made by whomever holds the power in any given supply chain.

But every supply chain professional in every company has a responsibility to craft a supply chain strategy that's right for that company in its particular circumstance. It's parallel with the responsibility of that corporation's management to craft an overall business strategy for a profitable future.

## Corporate Options in Differentiation

The commentary above notwithstanding, companies will take different philosophical approaches to details of strategy, and the supply chain executive would be a fool to ignore those details in favor of a more elegant supply chain strategy.

If the company is committed to being the lowest-cost provider, a high-cost, high-service supply chain model will be in constant conflict with top management's objectives. If the highest level of customer service is deemed to be key to corporate success, a supply chain strategy that slashes costs at every opportunity is not likely to last long.

And there are additional considerations. What if the corporate objective is to fatten up the company, building up the balance sheet to make it an attractive candidate for acquisition? The supply chain organization cannot go off on a tangent different from that overarching direction. What if the corporation is committed to growth through acquisition? The supply chain strategy must be geared to integrating products and customers into its structure with grace, style, and well-managed costs. What if the objective is to become a national entity rather than a regional operation? The supply chain strategy and plan must contemplate how and where to redeploy and add facilities, how to reconfigure facility missions, and what the transportation consequences might be for such a change.

The supply chain strategy and the organization must take into account any long-term corporate strategic direction — downsizing, a shift to offshore manufacturing, supplier base rationalization, a merger, product development, and marketing or manufacturing alliances.

## Is Outsourcing a Strategy?

Yes and no. It depends. Our opinion is that, in the world of supply chain management, outsourcing does not constitute a strategy. The design of a supply chain needs to be accomplished independently of who might actually execute transactions within it.

The key ingredients of supply management, manufacturing integration, transportation modes and roles, facility locations and missions, customer relationships, and the like should be designed in a "clean sheet of paper" approach. Once the strategic design has passed muster, then alternatives of execution may be considered.

If an outsourced solution set makes sense from standpoints of cost, service, flexibility, and capacity and capability to support corporate strategy — then go for it!

That said, there might easily be a corporate strategy that outsources non-core business activities, or functions not regarded as core competencies, for any number of valid business reasons. In those cases, a tactical outsourcing solution can mesh perfectly with a strategic corporate objective.

## Planning for an Uncertain Future

Truth be told, devising strategies for success is relatively easy. We're good at anticipating how to handle growth — even of the explosive kind. Creating strategies and plans for getting smaller is tougher.

But stuff happens. And sometimes it happens on purpose. The supply chain organization needs to be ready to support strategies for reduction, as well as to have contingencies in place in the event of business disaster.

A corporate strategy might be to "fire" its "C" customers and concentrate on doing business with a select top level. In an extreme case, senior management might elect to forego high-demand, low-margin business with a big box retailer in order to do a lower level of more profitable business with other customers. This would have staggering effects on supply chain activities.

Then there are always the worst case scenarios. The big box retailer might fire you before you can fire it. Your competitor might capture 20 percent of your business overnight. Your strategic plans need to recognize these possibilities and include provisions for shifting to new models overnight.

But there is a certain amount of guaranteed strategic change when there are frequent strategy reviews. That's especially true when an active vision drives strategic shifts. Consider an organization that begins life as a recording label, then morphs into a retail music store chain, and then takes on the challenge of being an airline, accepting the responsibility for managing passenger railroads along the way. Today, they're also making wines, and pretty decent ones at that. Brilliant? Zany? Impossible? Ask Virgin and its founder, Sir Richard Branson. Think for a moment on the supply chain aspects of those shifts. Then take into account that Virgin operates in eight business channels in 28 nations, on six continents. And it's looking at options in fuel and energy as well as in space travel.

## Strategy When All Bets Are Off

As the Virgin case illustrates, there are other levels and dimensions to the strategy question beyond handling growth and avoiding catastrophe. As Ram Charan brilliantly writes, business acumen also means interpreting the business landscape and attendant trends for re-directive strategy development.

Charan cites two examples: BP's environmentally focused repositioning against a back-drop of consumption up-ramps in developing economies, and Thomson Corporation's divestiture of its thriving newspaper and recreational properties in favor of online content delivery to targeted professionals. In both examples, he makes a case for the development, nurturing, and exercise of acumen-based thought and analysis.

BP, by the way, handily passed both Royal Dutch/Shell and ExxonMobil in revenues to trail only Wal-Mart in the Fortune Global 500 after taking the new tack. Toronto's Thomson has thrived in its new milieu, while the traditional newspaper companies continue to struggle in theirs. Their leaders, Lord John Browne and Richard Harrington, both had taken the rare step of radically changing course while things were going well — and both succeeded brilliantly.

The secrets? Not complicated. The execution? Incredibly demanding. Some luck always helps as well. The six-step questioning process behind insightful, thoughtful, and rigorous strategy development is straightforward:

- What is happening in the world today?
- What does it mean for others?
- What does it mean for us?
- What would have to happen first for the results we want?
- What do we have to do to be players in the sequence?
- What do we do next?

Companies that make a difference also display certain characteristics and attributes. They include:

- 1. Leaders who get it — who have vision, insight, and passion.
- 2. Organizations that consciously develop business acumen in their people.
- 3. Structural and individual discipline to raise the exercise considerably above intellectual daydreaming.
- 4. Context and world view that are able to relate seemingly unconnected trends and events into a cohesive framework.
- 5. Courage to act and to take calculated risks.

Other strategy success stories, based on strategic moves and predicated on this process, include GE and Jeff Immelt, Verizon and Ivan Seidenberg, and Apple and Steve Jobs. These kinds of bold moves inevitably have dramatic supply chain management consequences. We maintain that it is better to strain to meet this level of challenge than it is to comfortably go down with the ship in companies that can't face the prospect of major strategy shifts.

## Summing up

For large, diverse enterprises, the corporate strategy might not have a lot of specifics built into it. Instead they may pay attention to business units and product lines. Strategies shouldn't get carved in stone. At Procter & Gamble, for example, products get annual strategy reviews that discourage slick presentations and encourage open-ended debate — for as long as it takes to reach resolution. The key issues are simple to state and difficult to define — where to play and how to win.

Strategy is nowhere near as easy — or as fun — as it might appear from a distance. But it's necessary for a living, growing, evolving supply chain strategy to achieve long-term success.

A couple of words of caution — a relevant and realistic strategy is a prerequisite to designing the supporting tactics that can make it happen. In addition, the best strategy is worthless without effective action in its execution. Stated another way, an imperfect strategy enthusiastically implemented is worth 10 times more than a perfect vision half-heartedly pursued.

In the end, strategy is really all about focused action and decisions that map to an articulated vision. In the decision-driven organization, good managers understand that some decisions matter more than others. Because the ultimate goal is action in the right context, speed and adaptability are crucial. Practicing is more important than preaching.

# SUPPLY CHAIN ORGANIZATION(S)

When in doubt, reorganize!
*Whitney Massengill*

Civilization begins with order, grows with liberty, and dies with chaos.
*Will Durant*

Any fool can make a rule, and every fool will mind it.
*Henry David Thoreau*

There are enormous numbers of managers who have retired on the job.
*Peter F. Drucker*

## Introduction

It's all right to chatter on about key concepts in supply chain management. But sooner or later, we've got to face up to the question of how you get organized to deliver the goods. What kind of organization does it require to support, enable, and promote effective performance in the supply chain?

As you might expect, the answer is, It depends. It depends on what kind of company you're in, and on what its overarching and differentiating strategies are. It also depends on the organization's intrinsic culture, on precedent, on politics, and on the personalities of key players in the outfit. It also depends on how mature and progressive the company's supply chain vision is.

## Starting at the Top

We recently read a protracted discussion in a distinguished journal regarding the correct organizational placement of supply chain management. The debate centered on whether supply chain management should report to the chief information officer (CIO) or the chief financial officer (CFO).

How wild is that? We can scarcely imagine two worse reporting placements.

The CIO oversees the acquisition, development, and maintenance of the information technology and tools — both hardware and software — that enable and support operations, decision-making, and reporting throughout the enterprise. The CIO is no more qualified to lead SCM than an emergency phone operator is to head up a crime scene investigation.

The CFO may be marginally worse as a candidate. We need bean counters, to be sure. But in military service, the Inspector General does not get assigned to lead troops into combat.

Note the deliberate use of the term "lead." SCM isn't about reporting or administration. It needs leadership more than it requires management. SCM is about taking command of a company's moving parts — assuming responsibility for deciding how materials and products are acquired and made, how they are packaged and stored, how they are tailored to meet specific customer and market needs, and how they are delivered into customers' hands.

Supply Chain Management, in essence, is strategy made real. Supply Chain Management delivers on Marketing's representations. It meets Sales' commitments. It supports customers' business requirements, solving problems. In short, SCM delivers the physical side of the "promise of the brand" equation.

Another recent academic discussion we heard attempted to place SCM along an axis between Marketing and Logistics. The focus of the discussion was where to "position" SCM within the organization.

This shouldn't be all that complicated. Supply Chain Management should report to the top. SCM needs to report to the President, both structurally and conceptually.

## Defining the SCM Organization

We're not sure that this can be done, that the supply chain management organization can even be defined. The dilemma goes back to the politics, personalities, precedent, and vision points made above, at least to some extent.

Part of the problem lies in defining SCM itself. One school holds that much of what we call SCM today is the result of a kind of Darwinian evolutionary process. Traffic Management became Physical Distribution, which became Logistics, which became Supply Chain Management — all successive new names for the same thing. We differ, contending that Traffic Management became *part* of Physical Distribution, which became *part* of Logistics, which became *part* of Supply Chain Management. Thus, functions originally performed in the old Traffic Management may still be found in today's Supply Chain Management, but the two are not even remotely synonymous.

Still, there are some who aren't content to work with the definitions developed to date. They are trying to develop the "definitive" definition of SCM. One observer has posited that SCM is an integrating function that includes all logistics management activities and manufacturing operations. But what became of Sourcing and Procurement? Where are the customers? Where are the vendors in this definition?

The Council of Supply Chain Management Professionals (see the chapter titled

"Overview — Supply Chain Definitions") may have it about right. Under its definition, the supply chain organization encompasses procurement, manufacturing, suppliers, customers, and LSPs, along with the logistics and related planning, management, and execution activities. An argument might be made that most corporate activities, save for Finance and Accounting, Sales and Marketing, and IT, belong in the SCM organization. There are a few companies that have tried that approach, but they may have been premature in doing so.

One persuasive school of thinking has it that it's just not possible to sketch out an ideal SCM organization. Companies are too different from one another. Each has its own culture and history, industry characteristics, and strategic approaches to the role of SCM and visions of the future.

We agree. Drawing endless variations on arrangements of lines and boxes to define who reports to whom doesn't really answer the core questions in SCM organization. What's more important is the understanding of how SCM's functions and processes relate to core corporate functions and objectives — and then working like mad to maximize SCM's contributions to organizational success.

## Real-World Considerations

Specific local conditions will ultimately drive how organizations are actually structured. An integrated SCM perspective doesn't necessarily mean that there will be a singular command and control SCM organization structure. There may be dotted lines to operating functions in various corporate divisions or subsidiaries.

There may be more dotted lines to SCM functions that report elsewhere within the corporate structure. The SCM executive cadre may be consultants and advisors to divisional and international counterparts. It seems that when it comes to the SCM organization, the most successful leaders are those whose strengths lie in managing matrixed relationships. The likelihood of success therefore diminishes for those who can't live without command and control mechanisms in a tight structure.

As old-style, hierarchical organization structures continue to linger in the 21st century, those of us in the supply chain business need to embrace flatter, high-communication, high-collaboration organizational models.

## More Bad News?

Not really. These organizational developments are actually very good news. In its highest form, our organizational role in SCM includes the mandate to work and play well with others.

We'll continue to have all the usual responsibilities along with pressures to deliver higher performance at lower cost. But we'll also have the freedom and power to move across and through organizational boundaries. That could mean working closely with Sales on customer issues, both specific and general. That could mean working with Marketing on new approaches to markets and channels. Or it could mean working with R&D on product design and better time-to-market techniques, or with IT on the tools needed to enable best-in-class planning, decision-making, and execution in Supply Chain Management. It could even mean working with Finance and Accounting on the business impacts of projects and initiatives.

## In Summary

Certainly, it's a tall order. But the secrets of success in an SCM organization do not lie in lines and boxes on an organization chart that never gets pulled out of the file until visiting consultants ask for it.

The keys to this particular kingdom are contained in the following:

- Senior SCM management reporting to the top.
- An SCM vision shared by executive colleagues and bought into by internal practitioners.
- The comfortable ability, in all segments of the SCM organizations, to work with colleagues in other functional areas — on SC support for *their* problems.
- Technical capability throughout all SCM functions.
- Patience on the part of SCM leadership, if organizational maturity lies a bit further into the future.
- Multi-tasking, matrixed mentality in all corners of the SCM world.
- Shared vision for the integration of SCM strategies with corporate strategies — and clear understandings of how one supports the other.

## One Caveat

In thinking about organizational structures and how they inter-relate, it is critical to understand a company's "shadow organization." This amorphous and invisible group can scuttle your project — or make you a hero — without your even knowing it exists. You've got to know how to identify the decision influencers with secret veto powers and coax them onto your side.

This tactic is particularly important when change is in the air, as so often is the case in the supply chain world. Do a little research on the topic — the shadow organization can make or break you.

# INFORMATION SYSTEMS FOR SUPPLY CHAIN MANAGEMENT

A poor process done faster is not an improvement.
*Whitney Massengill*

Why shouldn't a PC work like a refrigerator or a toaster?
*Walter Mossberg*

The science of today is the technology of tomorrow.
*Edward Teller*

Computers can figure out all kinds of problems,
except the things in the world that just don't add up.
*James Magary*

## Information Systems — An Exotic Link in the Supply Chain

Not so very long ago, anything that involved computers was more art than business. The *artistes* involved had their own languages, and relatively few people could translate them into plain English. The technology was complex, sometimes deliberately so. Even today, there is an information and technology gap between what customers see that they need, and what the vendors are selling. Dr. John Maeda, a computer science expert, has said "Everything I touch doesn't work."

You know, instruction manuals were required to operate the early models of many consumer products, including the clock in the 1820s, the sewing machine in the 1840s, and the automobile in the early 1900s. Many owners of early automobiles had chauffeurs. Their function was not so much to drive as to keep the horseless carriage running. Information technology today is only slightly more advanced than the early versions of these products.

## The Make or Buy Decision

Most of the packaged software products used in supply chain management today could be developed in house. In fact, many companies have done so. Most software buyers, then, face a classic make or buy decision. Those who elect to build their own are often looking for greater security as well as exclusivity. They certainly have the opportunity to customize the solution to highly specific operating requirements. Sometimes they are unable to find an outside source at the right price. Other times, they can't find the specific skills needed from an outside source. However, in-house development often costs more and always takes longer. There is a high failure rate. Sometimes availability of resources poses a challenge, although in recent years the use of offshore resources has been a popular option.

Those who buy do so to save time or to save money — or to provide scalability against future growth. The number of package buyers continues to grow, but we should note that the possibility of failure does not disappear in the "buy" alternative.

## Options in Supply Chain Software

For most companies, the first choice to make is between enterprise systems and legacy applications. Enterprise systems are integrated software packages that are designed to handle most of the functions of a business. SAP, originally from Germany, is the largest, most widespread, and best-known of these enterprise resource planning (ERP) vendors. Legacy applications are generally independently developed software systems that are already in place. Over time, enterprise systems have added supply chain functionality and modules, rather than continue to interface with independent supply chain systems. So today, companies face a second choice, a decision between the enterprise system and "best of breed" in warehouse management systems (WMS) and transportation management systems (TMS).

Logistics service providers have unique options to consider. Should they offer their own IT systems, or should they rely on the systems used by their clients? Then, if they decide to offer their own, should they make or buy them?

There are some other options to consider as well. Today's marketplace also includes software solutions that go beyond the physical distribution functions commonly associated with supply chain management, such as customer relationship management (CRM), product lifecycle management (PLM), collaborative planning, forecasting, and replenishment (CPFR), and supply management and procurement.

When it comes to warehouse and transportation software, some packages offer special features and functions such as labor management systems (LMS), load building optimization, slotting optimization, transportation optimizers, and yard management systems (YMS). But they don't always have to be purchased as part of an integrated package; many can be purchased as a stand-alone package as well. No matter how they are acquired, each of these features can make vital contributions to an effective supply chain IT system.

The major suppliers generally offer a number of linked solutions or software suites. Eight of the top 20 vendors in this market space have WMS, TMS, YMS, LMS, OMS (Order Management Systems), and Visibility (Event Management) products. Another four offer all but one. The "best of breed" provider with only one functional product seems to be disappearing.

There are also solutions that may be used to simulate warehousing as well as manufacturing and transportation operations. This type of application is used to analyze the impacts of operations, layouts, and decision rules on overall performance. They may be either packages or custom applications, depending on the scope and complexity of the situation. While entirely legitimate and incredibly useful, they fall outside the population of "fundamental" information systems support, at least at the present stage of systems maturity.

## Sources of Advice

How do you find a source for software? A good place to start might be one of the many reference guides published by trade associations and independent analysts. One such reference is the Council of Supply Chain Management Professionals' annual guide to available software (www.cscmp.org). Another is a two—volume reference, *Third Party Logistics WMS Software*, published last year by independent consultant Phil Obal as a follow-up to his definitive 2004 book on WMS software selection. (For more information, visit www.idii.com.) Another possibility is to retain a management consultant to guide you through the software selection process. Whichever route you take, the main thing is to choose a resource with deep and broad knowledge of the field as well as objectivity, the latter being paramount.

## Success and Failure Factors

Whenever a change in information systems is undertaken, there is the promise of success (whether the promises come from a vendor's representative or from the internal IT department) and the risk of failure. What is the best predictor of success? Commitment. By that we mean the dedication of the entire organization, from senior management to the hourly worker. New systems work well only when people *want* them to. Remember, the best system in the world can be brought to its knees by people who don't want it to work.

There are other factors in a successful installation as well. For one thing, information technology must be closely coordinated with operations. For another, ample and positive training must be provided. Training is the best way to be sure that the system works and that people feel positive about the proposed change. If you've decided to go with an outside vendor, it's also critical to select the right software supplier. And finally, there's no substitute for thoroughly testing the system, with the vendor on-site just before and during the start up. The testing should include all modifications, process flows, and every other aspect of the system.

Unfortunately, IT initiatives sometimes fail. One common cause of failure is political unrest within the user organization. Others include poorly prepared specifications and, if both the technology and processes are new, insufficient education and training. In other cases, expectations are not well managed. Subsequent "scope creep" extends the initial parameters, stretching out development and installation times. In still other situations, the downfall is last-minute modifications; these are seldom done well under pressure.

## The Requirements Definition

Whether you are the buyer or seller of IT services, the most important step in the process may be to draft a clearly stated description of requirements. By all means, avoid technical

123

jargon and describe the situation in plain English. For example, if you were creating a sample checklist describing the requirements of moving product from inbound staging to storage location, the list might look like this:

\_\_\_\_ Directed put-away
\_\_\_\_ Exception handling
\_\_\_\_ Updating of inventory records
\_\_\_\_ Confirmation of put-away
\_\_\_\_ Cross docking

The requirements definition must consider customization. To what extent must the software package be customized? What is the ratio of standard code to customer-specific code? A 90/10 answer leads to a very different development approach than a 10/90 ratio.

The buyer should also consider the version number of the software package. Version 1.0 is a very new product, and the first buyer is certainly a beta tester, a polite industry term for "guinea pig." No matter what the version number, the buyer should ask for the planned date of the next release. If a newer version will soon be introduced, it may be worth waiting for. It may also contain critical features and functions that the salespeople have touted.

As a software buyer, consider whether there is a user group for the software product. Communication with that group can be very helpful.

## Choosing a Software Vendor

Once the requirements have been defined and some proposals have been received, the buyer must assess the vendor response. This task may take longer than you think, since evaluating every feature of the proposal usually requires a team effort. Follow-up questions will be sent back to the vendor in order to be sure that the proposal is completely understood. When the field has been narrowed to no more than three finalists, schedule demonstrations and customer site visits so you and your team can see how all the program's features work. Keep in mind that it should be simple to grasp and easy to train. As a buyer, you should consider the product's market penetration in your industry.

When decision-makers are located in more than one city, Web conferencing can be a vital part of the demonstration. As you consider questions to ask the prospective vendor, here are some tried and true ones:

*What is your primary business?*
*Can you supply some customer references?*
*How much support service is programmed into your proposal?*
*If things don't work out, how do we unscramble the eggs?*

## The Half-Million Dollar Question

As you qualify vendors, there is one question that's more important than any other, and it needs to be posed (in one of two variations) to both software vendors and their customers. Here's what to ask the vendor:

*"If I handed you $500,000, how would you use it to further develop your product?"*
Here's what to ask the vendor's existing customers:

*"If you could spend $500,000 on enhancements to this product, what features would you add or improve?"*

## Keep It Simple

Easier said than done. The landscape keeps changing. Execution system vendors are enhancing what is embedded in their offerings. Enterprise solution developers are touting their products, especially as they add functionality, as high-value substitutes for the best-of-breed offerings.

The best-of-breed vendors are adding performance management modules to their packages. They are even integrating manufacturing functionality. This feature may hold a lot of appeal to those who get the picture of manufacturing synchronization in supply chain operations.

Managing the supply chain is essentially a straightforward business, even in more complex global networks. Don't let systems make it complicated when it doesn't have to be! If a vendor or advisor can't explain an IT product or service in plain language and make a clear business case for its benefits, consider that a red flag. Get rid of that vendor and find someone who can.

# HUMAN RESOURCES — YOU WIN WITH PEOPLE

The growth and development of people is the highest calling of leadership.
*Harvey Firestone*

Nobody motivates today's workers. If it doesn't come from within, it doesn't come.
Fun helps remove the barriers that allow people to motivate themselves.
*Herman Cain*

The most important thing about motivation is goal setting.
You should always have a goal.
*Francie Larrieu Smith*

The worst sin towards our fellow creatures is not to hate them,
but to be indifferent to them; that's the essence of inhumanity.
*George Bernard Shaw*

## From the Gridiron to the Supply Chain

The legendary college football coach Wayne Woodrow (Woody) Hayes was a world-class recruiter. His book, *You Win With People*, reflected his philosophies about the importance of attracting, motivating, and keeping the right kinds of people. The parallels are clear in any endeavor, supply chain management included.

The best supply chain operators understand the fundamental importance of:

■ *Recruiting the best in all supply chain management functions, and testing to determine their "fit" in the organization.*

- *Creating a stimulating and rewarding work environment.*
- *Compensating fairly.*
- *Measuring and monitoring performance, and providing counseling based on results.*
- *Developing skills and capabilities within functions and individuals.*
- *Pruning low performers to revitalize the organization.*
- *Leading rather than managing.*

## Context for the People Equation

Of all the elements of supply chain management, leading people is perhaps the most challenging. Nowhere is that more true than in transportation and warehousing, which are among the costliest operational links in the chain as well as the most people-heavy.

As for why leadership and other human resources (HR) skills are so critical to supply chain management, it has to do with the nature of the work. For example, close supervision of warehouse workers is impractical. The best order selectors are "loners" and self starters. The same thing is true of truck drivers. Other supply chain functions have unique characteristics as well, but all have in common the need for good HR practices. We'll concentrate our examples in physical distribution, keeping in mind that the core messages are universal.

Upward mobility remains common in supply chain operations. A significant number of supervisors and managers began their careers as order pickers or forklift drivers. Nonetheless, the transition from worker to supervisor can be difficult. Some promotion decisions ignore leadership potential, and relatively few companies provide adequate training and support for the individual in transition from follower to leader.

Supply chain occupations — particularly in warehousing and trucking — may not be glamorous, but they demand much more from workers than the typical manufacturing job. For one thing, they require constant learning, as the worker adapts to new tasks and changing processes. But logistics workers often fail to get respect or even attention from senior management.

## Recruiting Your People

Recruiting is just as important in building a logistics team as it is in developing a football team. Most companies go about the task of finding entry-level people in one three ways: advertising, "temp-to-perm," and referrals. Of these, advertising will attract the largest pool of candidates, but it's an unfiltered pool. Many of those candidates will turn out to be unqualified for the job, and it will require a considerable amount of time to sort through the crowd.

"Temp-to-perm" represents a somewhat quicker route. Many employers bring in entry-level people through a temporary employment agency, and then promote those who do outstanding work to permanent status. This method allows the employer to evaluate each employee on the job before deciding whether or not that person is a keeper.

A third source of people is referrals from the existing staff. Good workers will very seldom refer a bad person, so this method is very likely to produce an above-average pool of labor.

The next step in the recruiting process is conducting interviews. It is generally advisable to delegate the job of interviewing to human resources specialists, particularly for opera-

127

tional positions. HR specialists are trained to ask questions that probe for attitude problems that make a candidate a poor employment risk as well as to avoid questions that are improper or illegal. Asking line managers or supervisors to handle the interviews increases the risk of bad hiring decisions, particularly if the facility is experiencing a labor shortage that's creating additional pressure. That said, when recruiting for expected growth or expansion, some companies opt for a combination of HR and management interviews in order to get both the capabilities and culture "fits" right.

In another approach, Southwest Airlines "auditions" candidates rather than over-relying on the interview process. The "auditioners" carefully observe candidates' behavior while outside interview settings, including when *en route* to the interview.

Regrettably, screening for substance abuse has become a necessity in the recruiting and hiring process today. The topic is discussed more fully in the chapter on Securing the Supply Chain.

## Getting Started

Many managers fail to realize the importance of the first day on the job. As anyone who has experienced a disastrous first day will attest, there's no substitute for starting a new worker off on the right foot. The first day usually includes orientation, as well as an opportunity to "learn the ropes" from somebody in the workforce. If management doesn't control who that "somebody" is, your workers may get an orientation that's less than positive, if not downright destructive.

The last phase of the recruiting process is the probationary period. In nearly every company, workers remain on probation for 60 to 90 days. During this time, management has the right to terminate that worker if performance does not meet expectations. This is management's last chance to confirm that it has made the hiring decision.

No matter how carefully designed a company's recruiting and interviewing process may be, it's inevitable that an occasional hiring mistake will be made. Those mistakes should become apparent during the probationary period, and it is essential to uncover and correct those errors before the worker reaches permanent status. This is especially important in a union operation, where the termination process may involve numerous and complex protocols.

## Motivation, Training, and Discipline

Both managers and supervisors should practice the "seven Ts" — Take Time To Talk To The Troops. The distribution center is the ideal place to practice what Hewlett-Packard co-founder David Packard called "management by wandering around." Some managers maintain a set of index cards to help them remember key facts about each employee they're likely to encounter in the workplace setting.

On-the-job training has become both a necessity and a motivator. Some organizations have a training department, and those that don't rely on peer training. When neither is available, the natural approach is a "buddy system." However, as with the first-day orientation, if management does not control who the trainer is, the results may be disappointing. At one retail organization, the best workers receive the title of "ambassador," and they have the task of training the part-time workers who are brought in to handle peak season volumes. Ambassadors are selected for their natural teaching ability as well as their attitude and job skill. The best training programs have a grading system, and it is important to decide how grades are given and who will give them.

Twenty-first century operating discipline is based on the practice of catching people doing something right and reinforcing good behavior. It is better to ask than to order, just as it is better to lead than to drive. It is essential to praise in public and correct in private, always being careful to avoid ridicule. In a supply chain operating environment, it is better to emphasize effort by teams rather than individuals, simply because teamwork is usually a requirement for success.

Discipline includes self-discipline, and time management is a key element. Successful managers build a reputation for getting things done, and getting them done on time. Staying organized is essential in supply chain operations at all levels, and that starts with each individual manager. Because no one has time to get everything done, the ability to delegate is another hallmark of successful management.

Another key element in motivating and retaining people is good communication. Each organization needs to figure out what communication styles and techniques work best for its individual culture. UPS uses a program of daily, and sometimes more frequent, three-minute meetings to get the word out while keeping the focus on speed, sense of urgency, and the criticality of schedule adherence.

Likewise, compensation is crucial, and more important than some in the touchy-feely business would have you believe. There's not time or space here to cover the myriad issues surrounding compensation, but some companies reap benefits — motivation and retention — from being just a little bit non-traditional.

Lincoln Electric, the welding equipment maker, has been cited for decades for its unique gainsharing plan. Whole Foods Market, a more recent player, builds temporary hourly rate increases into the wages of store teams that have delivered savings, which also helps in the recruiting process.

## Elements of Motivation

Remember that different individuals in different economic positions, and in different life stages, will respond differently to a given motivational technique. What effectively motivates a manager may not make much of an impression on an hourly employee. Abraham Maslow developed a hierarchy of needs, each of which needed to be met before an individual could reasonably be expected to respond to stimuli aimed at the next level up. In short, someone struggling to pay the rent and put food on the table would not likely be motivated by a public recognition ceremony. Maslow's pyramid is illustrated on the following page.

## Developing and Retaining People

The best logistics organizations use appraisals as a tool for staff development. Building a good team requires grading your people, promoting those who are successful, and providing constructive feedback for those who are not meeting expectations. Most managers appreciate the importance of the appraisal interview, but some avoid it. Those who dislike appraisals tend to blame the system rather than the actual interview process. In fact, most people want to be graded and appreciate the opportunity to learn just where they stand.

Part of the development process involves the identification and orientation of replacements. New York City Mayor Michael Bloomberg became known for demanding that

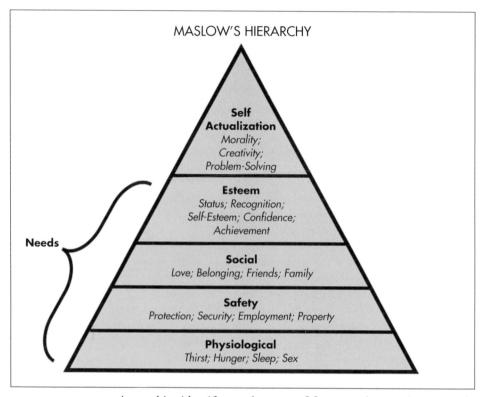

every manager reporting to him identify a replacement. Many people are reluctant to do this, perhaps out of insecurity or perhaps out of simple laziness. However, Bloomberg insisted upon it, and he achieved compliance by warning that those who could not identify a replacement were not eligible for promotion.

Good companies promote from within wherever possible, and supply chain organizations have an unusually good record for doing this. A policy of promoting from within can be a great morale builder, but it carries risks as well. For example, it's all too easy to run afoul of the Peter Principle ("In a hierarchy, every employee tends to rise to his level of incompetence"). There are plenty of warehouses in which supervisors still spend much of their time handling routine repetitive tasks. Sometimes this is a training problem; other times, it's a clear manifestation of the Peter Principle. Either way, failure to correct the condition can have significant consequences.

Retention is the process of keeping "A" players on the team. That's not always as easy as it sounds. When they're unhappy with one or more aspects of the job, it is natural for talented people to look for a better place. And even when times are good, your best people may be tempted by lucrative offers from other companies. In either case, when you lose a team member, find out why. This is usually accomplished through exit interviews.

The exit interview may reveal internal problems, such as a poor supervisor. While some worker turnover should be viewed as normal, churning of people usually indicates either job satisfaction problems or management weakness. Note that turnover among long-haul truck drivers now surpasses 120 percent per year. In other words, the average driver stays on the job for about nine months. Management people in the best trucking companies are trying to discover the root causes for this condition, and they are working aggressively on compensation and environmental solutions to improve driver retention.

When companies need to downsize because of declining volume, layoffs of good people are inevitable. It is essential that these be handled with compassion. Outplacement services should be offered wherever possible. The best-managed companies do everything possible to combat negative thinking and control rumors.

## Moving From Worker to Administrator to Leader

There is a difference between an administrator and a leader. The administrator organizes, plans, controls, and handles staffing matters. The leader inspires others to change. The leader has a well-articulated vision and ability to inspire trust. In supply chain operations, the line supervisor position is often the incubator for future leaders. Control is difficult in the operating environment, and routine or repetitive tasks are the exception rather than the rule. In the absence of close control, motivation becomes a necessity, and only a leader can provide that.

When working associates are promoted to supervisory positions, their ability to quickly learn the process of leadership is usually difficult to predict. Every outstanding leader possesses these seven traits:

- *Excellent communication skills.*
- *Vision.*
- *Empathy.*
- *Coaching skills.*
- *A common touch.*
- *A very positive attitude.*
- *Self-control.*

Retired General Electric CEO Jack Welch might add to that what he calls the four "E" characteristics of great leaders: Energy; ability to Energize others; Edge, or the courage to make tough decisions; and Execution, or the ability to get things done.

Not long ago, relatively few business schools or business writers recognized the distinction between administration and leadership. Even the prized graduate degree is a Masters of Business Administration. Today nearly everyone recognizes that leadership is the essential ingredient for business success.

## The Looming Crisis

The looming retirement of the baby-boomer generation, coupled with continued business and economic growth, is creating a nightmare scenario. There are simply not going to be enough skilled people to fill all the openings. (Yes, even with all the outsourcing and off-shoring, and even with galloping technology advances.)

The North American workforce is aging, although not as rapidly as the workforce in Europe, where economic growth has been merely creeping along for years now. Immigration, legal and otherwise, is unlikely to continue to fill the gaps forever, and managerial ingenuity is going to be tested as never before.

Executive succession planning will be impaired, and focus will shift to simply finding enough warm bodies to get the job done.

The entirety of solutions remains unknown. But Intel has taken an early lead, with an organized program to "retain" retirees. Instead of the storied gold watch, Intel gives new retirees a PC, a printer, Internet access, and tech support. It is consciously building a pool of talent and resources to be available on a project basis to serve as consultants, and to beef up support for escalating demands over the next 20 years. Others — including Pratt & Whitney and several telecommunications companies — are taking similar, if less organized, tacks.

In summary, remember that organizations are very much like football teams; the winner is the team with the most talented and best-motivated people. The job of building a team is ultimately the responsibility of the head coach. If you think it is OK to let the Human Resources people take complete responsibility for it, you could be missing a critical opportunity.

# SPEED

THIS WEEK WE MOVED THIS PRODUCT WHICH WE HAD MOVED LAST WEEK TO WHERE IT WAS THE PREVIOUS WEEK BUT WE'RE GETTING MUCH FASTER.

© Gene Gagnon
Reprinted with permission

Everywhere is within walking distance if you have the time.
*Steven Wright*

In skating over thin ice our safety is in our speed.
*Ralph Waldo Emerson*

To succeed, jump as quickly at opportunities as you do at conclusions.
*Benjamin Franklin*

Ralph Nader's *Unsafe at Any Speed* was useful, in its day.
*Lisa Lewis*

## What and When Was the Tipping Point?
We are indebted to Malcolm Gladwell for sharing his insights into how and why significant change occurs in his fascinating and frightening book *The Tipping Point*. He also scared us nearly to death by exposing some hard truths about decision-making in *Blink*. More about that later.

We won't subject the current drive for supply chain speed to a rigorous "tipping point" examination and reconstruction. But it should be clear that three major companies have driven it to a top-of-mind position among practitioners, academics, and consultants.

First came Fred Smith and Federal Express in 1973, and its galvanizing 1979 slogan, "When it absolutely, positively has to be there overnight!" These revolutionized both how business transported small parcels and large documents, and how mid-management and consumers thought about radically fast movement of goods. Later, the company changed its name to FedEx, which is, not coincidentally, much faster to say than its predecessor.

At about the same time, an unknown merchant in Columbus, Ohio, turned the retail fashion industry upside down by implementing a logistics-driven distribution system. The new paradigm focused on converting European-styled garments into Chinese mass production that was transported by air cargo to Columbus for processing, and immediate reshipment to Limited stores all over the United States. The technique, which slashed time to market for cutting-edge fashion, gave Limited Brands a significant jump on the competition, and fueled substantial growth — all through the power of supply chain speed.

Then the sure-to-fail Amazon.com phenomenon struck — and stuck. Emerging online in 1995 amidst the thousands of other dotcoms (many of which later morphed into dotbombs), Amazon raised the expectations of Americans, and later the world, about the online shopping experience. As a result, we now expect to be able to order *anything* online and have it arrive on our doorsteps in a ridiculously short time. Whether we wanted an item that quickly was — and is — beside the point.

Meanwhile, behind the scenes, people were beginning to figure out that supply chains encompassed more than the integrated activities of a company. The breakthrough came when practitioners and management realized that supply chains consist of interlinked sets of suppliers and converters and customer relationships.

Even when well-known companies such as Wal-Mart and Dell command public identities, they represent all the others in the chain. They are the public face of competing supply chains, and not simply individual competitors against other companies.

Somehow supply chain speed seemed to be at the heart of the competition. And speed was on everyone's mind.

## Elements of Supply Chain Speed

Supply chain speed takes several forms and has many purposes. Perhaps the most obvious is fulfillment speed — how quickly an order is filled. Not just processed and released or picked and packed, but how soon it is delivered into a customer's hands. The importance of integrated performance among supply chain partners is immediately clear. When it comes to satisfying customers, the musical "Chicago" offers genuine insight in the Kander and Ebb song, "I Can't Do It Alone."

But why is this speed so essential? For one thing, all the competition is promising — and delivering — fulfillment speed. Some because they can, and some because speed can be a vital competitive tool. In some segments of the technology business, for example, an order might be placed with two competitors. The one that arrives first is accepted and received. The one that shows up second is rejected and returned.

For another, companies are trying to operate today with smaller inventories than in the past (unless Far Eastern sourcing is involved). Rapid replenishment from suppliers becomes vital so they can maintain *their* stock positions and customer service levels. For example, auto dealers' service writers routinely promise the completion of repairs by 5:00 p.m. the same day, knowing all the while that the parts needed aren't in stock. The writer also knows that more than one local parts wholesaler can deliver the replacements in less than two hours.

The suppliers that consistently deliver quickly and on time tend to be rewarded with keeping the business, if not getting more, assuming that quality and accuracy are perfect.

134

## Beyond Filling Orders

Supply chain speed isn't just about physical movement, although the velocity of inventory turns, given the limitations imposed by lengthening replenishment cycles and uncertainties in delivery timing, is a constant target for increase. Speed of information and speed of transactions represent a huge component of the overall speed equation.

When orders can be taken electronically and acknowledgments returned through the same channels, when payments can be made electronically, when the Internet is used to provide access to transaction initiation and status review ... well, the world has changed. Furthermore, the pace has picked up considerably. These and other tools and techniques are being aggressively used to cut transaction times and reduce order processing time cycles. The impact on cash-to-cash cycle time, where the rubber really meets the road in financial performance, can be enormous.

## Moving Past the Tactical

In another arena, speed to market has emerged as a critical factor in supply chain performance and competitive advantage. This does not entail the lightning-quick performance and lock-step integration of warehousing and transport, as fulfillment does. But it does involve faster product development cycles, increased involvement of suppliers in the development process, collapsed timelines for packaging and marketing activity, white-knuckle scheduling through production, and extraordinary planning and coordination of launch communications and movement.

Flawless execution at this stage can keep a company in the spotlight for a long time, while the competition is still struggling to get an audition.

Speed to market begins to illustrate an important characteristic of supply chain speed. It is really about cultural attitude and behavior with the mechanics of fulfillment really being a manifestation of core strengths and values.

That's right. Organizations that exercise, expect, and demand speed in their interactions and relationships are the winners in the supply chain speed race. It's all part of a whole. Speed to change. Speed to make decisions. Speed to react. Speed to proact, to plan, to set new courses, to evaluate and anticipate, and to *act*.

These are all components of supply chain speed. Small wonder that organizations that are good at all those tend to be good at the nuts and bolts of transactional speed, operational speed, and fulfillment speed.

We'll take the case a step further and suggest that organizations that aren't good at cultural speed and hence embracing and making change might not understand the context for operational speed within their own four walls. They might not understand what it takes to sustain satisfying relationships that depend on performance speed (getting products to customers on *their* timetables). Maybe future research can look into the issue.

## Don't Forget the Human Dimension

This new age of supply chain speed requires operations to run well, 24/7. At peak seasons, it often feels like each day has 30 hours, and each week has nine days. The demands and expectations for people performance escalate in all facets of supply chain operations, from customer service centers to order entry, and ultimately in pick/pack and shipping operations in the warehouse.

Traditionally, we don't do well at planning and managing off-shift operations for either white collar or blue collar functions. Performance is typically low, along with quality and morale, while turnover is predictably high.

The problem results in part from the fact that we just don't treat people as well on the off shift as on the prime shift. When lighting, heating, cooling, and ventilation; lunch and break facilities; and parking areas are not as attractive for the nighttime employees as for the day workers, those who handle the off-shift operations will feel, and behave, as second-class citizens.

This may be the next great challenge for businesses: finding ways to treat all employees on all shifts in all functions like the valuable first-class assets they really are. Time will tell if we are up to that challenge.

## Back to Fulfillment Speed

So here's our fundamental position: speed is good and speed is necessary. That mantra runs contrary to the slogan of state highway patrols all over the United States: "Speed kills." Although that would be something of an overstatement in the supply chain world, it's also true that indiscriminate speed can fall short of the purpose.

When we become enamored of raw speed, when we fall into the trap of speed for speed's sake, or when we feel compelled to deliver speed in every instance because we fear that's what our competitors are doing, we are on a slippery slope. And a costly one.

Some things don't need the ultimate in speed. You know it, your customers know it, and their customers know it. They know it in their heart of hearts, whether they'll cut you any slack or not. Body parts for collision repair, for example, are entering a process that takes days, if not weeks, to complete; they don't need to be at the shop the next morning. Summer clothes don't need to be delivered before spring. The eiderdown jacket from the outdoor outfitter doesn't need to be in your hands until the snow flies, either.

Some things *do* need speed. They include out-of-stock goods, sell-one and make-one JIT items, mission-critical service parts for all sorts of equipment and machinery, and communications network components in the wake of a storm.

Too few companies know how to evaluate and discriminate among these possibilities. Too few companies know how to apply different — and appropriate — levels of speed to them, and how to communicate the cost consequences and benefits to their customers.

## Biting the Bullet

We owe it to our customers to talk straight with them about the costs of their service levels and the alternatives. Few of us have the courage to pull it off, to tell them that the speed of service they are demanding comes at a cost.

Think about it. What could it mean to your cost structure if you could ship some things in two days instead of one? What if you could aggregate enough to shift some things from LTL to truckload movement? Or from truckload to rail? Could you use less expedited air? Are all your value-adding activities really adding value? How much of the savings could you pass on to your customers? And what would that do for your price competitiveness?

We're not suggesting that anyone arbitrarily apply the one-size-fits-all approach to customers in reducing speed and service. But finding the right balance of speed and service for the right mix of products can be a win-win for you and the customer. A thoughtful manager who talks straight and knows *when* and *how* to apply supply chain speed can win out over the pedal-to-the-metal, speed-at-all-costs gang.

## Stopping at the Edge of the Cliff

Hold it! Let's not get too carried away here. Nobody wants to go back to the bad old days of "Please allow 8 to 10 weeks for delivery." Or 52-week lead times for critical industrial components. These were hallmarks of the old economy before we understood the possibilities offered by effective supply chain management.

The United States wasn't really competitive back then before the Japanese sounded their industrial wake-up call. The global economy did not yet exist. And we — as individual consumers and as business partners — took what "they" would give us — in quality, in quantity, and in time.

Those days are long gone, thank goodness. Now, we would like to have that book in less than a week, please.

Just not before 10:30 tomorrow morning.

# FLEXIBILITY

Whatever you are, be a good one.
*Abraham Lincoln*

New ideas stir from every corner. They show up disguised innocently as interruptions, contradictions and embarrassing dilemmas. Beware of total strangers and friends alike who shower you with comfortable sameness, and remain open to those who make you uneasy, for they are the true messengers of the future.
*Rob Lebow*

Weep not that the world changes—
did it keep a stable, changeless state, it were cause indeed to weep.
*William Cullen Bryant*

It so happens that the world is undergoing a transformation to which
no change that has yet occurred can be compared, either in scope or rapidity.
*Charles de Gaulle*

## Why Flexibility and Why Now?

"Flexibility" is one of those words that can mean whatever we choose it to mean. It has, in our view, become shorthand for doing the things that it takes to succeed in the fast-changing world of supply chain management. Like many old things that have become new again, it has gained favor, along with some measure of fervor.

"Agility" and "flexibility" are terms that had their beginnings in manufacturing in the early '90s, and then made their way into the supply chain, touching on strategy and marketing along the way. We might endlessly debate the relationship of supply chain flexibility to supply chain agility, but that's best left to the academics. There's been loads of research (Michigan State, MIT, Cal, Toronto, et al.) and some original thinking on the subject by the Supply Chain Council, Remko van Hoek, and others. For now, we are more interested in a practical view of flexibility, and what it can mean to a supply chain.

The distinction between agility and flexibility is largely artificial. One might consider agility's market sensitivity, reliance on information, process integration, and partner-leveraging to be all a part of one 21st century model. That model then includes defined attributes of product flexibility (customization), volume flexibility (demand-based capacity management), new product flexibility (launch and time to market for new products), distribution flexibility (the ability to reach or provide access to new markets), and response flexibility (the capability to be quickly driven by needs and demands of customers and potential customers).

We might not be so interested in the idea of flexibility if there hadn't been so much change in the nature of the demands placed upon supply chain performance. But the days are behind us when factories could run the same product for days on end and ship in railcar quantities. Not to mention the now-archaic commonplace of warehouses holding excess product, shipping pallets out in full truckloads only later and over some period of time.

Today, the pace has quickened to approximately Mach 2.

People are no longer exaggerating when they talk about a lot size of one or mass customization. We are expected to fill orders for quantities of one or two units, not cases, and to ship mixed pallets of products. Customers want special markings and labels, store-ready preparation, and kitting. Parcel shipment has become a major, if not dominating, factor in our lives. In short, the concepts of lean, quick changeover, short runs, customer and channel-specific processes, and flexibility are no longer pie-in-the-sky best practices; they've become requirements for survival.

Flexibility is admittedly the key ingredient in a recipe for enterprise resilience (see the chapter on Resilience). But our purpose here is to look at the application of flexibility in ongoing day-to-day operations.

## The Conventional Wisdom, and Some Definitions

To some, the concept of flexibility can be reduced to a handful of techniques in supply chain operations: redundancy, interchangeability, supply management, and postponement. All of these do play a role in at least creating possibilities for flexibility. They read like conventional wisdom, which is usually a term of derision. But in this instance, they might be right on target. Let's look at each one.

▪ *Redundancy* is simply capacity that would be deemed excess unless and until it was required by either a catastrophe or a demand spike. Redundancy might also involve bricks and mortar facilities, capital equipment, and people.

▪ *Interchangeability* means using the same equipment, layouts, processes, and standards throughout the network, so that any activity might be seamlessly re-routed.

▪ *Supply management* involves a number of carefully balanced initiatives to develop alternative supply sources, to manage redundant supply capacity for reallocated demand within the network, and to draw up flexibility contingency plans within the supply base.

▪ *Postponement* could be called the holy grail of flexibility, albeit a more attainable one than the Arthurian original. Among other things, postponement either allows production to skate on quick changeover and short-run tactics, or amplifies the capabilities that result.

Just imagine the gains in efficiency, consistency, and inventory management you'd achieve if you could make dozens of customer-specific SKUs in one run, labeling them only when orders are received and treating them as a single SKU until then. Consider the asset investment ramifications of not having any finished-goods inventory, assembling components only upon receipt of an order.

Picture an apparel retailer that can wait until the early returns are in before dyeing goods in this season's hot new color — and avoid dyeing them in this season's not-so-hot new color. Retailers would be ecstatic if merchandise could be held in a master distribution center a short distance from a network of stores until demand patterns are established to warrant shipment.

From batteries to paint, from T-shirts to shoes, from frozen peas to PCs, postponement means a big deal in the flexible world.

But there's more.

## Other Contributors to Flexibility

Let's not forget those things that make manufacturing flexible. It's important that these be institutionalized in the supply base or in internal operations (see the chapter on Manufacturing Integration). These improved processes form the foundation for all other flexibility initiatives. They cannot be short-changed if one's interested in the long haul.

One great way to develop redundancy is to contract with third parties for capacity. Usually, this is done to accommodate seasonal peak periods. It is typically not cheap, but is most often far less expensive than carrying redundancy year-round. The redundancy can involve supply, manufacturing, transportation, or distribution space.

Defining processes, including resource requirements, for so-called non-standard products and activities can be a life-saver. Typically, the elements aren't really non-standard, but because they represent such a small minority of transactions, they get lost in the shuffle of designing new systems or facilities.

When they do show up in real life, if the workarounds haven't been specified, they can bring an operation to its knees — and usually at the worst possible time. The investment of solving these problems in advance is worth its weight in Valium.

Another key to operational flexibility is to design materials handling and control systems with adaptability in mind. A couple of things tend to happen after new facilities and systems are brought on-line. One is that customer and order profiles change, often even before implementation has been completed.

The average order no longer consists of "x" pieces in "y" line items. The average number of totes in an order train is no longer "z," but has become bi-modal, neither mode processing efficiently through the two-mile conveyor system. In addition, because a significant percentage of orders now arrive complete at the first pick module, they can dispense with the half-hour ride to the sorters.

And so it goes, as the late sci-fi author Kurt Vonnegut would say. Ensuring that mechanized systems are not too rigid and are relatively easy to re-engineer is critical to the flexible life.

Then there could be more customer issues. As time passes, individual customers will diverge in their requests and demands for special handling. It is no longer OK to tell a customer "We don't do that here." That means your mechanical systems and processes must be set up to do essentially the same thing in different ways.

A vital enabler to successful organizational flexibility is the ease with which information systems can adapt to change. A sure warning sign is when a company decides that something "can't be done" because "the system won't let us."

The bedrock foundation for any and all of these approaches to flexibility is, however, cultural. Flexibility is only a word to organizations that try to force all transactions and relationships through a one-size-fits-all model. The old idea of high-volume standardization equating to "efficiency" doesn't work in customer-focused demand-driven supply chains.

## Recap

Summing up, flexibility requires a few things, all vitally important:

- The ability and willingness to stop on a dime, and change direction when either strategy or tactics indicate.
- The capacity and desire to alter both physical and intellectual processes when customers and markets require the next level of execution.
- The capability to maintain excellence in parallel processing paths for customers and channels with differing requirements — simultaneous execution of diverse game plans.
- The discipline to set up and test alternatives in sourcing, manufacture, transportation, warehousing, order processing, information systems, and communications — both as capacity/capability solutions for seasonal and other peak periods, and as provisions against future needs to change.
- The routine integration of flexibility techniques into operations, throughout the realm of supply chain planning and execution.
- A culture that goes beyond embracing change to become one that seeks change and understands how to leverage fragmented, diverse, and focused solutions for long-term marketplace success.

## An Inevitable Conclusion

In the end, of course, there's more to flexibility than its vocabulary. Like most worthwhile efforts, there's loads of hard work, persistence, stamina, commitment, and resources involved. What a payback, though!

# RESILIENCE

He who limps is still walking.
*Stanislaw J. Lec*

Perhaps catastrophe is the natural human environment,
and even though we spend a good deal of energy trying to get away from it,
we are programmed for survival amid catastrophe.
*Germaine Greer*

Calamity is the perfect glass wherein we truly see and know ourselves.
*William Davenant*

My downfall raises me to infinite heights.
*Napoleon Bonaparte*

## The Wake-Up Calls

Terrorist attacks, natural disasters, armed conflict, ethnic violence, floods, famines, hurricanes, tsunamis, typhoons … the signs are all around us. Have we reached the prophesied End Times? Probably not. But like everything else in the 21st century, the pace, scale, and intensity of supply chain interruptions are on the rise.

Given that intensity, we can no longer afford the luxury of 19th or even 20th century responses. Supply chains for all classes of commodity, material, and product are too competitive, too global, and too necessary for social and business survival. Food must get to hungry people, and clothing to those without. Goods must be produced and reach their markets, and the myriad of business enterprises involved must keep operating and paying their employees, so that they, in turn, can continue to buy what supply chains bring them.

These parlous conditions have prompted much discussion about how to make enterprises — and their supply chains — more resilient. Truth be told, there's a big difference in degree between an organization's being flexible (see the chapter on Flexibility) and being resilient. But 9/11, Katrina, and other events are forcing us to focus on resilience — the capability of bouncing back from major events.

Dr. Yossi Sheffi of the Massachusetts Institute of Technology (MIT) is one of the leading researchers on this topic. In a miracle of timing, his book *The Resilient Enterprise,* the product of three years of research at MIT's Center for Transportation and Logistics, was published immediately after the most destructive U.S. hurricane season in memory. Dr. Sheffi has rightfully captured the attention of business leaders, who have quickly come to grasp how critical supply chain operations are to business resilience.

## We Know How to Plan for Hurricanes, Don't We?

One would think so. But this isn't really about hurricanes; they merely served as the latest reminder of the importance of resilience. "Plan" is the operative word here. Resilience isn't simply about working hard and getting things back in order after an event. It is about planning. And relationships. And attitude. And selectivity. (See the chapters on Relationships in the Supply Chain and Supply Chain Planning.) Let's explore some new views on how to prepare for an unknown but challenging set of calamities.

## Scope and Range

First, it's important to know that the situations and events that can cripple vulnerable organizations aren't limited to natural disasters and terrorism. And they certainly aren't confined to the internal workings of a company. There are plenty of other threats out there, including the operational or financial failure of a supplier, new competition, quality failures, product tampering (internal or external), theft, unintended consequences such as chemical or drug interactions, financial irregularities, technology change, and the loss of a dominant customer or channel.

Further, disruptions aren't confined to supply chain operations, although supply chain execution can be a part of the solution. The PR disaster and loss of customer confidence that result from product tampering may have nothing to do with supply chain failure or collapse. But the solution — isolating the tampered products to minimize the chances of recurrence — relies on reverse logistics capabilities.

## Facing the Future Before It Has Been Defined

For those inclined to think in terms of how to react to bad news, wake up! Resilience isn't about reaction, but rather, *proaction.*

Developing a resilient enterprise starts with taking an organized and rigorous approach to identifying vulnerabilities and the related possibilities for disruption. These may be categorized by type of vulnerability and degree of hazard.

There is more than one way to define and quantify supply chain risk. One approach would be to begin by categorizing risks as those specific to the individual company, and those that are faced by all players in a given market. There are then three elements of risk profiling that incorporate both categories:

■ *Supply side risk.* This would involve a visual, text, and data profile of the supplier base with its production and distribution nodes and networks.

■ *Demand side risk.* Again, this would involve a visual, text, and data profile of customer demand points to create a visual and quantitative picture of the outbound supply chain.

■ *Supply chain network risk.* This would be a similar picture and description of the production and distribution network and products.

Vulnerability mapping also considers whether the potentials are internally or externally generated. Disruptions may originate in these three organizational areas:

■ *In supply.* A disaster or even something as mundane as a lack of capacity for either growth or response can bring down a supply chain.

■ *In demand.* Any number of factors could cause demand for a product to plummet — think of skyrocketing fuel prices that cause SUV sales to collapse or an airline bankruptcy that results in the cancellation of orders for dozens of expensive new planes.

■ *In internal operations.* An example of an internally caused disruption would be the discovery that someone had hacked into the corporate information and communications systems, crippling operations and triggering panic throughout the supply chain.

## Getting a Grip on the Possibilities

In any case, the potential threats seem nothing less than overwhelming. Scores of showstoppers can appear on the vulnerability radar screen. How to grapple with them?

The venerable Johari window provides a useful tool here. Vulnerabilities may be placed in one of four boxes aligned along axes of probability, from low to high, and impacts from light to severe. For global enterprises, this exercise can become incredibly complex because process and flow relationships are built into the evaluation.

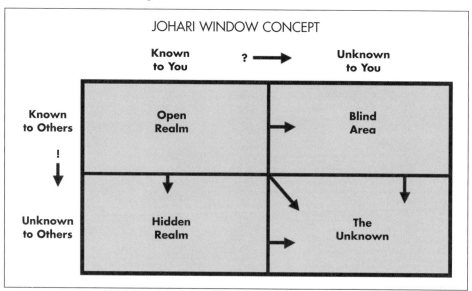

*Note: The Johari window was developed in the middle of the last century to illustrate interpersonal relationships and communications. Its structure has since been adapted for many business applications.*

The point of the exercise, of course, is to identify what can go wrong, the chances of its happening, and how much devastation it would wreak.

Colgate-Palmolive approaches the subject broadly and pre-emptively. It has set up a system of *daily* early warnings to spot and correct brewing trouble, from labor unrest to theft and counterfeiting.

## What to Do About Them

Once you've identified — and classified— the threats, the next step is to translate them into actionable items aimed at both preventing the disruptions and at reducing their impact and enhancing your company's prospects of a speedy recovery should they occur.

Both elements are vital to resilience. Events such as monsoons may not be preventable, but devising workarounds and developing alternative sources can go a long way toward mitigating their effects. The likelihood of a calamitous fire may be reduced through a number of actions, but the bypass and recovery paths still need to be defined.

Interestingly, the MIT research has shown that, while the likelihood of a specific event in a specific location may be rare, the chances for that event to occur *somewhere* in the supply chain remain relatively high. Extending that notion, the probability of some major event, somewhere in the chain, is extremely high, and warrants the prudent exercise of resilience planning throughout the company.

Not so amazingly, failure to prepare for even low-probability events or to address conditions that might mitigate their impact actually raises the probability of calamitous outcomes.

## Some Tactics and Techniques

Here's where the intense application of flexibility and resilience solutions comes into play. The categories of flexibility are simple enough to state, but they can be complex and fragile in their execution, particularly when one is contemplating the issues of corporate survival and failure.

Besides knowing how to identify, evaluate, and plan for threats, it's important to build processes and triggers to help in identifying incipient disruptive events. Programmatic initiatives to assist in prevention and recovery include:

- Interchangeability of plants, of people, of parts, and of processes. This allows seamless rerouting to operations unaffected by a disruptive event, without the need to redesign or otherwise overcome, non-standard processes or components.
- Redundancy in capacity, in power backup, in information processing, in employee skills, in inventory stocks. This allows rerouting orders, processes, materials, and people to points of either need or available capacity in the maintenance of supply chain execution.
- Postponement of final manufacturing and shipping steps for mass customization solutions. This permits shifts of production, for example, to an unaffected facility, needing only the parts and labels that are customer/market/country-specific to be moved to the "new" producing location.
- Strategic supply management to find the right balance among tactics of multiple sourcing, single-sourcing, and intimate supplier relationships to overcome disruption. The key to making this work lies in the quality of communications and working relationships among the supply chain partners. Some of the related solutions are programmatic (e.g.,

supplier-level contingency and business continuity planning); others are motivational (e.g., rallying 'round the flag in times of turmoil and distress).

■ Customer relations management to protect key customers from the worst effects of the event. This entails the quality of public and private communications regarding consequences and next steps, and a demonstrated commitment to helping customers recover. This relies on the pre-existence of strong, organization-wide relationships.

■ Collaboration on security initiatives with supply chain partners, within industry groups, and with government agencies (notably in the Customs-Trade Partnership Against Terrorism program developed by U.S. Customs and Border Protection, now part of the Transportation Security Administration).

## Organizational Implications

Does all this mean that a company needs to appoint a CRO, a Chief Resilience Officer? Dr. Sheffi contends (correctly, we believe) that resilient enterprises seem to have resilient qualities built into their DNA — that the culture breeds and promotes resilience. We lean in that direction as well. And we hardly think that adding another position to the executive infrastructure is the best way to promote resilience. However, it does seem that the executive who leads supply chain management would be the logical candidate to head up any resilience planning initiatives.

## In Summary

In just a few short years, resilience has become a fundamental requirement for business survival in a complicated, interdependent, and dangerous world. If you look on the bright side, getting good at the components of resilience also means being good at the things that can make a positive competitive difference. Catastrophic events, managed well, can give an enterprise a very public opportunity to shine in front of its very best customers. And how many opportunities does one get to advance the cause of "customers for life"?

# VISIBILITY

The music is nothing if the audience is deaf.
*Walter Lippmann*

Vision without action is a daydream; action without vision is a nightmare.
*Japanese Proverb*

The power of imagination created the illusion that my vision
went much farther than the naked eye could actually see.
*Nelson Mandela*

Where secrecy reigns, carelessness and ignorance delight to hide ...
*Daniel C. Gelman*

## Whatever Happened to Visibility?

Supply chain visibility was all the rage at one time. The trade publications were chock full of articles and interviews. Conferences were held on the topic and keynote addresses spoke to "visibility" to no end. Experts sprang up overnight, and consultants mined the hot new topic for all it was worth.

What it was worth to them was, perhaps, plenty. What it was worth to others is harder to say. The furor seems to have died down, beginning approximately in 2001. Why? What happened?

Dr. Lawrence Lapide, research director at the Massachusetts Institute of Technology's Center for Transportation and Logistics, offers some interesting observations on the topic. Lapide contends that the major shortcoming was that the term "visibility" had no particular meaning.

Further, Lapide argues that visibility never was the real issue. What's important is what one does about things — conditions, events, trends — that have become visible. At the end of the day, informed action trumps information alone. We can only agree and applaud.

## Is There More?

It's not that visibility, however defined, hasn't any merit or use. Some dozen years ago, a leading apparel retailer, with genuinely global sourcing and very dense national distribution, conceived a vision for a "glass pipeline" that would provide total supply chain visibility. It knew what it wanted, but it did not have the tools and resources to achieve it. Like so many pioneers and visionaries, it was ahead of the wave.

Today's world is different, and we think that one reason that the visibility furor died down is that visibility is here. In fact, it's so commonplace that we often take visibility for granted. We might raise Dr. Lapide's fundamental question, though: "What is anyone *doing* about what has been made visible?"

## Part of the Visibility Challenge

Here we go, throwing rocks at the techno-geeks, again. But it must be said: It's a mistake to let the Information Systems community try to define these things. It took them forever to learn that a one-page summary of exceptions was preferable to a data-rich report of several hundred pages .

Similarly, mere visibility or the presentation of data doesn't have much meaning. It takes some work and planning to construct systems that transform and translate data into information. It is visible information, not visible data, that can be acted upon to correct or prevent problems.

There's another component to the equation. It's that information really needs to be the input stream to intelligence, if resulting actions are to be on target and effective. Sometimes enough context and logic can be built into systems — think decision trees that permit the leap from data and information to intelligence (even though further analysis by weak and inefficient human brainpower may still be needed). Information without context is messy and tricky, and actions based on such can have unintended consequences.

This challenge still exists in the worlds of data and information; imagine how difficult it was to address a few years ago.

## Developments in Visibility

We submit that visibility is here — at least at the data level. It has become table stakes for software providers in all facets of the supply chain business. Maybe this development was a natural evolution, maybe it gained momentum from the visibility craze, or maybe it got a big push from the parcel carriers.

As is often the case, event visibility and event management were developing in manufacturing applications before they surfaced in other business segments. But the supply chain world has made great strides in this area to date.

We were suitably impressed a few years ago when FedEx and UPS demonstrated that they could track the precise status and location of a package. Of course, nowadays you can do it yourself, online, using their systems.

Then it became "normal" for logistics service providers in the fulfillment business to be able to present the status of any order, at any processing stage, to their customers. As you might expect, the customers can now look for themselves, using the LSP's Internet-enabled systems.

Visibility has become an integral component of all of the big application areas: customer relationship management (CRM); collaborative planning, forecasting, and replenishment (CPFR); warehouse management (WMS) and yard management systems (YMS); transportation management systems (TMS); and product lifecycle management (PLM).

The last apparent holdout has been reverse logistics (RL). But it too has joined the parade, judging from recent announcements of visibility enhancements to RL software (the latest by Newgistics). For several years, other RL software has possessed the capability to highlight cues and pointers for quality and recall possibilities, based on automatic analysis of transaction volumes, patterns, and trends.

Some level of visibility is just about everywhere. And perhaps more importantly, there has been a general trend toward providing useful information rather than mere data.

## Actionable Information

It's not helpful to know an on-hand inventory quantity. But it's vital to know that you have only three days' supply on hand. Yet that piece of information in itself is not relevant if a three-month supply is scheduled to arrive tomorrow. That information, in turn, is not all that useful unless there is evidence — visibility — that the truck carrying the new shipment is on time and within a hundred miles of its destination.

If more product is not on the way, or if the expected delivery is not enough to cover the anticipated demand, or if demand has increased, then the system should automatically generate an electronic purchase order for expedited delivery. Or conversely, if the on-hand quantity represents a three-year supply, the system should automatically cancel any open orders unless it's a new product ramping up for introduction in the marketplace. In both cases, visibility has triggered informed action.

Other illustrations include notification of status — holds, diversions, port and customs clearance, and the like. In the case of goods sourced offshore, this allows for corrective or ameliorating actions to be initiated in hopes of heading off a crisis.

## Really Actionable Information

Not all visibility is limited to the world of traditional information systems. The *kanban* system popularized in manufacturing relies on a card — a visible signal for replenishment action. A modern application of the principle developed by Visible Inventory, Inc. provides visibility to inventory status at the SKU or bin level. Beyond that, it relies on built-in sensors to determine whether quantities are at reorder points, or at critical levels that require replenishment orders.

## Marrying Metrics and Visibility

Visibility has more recently provided an impetus to the aggressive analysis and use of performance measurements. That's in large part the result of the development of some Web-based visibility tools. It's also the result of the integration of performance information into many WMS and TMS products.

Some fear that the idea of greater transparency in supply chain performance is more dream than reality, but the pieces of the puzzle are beginning to appear. The next challenges are to learn how to be selective in what is presented, in what detail, and to whom, and to reinforce the information processes with actions that have meaning and staying power.

## The China Syndrome

Late-breaking news from the offshoring front suggests that visibility may once again be in need of attention. Sooner or later, that attention will be paid, but there are challenges to be overcome.

An international shipment can involve dozens of physical and informational touch points, along with performance variability of perhaps as much as 40 percent. It migrates from the category of frightening to terrifying when some of the operating partners in a global supply chain don't offer integrated visibility in their systems.

As a consequence, we've regressed to some extent in the age of globalization, stimulating a renaissance of management by hope and other dangerous tactics.

## Back to the Beginning

There's an old saying, "We are drowning in data but thirsty for information." Visibility is much more useful when there are flags to mark what is actually important.

Now that we've got more visibility than ever before, it may be time to get introspective about whether we're doing more problem-solving than ever before. Success in this arena starts with individual intellectual curiosity — yours! Corporate attitudes and visions are important foundations for individual efforts, though.

We suspect that the companies in which being proactive and flexible are emphasized and rewarded are the same companies that are taking advantage of information visibility. They are probably moving up to the level of intelligence for the most effective use of visibility.

# MIGRATORY SUPPLY CHAINS

A man must carry knowledge with him if he would bring home knowledge.
*Samuel Johnson*

My favorite thing is to go where I've never been.
*Diane Arbus*

A permanent state of transition is man's most noble condition.
*Juan Ramon Jiminez*

Consistency is the last refuge of the unimaginative.
*Oscar Wilde*

## New Kinds of Migrants

A new term has crept into our lexicon: the migratory supply chain. But despite the similarity in name, these supply chains have little in common with robins or monarch butterflies.

What is a migratory supply chain then? It's perhaps best explained by way of example. For many, the migratory supply chain has been epitomized by the one operated by Sun Microsystems. Sun specializes in complex, often uniquely-configured systems with many components, individually sourced in different low-cost locales. Any given order will, therefore, have a different supply chain profile from other orders.

That means Sun's supply chain execution will migrate from order to order, with different transport components being marshaled in different sets of countries to move all of an order's components to the point of installation.

When the central authority receives word that all elements for an order are ready to ship, it notifies the various carriers in the various modes — the result being a complete and coordinated order delivery.

As complicated as that may sound, there's another factor that sometimes comes into play in migratory supply chains. If there are multiple production points, the low-cost sourcing location for a given component might also change. So, the dance of the migratory supply chain can go on, with a surprising number of variations.

## And Another Thing ...

The migratory supply chain concept is not limited to companies producing complex products with multiple and mixed sourcing points. Continuing shifts away from purely domestic manufacture create another kind of migratory supply chain.

For example, a company that's moving some manufacturing to Mexico needs to redesign its supply chain and restructure its distribution network. The flow of raw materials will take on different sizes and directions, with some going to Mexico and some going to the mother operation.

A number of things might then happen. One is that the experience could be enormously successful, prompting the company to shift even more work to Mexico. Another is that cost and quality considerations might lead the company to decide to source some components in Asia while others remain in Mexico. Either way, the supply chain must migrate to new structures and dimensions.

## The Speed Issue

Often, the migration needs to happen quickly. And, of course, even the smallest change will ripple quickly through the chain, demanding more adjustments. We used to suggest that a distribution network structure needed re-examination once every five years. Now it is clear that reviewing the overall supply chain structure is a never-ending responsibility. The changes are that many and that fast.

## The Pendulum Swings

Sometimes a clear-eyed analysis shows that the move to Mexico, or Vietnam, or Haiti has resulted in quality or dependability problems, which are only complicated by eye-popping variations in delivery timing. We move production back to the last point, and the supply chain must migrate once more.

We keep on moving. We move because markets and sources move. We move until we think we've got it right. Then something changes, and we move again. The supply chain migrates right along with all the moves.

Globalization has truly let the genie out of the bottle, with seemingly infinite possibilities for movement — and migration.

## Another Flavor of Migration

Let's take the case of a global operator with relatively stable but far-flung sources of supply, a relatively well-established network of retail outlets, and a domestic physical distribution operation that has been honed to world-class status. What does a migratory supply chain mean to this company?

Everything! It would be competitively dead without the capability and capacity to frequently migrate its supply chain to and fro and back again.

One wag with some insight into that company's operations has remarked that it doesn't have a supply chain strategy — it has a collection of contingency plans. It has to!

When the hottest-selling item of the season absolutely, positively has to be in the stores by a certain date, it must know when *not* to risk the slow boat from China and move goods by air. Conversely, it also needs to know when to stop air expediting and resume movement by water.

When port congestion ties up operations in California, it has to be able to pull the trigger and shift to ports in the Pacific Northwest (whether U.S. or Canadian). All of these options have ramifications for ground transportation — truck, rail, or both — based on cost, speed, and availability.

It gets even more interesting. The new Lazaro Cardenas port in Mexico opens up another alternative to Long Beach and Oakland, with the result that U.S. railroads are investing billions in getting ready for it.

But there's more in play, even today. The retailer must be able to restructure its supply chain to divert shipments to East Coast ports with little notice, and it does this routinely, moving goods through the Panama Canal or the Suez Canal in Egypt. Whether the goods arrive in Charleston or Savannah depends somewhat on what's happening at the Port of New York/New Jersey. If the port of arrival is shifted, the plan for ground transport will require serious adjustment to accommodate these migrations.

The retailer does all this several times a year, based on dynamic conditions in its supply chain, and on local developments with its principal ports of entry. It has been doing it for some time, since well before the term migratory supply chain popped up.

## Looking Ahead

Only time will tell whether the term "migratory supply chain" takes hold. But whatever we call it, the phenomenon of conscious supply chain migration is here to stay.

Demanded by good planning and the imperative to satisfy customers, enabled by better information, and fueled by globalization, the migratory supply chain is a bigger and bigger fact of supply chain management life for a growing number of companies.

Despite all the uproar about China, we've only begun to scratch the surface of what is possible in globalized supply chains. The trend is fairly clear — more, more complex, and faster. Migratory supply chains may be the only way to keep up.

This much we can pretty well guarantee: Whoever is standing still will *not* get the license plate number of the supply chain that runs them down.

# SUPPLY CHAIN PLANNING

It's better to be prepared for an opportunity and not have one
than to have an opportunity and not be prepared.
*Whitney Young*

In baiting a mousetrap with cheese, always leave room for the mouse.
*Saki (H. H. Munro)*

No more prizes for predicting rain. Prizes only for building arks.
*Anonymous*

Competition means decentralized planning by many separate persons.
*Friedrich Hayek*

## Facing the Truth

The Queen Mother of the "P" words is planning. In reality, supply chain people are usually not big on planning. We are reactors, problem solvers, fixers, and deliverers. We typically wait to receive the orders before we devote all of our energies to fulfilling them. When things go wrong, we spring into corrective-action mode.

Both our peers and our superiors tend to think of us that way. We are operatives, the ones who make things happen. Doing our jobs well is expected, and saving money is highly appreciated. But planning belongs in another department. As for strategic planning, well, that's for generals and board chairs.

## Strategy and Tactics

To a great extent, supply chain management is more a set of tactical activities than a strategic exercise. In the military, there is a distinction between long-range plans and battle tactics. In football, the tactics involve blocking and tackling, and the game plan is the strategy. The tactician is focused on doing things right; the strategist is more concerned about whether people are doing the right things.

A surprising number of companies seem to function without a strategy; their only visible tactics are to produce earnings that are within ranges of expectation. Once again, the mathematician C.L. Dodgson gets right to the heart of the matter with his observation in *Alice in Wonderland:* "If you don't know where you're going, then any road will take you there."

## Planning Pokes Its Head Into the Room
Whether the emphasis is placed on the tactical or the strategic, planning constitutes a critical part of the success equation in modern supply chain management. Like it or not, we've got to get metaphorically outside of the house and extend the horizons of our defined world.

If we apply a layer of planning to our tactical operations, we'll surely do a better job of order fulfillment or problem solving or whatever. The execution of a strategy without the corresponding planning is too much like driving blindfolded in the Daytona 500 — you might get the hang of it eventually, if you've not been killed in the first turn.

## Planning Applications
We've explored some planning applications in earlier chapters. Distribution network design is fundamentally a planning exercise in determining where to put what kinds of facilities to serve which customers. Inventory planning derives from the same effort — it calculates how much stock of what type needs to be how near to certain markets and accounts. These both rest on the planning assumptions that describe and define the service levels required to retain old customers and acquire new ones, while maintaining and building market share.

Planning, as we have noted, represents *the* critical success factor in implementing new information systems. Actually, planning is also the cornerstone of any change initiative, whether technological, process, or cultural.

Almost everything we work at benefits from planning — new equipment installation, facility relocation, and training programs, to name a few. They all need planning and documentation as well as active management, followup, and evaluation. That also goes for descriptions, definitions, resource identification and commitment, budgets, business cases, timelines, risk analysis and mitigations, go/no-go decision points, and exit strategies.

The communications that accompany development and change initiatives are worthy of sub-plans all their own — message creation, target audiences, planned outcomes and responses, and validation processes.

Planning for labor in all aspects of supply chain operations is vital, for reasons of both cost management and service performance. This needs to be done for the short term to meet expected peaks and valleys of activity as well as for longer planning horizons to prepare for longer-term growth or shrinkage, or even changes in transaction mix. Those changes, in turn, must lead to plans for training and development, and for recruitment and retention. Indeed, succession planning in the management and executive ranks holds as much importance in the supply chain as in the rest of the organization.

These plans are growing in importance as entire companies begin to face up to the imminent collapse of skilled resource availability with the retirement of baby-boomers.

Likewise, capacity planning takes on near- and short-term dimensions for both facilities and transportation. In this arena, planning for peaks may involve planning for LSP support, and planning and executing an RFP evaluation process.

Improvement programs and initiatives need planning: opportunity sizing, analytic tool and approach definition, and resourcing, for example. Setting up supplier relationships, even defining the sourcing philosophy and processes, requires more planning. Creating customer relationships with purpose requires still more planning (particularly if understanding *their* business drivers is included).

The 21st century's newly recognized critical success factor of enterprise resilience completely depends on planning, planning, and more planning (see the chapter on Resilience).

There's no end to the applications of planning in supply chain operations. Certainly, there's more involved than the applications cited above, which merely illustrate the scope and range of operational planning in the supply chain.

Can planning be overdone? Yes, but it doesn't happen as often as we'd like to believe. The level of detail, the rigor of analysis, and the depth of communications all need to be crafted to fit the situation. Empty *pro forma* plans with more focus on structure than on reality can be positively dangerous. Take note — there are very, very few things in our tactical, operational world that should be attempted without organized planning.

## Relating Operational Tactics and Strategies

Now that we've made a case for broader and deeper planning at the operational level, let's move out of our comfort zone and into the realm of pure planning. Because we are so often sidetracked by tactical issues, it becomes easy to ignore planning at the strategic level. Yet the companies that succeed are the ones that emphasize the development of sound strategies, followed by execution.

Although some might argue that the most successful corporations are those blessed with luck, we maintain that creative strategies, accompanied by superb execution of those plans, have a lot more to do with it. As Louis Pasteur, the 19th century French scientist, keenly observed, "... chance favors the prepared mind." Saying "It's better to be lucky than to be good" is a dangerous position to take, imputing little worth to vision and discipline.

## Making the Link

In the leading companies, strategy closely relates to operations when it comes to both implementation and ongoing achievement. In developing a strategic plan, seven critical questions — all with operational implications — must be addressed:
- What changes are contemplated by and for our existing customers?
- How will these changes influence our marketing plans — and our day-to-day operating relationships?
- What might we change to successfully approach new customers and markets?
- What changes are under way or under consideration by our most significant competitors?
- Where are current industry trends likely to peak, and how will that affect our current practices?

- What are our internal and external vulnerabilities, and are our strengths sufficient for new demands?
- What are the most critical issues our company faces?
- What changes will most influence our company's profitability?

In most cases, the environment is the same for every competitor; however, the successful ones are those who are best able to anticipate changes and take pre-emptive action. For example, previous decades have seen a conversion of logistics service companies from largely union operations to primarily non-union. The successful firms saw the change coming and were successful in adapting before the situation reached crisis proportions. Most of those that did not adapt are no longer in business.

It is easy, but dangerous, to ignore competitive activity. For example, some staffing services now offer a complete materials handling service on a piecework basis, making them direct competitors of traditional warehouse service providers. At the same time, a few warehousing service companies have entered the staffing business, offering temporary workers not only to their own customers but to others.

Outsourcing and globalization are two strategic moves that influence supply-chain managers and their related operations even to the extent of floor-level planning. With the continuing transfer of manufacturing activity from domestic sites to overseas locations, the flow of materials has changed radically in geography, mode, and units of measure. This creates new challenges and opportunities for those who manage the flow. ("Challenges and opportunities" is the language of consultants, and it's code for problems — big problems.)

The globalization of logistics offers another significant point of change. Unlike manufacturing, logistics globalization tends to favor the company that is playing on its own turf. The hometown player has a clear advantage, particularly when there are significant culture gaps.

## Digging Deeper — Strategically

When it comes to making decisions about corporate strategy, the questions supply chain organizations must answer look very much like the questions facing every other part of the organization. Those questions include:

- Are we generalists or specialists?
- What is our target market?
- Should we practice vertical or horizontal integration?
- Which of these is our growth imperative:
  - Earnings?
  - Volume?
  - Market share?

In preparation for development of a corporate strategy, you should recognize that there are only a few key questions that define the elements of a strategy. First, what is the business that we are *really* in? Second, who is our *preferred* customer? Third, what is our *special magic?* Next what do our customers think of us? And, finally, how will we survive?

Corporate strategists have long realized that the company's apparent activity may not be its real activity. For example, Southwest Airlines claims that it is a customer service company that happens to run an airline. A lamp shade manufacturer might decide that it is really in the light control business. A warehousing 3PL (or LSP) might understand that real estate development is its true financial lifeblood.

Good strategists target certain customers. Some seek to attract a few very large clients; others, citing concerns about becoming overly dependent on a few clients, seek out a large number of small accounts, none of which accounts for a significant percentage of total sales.

The top companies recognize and exploit their *special magic*, something that they can do better than anyone else in the business. They also recognize the importance of taking the pulse of the customers, not just occasionally but on a regular basis. Finally, the best strategists recognize the inherent fragility of every organization, and study the resilience gap to determine what steps they must take in order to survive when things go all pear-shaped.

## Strategic Planning Choices With Operational Consequences

An early strategic choice lies in whether to be asset-based or non-asset-based (or to paraphrase Shakespeare, to buy or not to buy). The vertical integrator is likely to build and own warehouse facilities and possibly also own and operate some transportation assets. The horizontal integrator will seek to avoid asset investment by renting or leasing its capital equipment.

Companies that focus on maximizing return on investment capital (ROIC) will strive to be asset-light. Other strategists believe that they can make money with good investments in real estate and capital equipment; hence, they will seek the advantages of vertical integration, all command-and-control issues aside.

Similarly, there are strategic choices when growth constitutes an objective. For some organizations, the primary growth engine is acquisition of other companies. Managing supply chain operations and planning their specifics in this environment can be very different from management in a company that is either not making acquisitions or not growing. For others, joint ventures are prime growth strategic vehicles. Still others prefer to grow with early startups.

Growth becomes more complicated when a local company chooses to go national or multinational. One strategy is to follow key customers around the globe. The alternative is to simply plant a flagpole and start selling. Either way, once the strategic decision has been made, operations become more complex in their execution.

The strategic resolution of the "who is our preferred customer" question also complicates "routine" planning and operations. Some companies actively pursue a few large customers. The ultimate end point of this approach can be to wind up with Wal-Mart, Home Depot, and Sears accounting for 95 percent of revenue. Others feel that the largest customer should never control more than 10 percent of total capacity. Still others look at the penetration of the top three or five customers, and they work hard to avoid becoming dependent on just a few companies. The supply chain ramifications are enormous.

The supply chain manager needs to understand the growth strategy of the company that controls that chain, not just his or her own. Supply chain management tactics in a company that grows by acquisition will be far different from the tactics used in companies that grow organically. And they will be different still in a company that is merely following the lead of its supply chain partners.

## Six Developments Driving Both Strategies and Tactics

In addition to outsourcing and offshoring, six practices have changed the way that supply-chain managers strategize, plan, and function. These practices are: cycle time reduction, postponement, improving return on assets (ROA), compression of distribution channels, partnerships, and shifting of control.

Improved technology, in both communications and transportation, has made it possible to deliver both goods and services at speeds that would have been inconceivable a few decades ago. Cycle time is the interval between the moment a buyer desires a product and the time that he or she receives it. Delivery times that were considered normal a few decades ago would be seen as downright unacceptable today. Management's ability — and supply chain management's capability — to meet current customer expectations has become a dominant competitive challenge.

Postponement constitutes the delay of one or more of the final steps in assembly, branding, packaging, or passage of title until the latest possible moment. By the way, postponement is not new practice — it was described in marketing textbooks in the middle of the last century.

What's new about postponement is its enthusiastic adoption in computer manufacturing as well as other corporate services. Examples include the hardware retailer that blends pigments to create a customized paint color in the store. Another example is the vegetable canner who establishes a casing and labeling line at a remote distribution center. Postponement reduces cycle time, but it does more as well. By allowing a single generic SKU to be converted into a variety of items, postponement can significantly reduce inventory investment as well as the risk of running out of stock.

Improving asset productivity usually involves sale and lease back of warehouses, handling equipment, and other corporate assets. Liquidation of excess inventory is another way to improve return on assets. One of the major selling points for logistics service providers is that they can provide logistics assets that never appear on the customer's balance sheet.

The compression of channels means disintermediation, the word that strikes terror in the hearts of many wholesale distributors. Corporate buyers may outsource logistics activities in order to reduce the number of layers in the process. When changing conditions leave the corporation burdened with idle assets, it may be sensible to reverse the outsourcing practice and use the empty trucks and warehouses that are now available, a tactic now known as "insourcing."

Some companies seek to support profitable growth through partnerships and strategic alliances. These managers try to break down the adversarial relationships that have infected procurement processes and customer relationships in many companies. The tradition has been to shop for the lowest price and to engage in frequent bidding contests in order to "keep them honest." The emphasis rests on transactions, and the most important thing in the relationship is the initial purchase price. Within the supply chain field, we see occasional but growing emphasis on strategic partnerships. These are not based solely on price, but rather on the drive to continuously improve quality and productivity — as well as total supply chain costs.

One of the mega-trends in the supply chain environment over the past 15 years has been the shift of control to retail organizations, and the resulting shift of power away from manufacturers. A few years ago, the logistics service provider focused on keeping its manufacturer client happy. Today, the emphasis has clearly switched to the retail consignee.

## Strategic and Tactical Adaptability

Part of the strategic planning process is adapting to the considerable changes that have taken place over the past decades. Not every competitor has been able to adapt successfully. For example, throughout most of the 20th century, consumer goods manufacturers commonly had dozens and sometimes even hundreds of warehouse locations in order to provide convenient service for customers in every city where their products were sold. In the grocery business, food brokers were instrumental in establishing warehouse locations. With improved communications and the development of logistics management as a profession, most manufacturers found that adequate delivery service could be provided from a much smaller number of locations.

Adaptability is not about random movement but rather the ability to observe new trends together with a willingness to change. Those managers who cannot adapt are unlikely to survive. Furthermore, the pace of change today is faster than before. Rapidly advancing technology gives us tools that no one contemplated a few decades ago. While their predecessors had to rely on phones and mail, today's supply chain executives have learned to use computerized management systems, e-mail and cell phones.

## And Your Point Is?

Strategic planning does not always involve making decisions. Sometime it consists of documenting choices that have already been made. A surprising majority of executives are not satisfied that strategic planning is really worth the effort. They may be right in the short term and dead wrong in the long term.

Unless strategy drives decision making, it may have only marginal value. If the carefully crafted strategy is as empty of meaning as the *pro forma* plan cited earlier, it can even be counter-productive to try to hitch anything else onto it. There's no point in creating a strategic plan just to say you have one.

The rest of the bad news? There's also no point in trying to build tactical plans if there is no real, flesh-on-the-bones strategy on which to base them. So, it all begins with strategy. Absent a strategic plan, the only tactics that make sense are staying in your foxhole and keeping your head down.

# RELATIONSHIPS IN THE SUPPLY CHAIN

The hardest thing in life is to learn which bridge to cross and which to burn.
*Laurence J. Peter*

Assumptions are the termites of relationships.
*Herman Hesse*

The bird of paradise alights only on the hand that does not grasp.
*John Berry*

Acquaintance (n): a person whom you know well enough to borrow from,
but not well enough to lend to.
*Ambrose Bierce*


## From the Cosmic to the Commonplace

The term "relationships" covers a lot of ground in supply chain management. There are strategic relationships, tactical relationships, transactional relationships, internal relationships, and possibly more. There are also relationships among members of the supply chain community. Let's tackle those first, with an off-the-wall reference that may not be so off-the-wall after all.

Our supply chain universe can be seen as clustered around three "estates," roughly comparable to the social divisions in pre-revolutionary France. We might, without stretching too far, term them the First Estate — the academic community (or the "clergy"); the Second Estate — the consultants and software developers (or the "nobility"); and the Third Estate — the working practitioners (or the "commoners"), led then as now by the *bourgeoisie* of visible, leading-edge advocates.

There is also a kind of Fourth Estate (or the "press") in supply chain management, but the trade press generally does not play the same watchdog role as its counterpart in the outside world. In fact, a disappointing proportion of the supply chain's Fourth Estate appears to be held in thrall to its advertisers, at the expense of independent journalistic endeavor. Only a few publishers seem to have escaped this trap.

We have not yet seen a supply chain Fifth Estate emerging, but the millennium is young.

For the moment, it's important to realize that relationships among the supply chain estates must be maintained for balance. Too much power and influence in any one camp and you risk derailing the Supply Chain Express.

The principal means for bringing the estates together and leveraging their individual talents and contributions lies in the field's professional organizations, mainly the Council of Supply Chain Management Professionals (CSCMP) and the Warehousing Education and Research Council (WERC). The personal networks built among leaders in the three estates (and sometimes with the Fourth on the periphery) at these groups' annual gatherings continue to harness the synergistic potential of their collaborative strengths.

## Velvet Glove/Iron Fist — The Governmental Dichotomy

Relationships among businesses with all levels of government — federal, state and local — are important as well. Governmental and regulatory bodies can provide restrictions and incentives, regulations and freedom, and roadblocks and opportunities for individual companies. They also provide venues for teaching and research. They can also help create the environments that incubate consultancies and technology development. (See the chapters on The Role of Infrastructure(s) and Supply Chain Regulation.)

Programs and actions at all levels of government can exert powerful influence on where supply chain operations are located, how successful they are, and how committed they become to maintaining a physical presence and investment in localities, regions, and countries.

These help to explain the phenomenon of "brain drain," headquarters relocations, some sourcing decisions, business flight from certain states, and continuing economic *malaise* in countries that should by all rights be prospering. Thomas Friedman's *The World Is Flat* and *The Lexus And The Olive Tree* both provide insight into these phenomena.

At the level where most of us work every day, there are vital relationships to build and nurture: between the company and its key suppliers; between the company and its customers; and among the company and academics, consultants, software providers and other practitioners. This relationship business keeps getting more and more complicated. Let's touch on a few key issues that are a little closer to ground level.

## Within the Supply Chain

Let's start with the working relationships between suppliers and customers, which some like to call "partnerships." The partnership notion has been much-abused over the years, and we're simply not going to go there. Calling business relationships "partnerships" doesn't make them so. Furthermore, there are limits to how many partnerships any company can effectively maintain. Certainly, you can't have partnerships with everyone in your supply chain, unless the chain consists only of you and two others.

Still, it is important to maintain high-trust, high-communication, mutually beneficial relationships with key suppliers and customers, whether they're called partnerships or not. Granted, there are some very successful mega-merchants that are able to dictate prices, terms, and processes to their suppliers by threatening to pull their business. But the fact is that very few of us are in the position of being able to tell our suppliers, "My way, or the highway." For the rest of us, creating and developing strong, positive relationships are keys to supply chain success.

What does this mean? For openers, it means communicating demand events and the direction of strategic plans. It also means linking information systems and jointly leveraging the potential for Internet and other electronic communications. It means working together to reduce costs and improve quality, and understanding capacities and capabilities. And don't overlook your responsibility to teach your partners the techniques needed to make it in the 21st century.

On the customer side, it means many of the same things, only working in another direction. You need to know about their strategies and directions, their event plans, and their needs for flexibility and resilience. The collaborative planning, forecasting, and replenishment (CPFR) process works both ways. Your customers need to know about your capacities and capabilities, just as you need to know theirs. And remember, it's your responsibility to educate them about ways in which you can help them succeed in their markets.

In an ideal supply chain relationship, both customers and suppliers get hooked up in ways that allow them to easily exchange information, demand data, and the visibility of status.

Wherever you sit in the supply chain flow, you can improve your positioning by understanding both the upstream and downstream business issues — and what the ultimate user or consumer wants and needs.

All of this takes fundamental talent, a positive attitude, and an overall culture of strong relationships. And it's got to be for real. As someone once observed, "You can only fake sincerity for so long." That's true in the supply chain world, for sure.

## Within the Company

Before a company attempts to build good external relationships, it must first put its own house in order. You can't really develop open communications with others if your organization is partitioned itself.

Within the friendly confines of your own four walls, Manufacturing and Distribution need to do more than communicate — they need to march in lock-step. Both functions need to be plugged into what's going on with Sales and Marketing. Sourcing and Procurement can't operate independently of other supply chain functions. Senior management must include the supply chain organization in the strategic information loop, while the supply chain organization must let the C-level officers know what it can do to support strategies. (See the chapters on Supply Chain Organization(s), Strategies and Supply Chains, and The Role of Infrastructure(s).)

This means joint planning and joint problem solving. It means cross-functional teams with a purpose other than political correctness. It means that everyone has, if not a voice, at least a hearing in product development and SKU extension discussions.

If all that's fairly scary, you're not ready for a prime time appearance on the stage of external relationships. They can't possibly succeed until your company is master of its own domain.

## LSPs, Consultants, and Worse

Once issues within the company and within the greater supply chain have been satisfactorily addressed, don't forget relationships with service providers. This need is particularly acute when logistics service providers (LSP) are involved.

Building a successful LSP relationship is absolutely essential to their successful use. Open and full communications are vital from the outset — beginning with the evaluation and selection processes (see the chapter on Logistics Outsourcing). Multi-level working relationships throughout both organizations provide the key to making processes work and to effectively solving the problems that inevitably crop up.

And the work doesn't end there. LSP relationships, like marriages, require constant effort and continued attention. The LSP also needs to know about upcoming events, changes in strategy, and new products and customers — things that were kept "secret" in the old days.

The arms-length, transaction-based, traditional relationship may get the job done at a low price in the short haul, but it does nothing to build a foundation for the future. You and the LSP need to engage in regular dialogue about where and how they can add value to what you are doing.

It's more difficult to have a relationship with consultants that spans functions and managerial generations. But the quality of relationships with consultants can have a profound effect on the quality and extent of outcomes. For best results, mutual trust and open communication are required. The more your consultants know about what's really going on and the more you can tell them, the better their chances of getting to the heart of the issues and devising on-target solutions. Capability is usually a given in the consulting relationship. Chemistry, on the other hand, provides an important indicator of how the relationship will go.

As for software providers, they are often portrayed as upscale used-car salespeople, without scruple or inhibition. That's unfair. When it comes to evaluating vendors, your job is to look for and assess the qualities that can make for a positive mutual relationship, all the way through a successful implementation.

Like all the other aspects of the supply chain, this is about more than simply making a purchase. It is about having a sustainable relationship with someone who can play a key role in your long-term supply chain success.

# METRICS IN THE SCM WORLD

Statistics are no substitute for judgment.
*Henry Clay*

Data informs experience; experience interprets data.
Without data, experience is short-sighted; without experience, data is dangerous.
*Whitney Massengill*

High achievement always takes place in the framework of high expectation.
*Jack Kinder*

... when you cannot express it in numbers,
your knowledge is of a meager and unsatisfactory kind ...
*William Thompson, Lord Kelvin*

## Revisiting a Not-So-Tired Topic

What, metrics again? Aren't we getting tired of hearing about metrics? We hope not. Whether you call them "metrics" or use the old-fashioned term "measurements," they are indispensable. They're how you keep score!

Without good, relevant measurements you don't know whether you're winning or losing. You can't tell if you're gaining ground or falling behind. Actually, without metrics you don't even know if you're in the game.

Some of the best recent writing about supply chain metrics has been done by our friend Kate Vitasek. Her work was serialized in 2004-2005 in *DC Velocity* magazine, and it's available through the magazine's Web site (www.dcvelocity.com). In addition, the Warehousing Education and Research Council (WERC) and *DC Velocity* have conducted research and published material about benchmarking in logistics.

Our take on the subject may be slightly heretical, but it follows below for better or for worse.

## Who Uses Metrics?

Winners in the Great Game of Supply Chain Management do. In both the United States and Europe, study after study has shown that companies that measure performance consistently outperform those that don't — and by an ever-growing margin. Simply put, the leaders measure, the laggards often don't, and the dominators definitely do.

But it's also true that some of the losers regularly measure performance. How can that be? Easy. They're measuring the wrong things. They haven't learned what to measure — what really moves the needle when it comes to supply chain and corporate performance. Interestingly, many of these outfits are downright aggressive and intense in their measurement and reporting. But all too often, their efforts yield little or nothing in the way of improvements because they have their eye on the wrong ball.

At the end of the day, any company that is even halfway serious about the Deming cycle of continuous improvement — Plan-Do-Check-Act — uses metrics throughout the process.

How about those that strive to be world-class? Does this focus pay off? According to research published in *Material Handling Management,* it does and big-time. Those who believe they are world-class or well on the way toward that status report that they enjoy the following:

- Order cycle times that are 29 percent shorter than those of companies that aren't making much progress toward the world-class goal.
- Customer delivery lead times that are 45 percent shorter than their non world-class counterparts'.
- On-time delivery rates that are 9 percent higher.
- Perfect order rates that are 8 percent higher.
- Warehousing costs that are 31 percent lower.

Yes, and all this with a fill rate of 95 percent and order and order line accuracy rates of 98 percent.

## Use and Abuse of Metrics

It's important that supply chain professionals understand that measurement must constitute a way of life, not just the corporate program *du jour.* Sporadic measurement is better than never measuring at all, but only just.

It's also critical to know what to measure — and what not to bother with. Measure and report on everything, and performance will collapse under the weight. It's vital to focus on the few critical measures that profoundly affect the business (or the function) and put aside all the other possibilities. Pareto principles apply here, too (see the chapter on Inventory Management). This holds true whether you're measuring corporate supply chain performance or pick/pack operations.

Of course, metrics only add value when you do something with them. It's important to communicate what you've learned. While we advocate the sharing of overall supply chain performance measures, associates also need visibility of the metrics over which they have direct control. A forklift driver who's kept informed about trends in units per hour is far more likely to be engaged in efforts to improve performance than one who's left in the dark.

One way to undermine the benefits is to over-emphasize the quantitative to the exclusion of the qualitative. What is the ultimate point of producing record numbers of substandard products? What is the real cost of rework? It's not simply the labor and material involved but the loss of customer confidence and a reputation in the marketplace for less than the best.

Tying activity performance standards to incentive pay for workers practically guarantees you'll see a noticeable decline — perhaps not fatal, but certainly as serious as shooting oneself in the corporate foot. It's amazing how many people get all worked up about piecework pay for children in far-off sweatshops but can't see the parallel in doing the same thing to adults here at home.

## Making Metrics Real

How should measurements and results be communicated? Clearly, early, and often, which is easier said than done. Whether the metric is "units per hour" or "on-time delivery" or "total supply chain cost vs. budget," performance stats need to be posted—or published—as soon as information becomes available and at intervals dictated by the natural business cycles. That is, measuring unit costs or total supply chain costs on a weekly basis might not provide much in the way of meaningful information, but weekly stats on group performance might prove invaluable. The trick is to find the time cycle that informs soon enough to permit corrective (or congratulatory) action, but which is also long enough to incorporate all the factors that affect performance over the long haul.

As for communicating the results, companies do this in a variety of ways, from corporate memoranda to hand-written production sheets pinned to a bulletin board. In any given workplace, the choice will be dictated by such factors as the source of the report, the audience, and the local culture.

One of the best is a dashboard set of measures, arrayed on a single 4- by 6-foot board, updated monthly and prominently displayed at the distribution center's entrance. The metrics typically span operational, cost, quality, and HR measures. They are presented in graphic format with gauges and needles and are color coded (with green for performance that's at or above target, yellow for slightly below target, and bright red for unacceptably below target) to make it easy for viewers to grasp the situation at a glance.

Our Dutch colleague Jeroen van den Berg has created an automated system based on similar principles. It features a robust data base, which feeds a simple set of dials representing various elements of performance.

## What to Measure

To a company contemplating which metrics to adopt, the vast array of options might seem an embarrassment of riches. But our view leans toward a few "musts" at the corporate level — the "cosmic" metrics, if you will:

- Cash-to-cash cycle time.
- Supply chain cost (as a percentage of sales).
- Perfect orders.
- Economic Value Added (EVA).

Although most will agree that supply chain cost and perfect orders are relevant measures of supply chain performance, they may need some convincing when it comes to EVA and cash-to-cash performance. We would argue that in the overall supply chain, we have enormous and diverse responsibilities, including sourcing and procurement, supply and supplier management, physical distribution, customer relationships, and loads more. We have — or ought to have — profound influence on trends in cash-to-cash. We are supposed to be about speed, about inventory management, about continuous improvement in all aspects of supply chain. Cash-to-cash should be a major measure of our operational and planning success.

The same reasoning applies when it comes to EVA. What we do in supply chain management is (or should be) focused on getting the most out of assets (or on maximizing the return on newly employed assets) — in other words, on adding value. As for measuring EVA, the time-tested DuPont Model is a phenomenal tool for displaying how supply chain management contributes to EVA. (See the chapter on Supply Chain Finance and Accounting.)

## Surely There's More

But the most important metric of all remains customer satisfaction. If you measure nothing else, measure customer satisfaction. And do it right.

Measure it often. And measure it using a variety of techniques, including telephone surveys, return cards, focus groups, and questionnaires. Wherever possible, use outside professionals to design and execute customer satisfaction measurement programs. Your organization may have the resources to conduct its own research, but the odds are that it doesn't have the objectivity. The independence of the evaluation is vital to its accuracy and usefulness.

As for why it's so important, companies that let their focus stray from customer satisfaction are likely to pay dearly for the lapse. Even in the best of times and with the best of performance, losing customers is inevitable. Losing sight of satisfaction levels only increases an organization's exposure to customer losses and the associated damage to the business. Replacing those customers is incredibly expensive, and regaining the lost business is an iffy proposition at best.

## And Still More

We haven't even touched on the almost infinite world of granular operational measurements. Books have been written, as they say, on the topic. The keys to success here are the usual — simplicity, focus, and visibility.

These measures range from "transactional productivity in putaway" to "relationship structures in sourcing and procurement" and include almost everything in between. But all elements of the supply chain — including the planning functions — can and should have active and relevant metrics.

There's a caveat, however: As you delve deeper into individual granular metrics, keep in mind that they are all part of a balanced approach to achieving corporate supply chain objectives. There needs to be an *arbeiter* who's responsible for ensuring that all the specific targets and measures do not have a negative impact on the surrounding operations.

As for what to measure, the specifics of granular measurement will vary, as you might expect, based on such factors as industry and market, supply chain position, strategic approach to SCM, and the closely related element of measurement culture.

## And the Winner Is …

Despite the demonstrated benefits of measuring performance, not everybody's doing it. In fact, only half of the shippers who responded to a survey conducted by the Aberdeen Group said they use supplier performance metrics. To us, that means that the other half are really in trouble.

That raises the question of what those companies that do use metrics are measuring. Respondents to the Aberdeen survey reported that they measured the following (listed here in descending order of popularity):

1. On-time delivery.
2. Quality of goods and services.
3. Service capability and performance.
4. Price competitiveness.
5. Contract terms compliance.
6. Response.
7. Lead time.
8. Technical capability.
9. Environmental, health, and safety performance.
10. Innovation.

Despite an apparent stagnation in the use of such metrics, interest in the topic reportedly remains high. In fact, software vendors are increasingly bundling performance management tools into their packages. Perhaps increasing metrics visibility (see the chapter on Visibility) will fan the flames a bit.

## Benchmarking

Benchmarking deserves a book all to itself. It is a powerful tool in skilled hands, supported by solid metrics. But benchmarking has been much abused.

There are busloads of consultants ready to "do" benchmarking for whichever client sees the process as a necessary first step to any improvement. The plethora of proprietary benchmarking databases can vary in quality from outdated to incomplete to woefully misleading.

There are a few managers and consultants who understand the process and the power of its application. Hewlett-Packard, for example, has not benchmarked itself against "peer" companies for some time. Instead, it regularly builds matrices of business units and business functions (e.g., servers and R&D) and compares the performance in each cell of the grid against leaders in other industries.

## What's the Point of All These Measurements?

In addition to assessing the current performance of an organization, department or function, metrics are also used to set targets — what "could be" for groups and individuals. And they let you know where you stand on the journey from "was" to "will be."

They also help to stimulate improved performance. But the purpose is not to drive people to meet the target just because it's the target. The larger aim of measured and reported objectives is to provide a window into failure, to help identify not only when but why the goal is still out of reach. Then, it becomes management's responsibility to clear away the obstacles and do whatever it takes to allow people to meet and exceed published expectations. Making measured progress along the way, of course.

In talking about metrics, Terry Pohlen of the University of North Texas cites Albert Einstein: "Not everything that counts can be counted, and not everything that can be counted counts."

# PERFORMANCE MANAGEMENT

Motivation will almost always beat mere talent.
*Norman R. Augustine*

Never be satisfied with what you achieve,
because it all pales in comparison with what you are capable of doing in the future.
*Rabbi Nochem Kaplan*

I feel that the greatest reward for doing is the opportunity to do more.
*Jonas Salk*

Productive work is the central purpose of a rational man's life ...
*Ayn Rand*

## When the Stage Is Set
We can do everything possible in strategizing, planning, benchmarking, measuring, adopting best practices, and reporting, yet a fundamental question remains: How can we get people and organizations to consistently perform at high levels? The answer may be complicated — it is certainly highly detailed — and its components are inter-related.

## At the Highest Levels
Elevating performance is closely related to the subject of metrics. But it's not about what the metrics *are* — it's about how they are *used*. When an organization can focus on a few mission-critical metrics, it has a couple of subsequent responsibilities. One is to report results — often, visibly, simply, and on a timely basis. The second is to plan what to do when targets are reached — and then do it.

So far, so good. Highlighting metrics, and shining bright lights upon them, creates an expectation that something will happen when targets are reached. It's not enough to report current status or even to relate status to a baseline. People need a target, something to shoot for. It's human nature to want to strive — to meet expectations, to reach the goal, to excel. This desire to achieve is not peculiar to Americans or limited to those brought up on the so-called Puritan work ethic. People from all over the world respond positively to clearly communicated expectations.

Failure to take visible action when a goal has been met will cause people to lose interest in doing what it takes to continue meeting targets. It's not a matter of having to bribe people to perform. It is very much a matter of demonstrating a positive link between cause and effect. That demonstration reinforces interest and commitment to contributing to sustained high-level performance.

It doesn't matter whether the measure and target are quantitative (more production, say, or perfect orders) or qualitative (zero defects or on-time deliveries). The details of the associated reward and recognition are less important than their consistent implementation.

The payoff might be a group pizza party, a quarterly bonus, a field trip, or desirable parking spots. Although the decision will vary from company to company, the key is to make the rewards as visible as the accomplishments.

Group rewards are appropriate, whether they involve group benefits or individual benefits delivered to all members of the group. This approach is particularly conducive to developing cooperation among team members and to fostering healthy competition among teams.

## On the Floor

The possibilities are nearly endless when considering individual performance. But the reward and recognition solution might be trickier.

There is a tendency among the techno-geek community to want to use performance standards to generate incentive pay for working associates, be they drivers, order pickers, or customer service reps. The concept is generally dangerous. It smacks of the bad old days of "efficiency experts." Worse, it suggests parallels with the bad new days of piecework in third-world sweatshops.

But we do need to have performance targets, and we must have ways to motivate people to achieve them — consistently. There's a fair chance that hitting the numbers will contribute to meeting the organization's higher-level group objectives. What to do?

Begin by setting equitable, achievable targets. Not "stretch" goals that can only be met when the sun is out and the planets are aligned. Not generous allowances that can be achieved all day every day without breaking a sweat. This sub-topic is worth a book all on its own — and in fact, books have been written. The specific standards can be engineered, derived from historical data or reasonable expectancies, or the product of MTM (methods time measurement) or MOST (Maynard Operations Sequence Technique)-like programs. The type you choose is not material. Just stay away from guesses and management estimates.

Follow standards establishment with timely, visible reporting by person. Recognize individual accomplishment orally and with gift certificates or T-shirts — whatever makes sense in the company's culture and environment. But even as you recognize individuals' performance, keep in mind that the emphasis should remain on group rewards for meeting group objectives.

Don't use day-to-day quantitative performance for disciplinary purposes. If you do, the program will immediately be discredited, and good performers' achievements will drop like a stone. The responsibility for getting individuals' performance to the desired level rests with the line supervisor. Likewise, the supervisor gets tagged with the responsibility for getting the group to perform — on average and as individuals — to the desired levels.

## The Purpose of Standards and Reporting
What the reporting process is really all about is highlighting both success and failure. At the same time, it also presents an opportunity for supervisors to interview high-performing associates to determine what factors account for their success. The answer might be a process, a short cut, an absence of obstacles, good weather, or the mix of tasks and transactions.

Failure presents an even greater opportunity. As with success, failure provides supervisors with an excuse to interview the less-successful employees to try to determine what went wrong. If the supervisor is able to identify the root causes for failure, two good things can happen. First, it demonstrates to the worker that the company's intentions in setting up the measurement program were pure — that it's not a thinly disguised disciplinary tool. The effects of this realization on morale and employee commitment can be enormous.

Second, it provides a forum for workers to inform their supervisors about those things that hamper their performance — barriers, obstacles, problems, events, bad processes, upstream failures, downstream disconnects, insufficient tools, lack of information, and poor communications. Supervisors then have the opportunity to analyze, prioritize, and remedy those problems.

In addition, continuous reporting of performance to targets provides a way for both working and supervising employees to track the effectiveness of their problem-solving and repair efforts. This approach, which is powerful indeed, is a far cry from the old system of punishment, rewards, and incentive pay.

## The Metrics/Standards Disconnect
At this point, we hope it's clear that there is a big difference between performance metrics and performance standards. In the world of metrics, we are generally after outcomes, ideally outcomes that bear directly on customers and profitability.

In the realm of standards, we are working with details that, in the aggregate, contribute to the outcome metrics. But standards also help us devise better processes and to understand and improve costs, as well as plan the labor component of supply chain management.

By way of illustration, we might want to have standards related to numbers of stops, miles driven, parcels handled, or number of orders delivered. The performance metric, by contrast, would likely be on-time delivery percentage. In a DC, we might have standards for picks per hour, putaway productivity, fill rate, and the like. But a performance metric might be cost per order.

## Exceptions
All the above notwithstanding, there are times when performance standards are used in other ways. For example, many operations have — or should have — a minimum production or quality standard. Inability to meet the minimum, assuming adequate training, can indicate a mismatch of skills and job demands. For example, in a DC, people without suf-

ficient hand-eye coordination, with poor small motor skills, or with alphabetic or numeric processing problems may simply be miscast in their assigned roles. Consistent performance below minimum standard will show this.

Other problems may manifest themselves in low productivity or quality. In those situations, documentation becomes important. But the issue is not failure to meet standards. Consistent shortfalls indicate that something else is wrong and that further analysis is necessary.

## In Closing

It's borderline magic. The way to get people to meet or exceed targets, goals, standards, or objectives is not to push them to strive for excellence. Instead, it's simply to remove the obstacles that get in the way of stellar performance. Once the barriers have been dismantled, they'll strive on their own to do what is expected and needed.

# FRAUD

I do not mind lying, but I hate inaccuracy.
*Samuel Butler*

The lie is a condition of life.
*Frederick Nietzsche*

A criminal is a person with predatory instincts
who has not sufficient capital to form a corporation.
*Howard Scott*

There is only one social responsibility of business — to use its resources and engage in
activities designed to increase its profits without deception or fraud.
*Milton Friedman*

## Introduction

Our friend Whitney Massengill has observed, "A gang armed with guns can easily steal thousands. A gang armed with pens can just as easily steal millions — and the prison terms are shorter." Enron may have provided the ultimate proof of concept, but the supply chain world has been plagued by fraud and deceit since long before supply chains were known as supply chains. The manifestations, while often physical, are also found in the cooked books.

Not so long ago, it was stunningly easy to put an extra case or pallet on a truck for the driver to sell, splitting the take with the inside man. Today's information systems may make detection quicker, but collusion theft has hardly gone away. And in the meantime, modern forms of fraud have emerged, many of them complex — even elegant — in their design and execution.

## The Classics of a Golden Age

It seems that fraud, in its infinite variety, has been around about as long as the human race. Some would cite Homer's Trojan Horse as an early example of logistics fraud, illustrating the need for inbound inspection. Maybe the good ol' days weren't so good after all.

The Teapot Dome scandal that engulfed the Harding administration involved shady doings around oil reserves.

Product adulteration or dilution has been practiced since the earliest times; it is not a modern phenomenon limited to the narcotics trade. Back in the day, it might involve such commodities as sugar, coffee, flour, and liquor.

Outright theft, of course, remains a staple occupation in some locales within our globalized supply chains. Some shippers deliberately send extra truckloads of product into known high-theft areas, knowing that they can expect to lose a predictable percentage of the cargo to hijackers.

An interesting variant of the extra-case scam involves unscrupulous suppliers who would ingeniously stack pallets with a case or a bag missing from the inside of the stack. The omission is not visible until or unless the pallet is broken down. But by then the goods have typically been paid for, and the missing case has disappeared into someone's personal supply chain.

Truth is, some of the more spectacular frauds in business history have had a supply chain management flavor.

## In More Recent Times

In the annals of corporate misdeeds, the recent Enron scandal has overshadowed all others, and, of course, it had nothing to do with the supply chain. But what about McKesson & Robbins? In 1938, the giant wholesale distributor got caught up in a case of accounting fraud that involved a non-existent $10 million worth of inventory in Canadian warehouses that also didn't exist. The sum of $10 million was more than pocket change during the Great Depression. While considered at the time to be accounting fraud, the case might be more accurately described as a conspiracy between physical supply chain operations and accounting to perpetuate fraud. In the '80s, a large public accounting firm was brought down — foreshadowing Arthur Andersen's collapse — when entire manufacturing and storage facilities were belatedly discovered not to exist.

The '60s saw plenty of scandals as well. Billy Sol Estes, politically connected with Lyndon Johnson, managed a double whammy in the first half of the decade. First came the improper purchase of cotton allotments, aided by payoffs to Agricultural Adjustment Administration minions and complicated by the suicide of a principal antagonist. Then in a notorious exit from the public arena, Billy Sol was found to have extracted enough money to fund the illegal allotment transfers by using phantom fertilizer tanks as collateral. He was released from prison in 1983.

In 1963, in news largely overshadowed by the Kennedy assassination, Tino De Angelis, principally financed through loans guaranteed by American Express, was found to have storage tanks full of water. That wouldn't have been a crime, except that the tanks were supposed to be full of salad oil. AmEx was not pleased. Nor were Manufacturers Hanover Bank (among about four dozen banks), Bunge Corporation, Williston and Beane, and Ira Haupt Brokerage Company, all of whom got taken. Foreshadowing events that would unfold nearly four decades later, a major public accounting firm was ultimately accused of negligence.

It seems that De Angelis couldn't help himself. Earlier in his career, he had gotten away with selling bad shortening to post-war Europe and spoiled meat to U.S. school lunch programs. Encouraged by his apparent success, he then put together an ultimately failed plan to corner the world market in soybean oil.

Tino, only momentarily the pride of the Bronx, himself got taken, but to the pokey, for several years. Upon release, he attempted to recover his lost fortune with a Ponzi scheme, which required more credibility to pull off than Tino possessed.* The price tag of this oil escapade was a trifling $175 million, which would approach $2 billion in today's money.

## Where Were the Auditors?

Uncovering fraud is not an arena in which the mild-mannered certified public accountant (CPA) has typically excelled. It's not that CPAs are naïve or feeble-minded, but these aren't really the things they've been trained to run to ground. The auditing firms have been generally more concerned with matters that have material impact on the balance sheet or income statement — *known* material impact, that is.

Furthermore, because CPAs most often were not operations people, they didn't always know what to look for when physical inventories were involved. In one celebrated case, the fraud was so extensive that the company in question loaded bricks of approximately the right weight into sealed cartons ostensibly containing technological equipment. The physical inventory disclosed the right number of cases, and it never occurred to anyone that something else might be inside.

In another major event, the headquarters inventory was fine. But no one deemed the relatively tiny store inventories worth examining. Regrettably, fictitious transactions had moved mountains of non-existent product into phantom local stocks, creating enormous but false sales volumes.

## Prevention

Over the years, companies seeking to prevent fraud have tried solutions as high tech as biometric screening and as low tech as intuition — with approximately equal results. We vividly remember the very large international technology distributor that invested a lot of money in screening devices through which each and every employee, visitor, vendor, contractor, and consultant was required to pass. No one could enter or leave the DC at anytime or for any purpose — the start or end of a shift, in and out for lunch, or in and out for breaks — without undergoing screening. The distributor's concerns were well-grounded because its products were both valuable and highly desirable in the consumer market.

While the working associates were queuing up to pass through a "security" process that would have made a TSA screener proud, however, two mid-managers were successfully conspiring — until they were caught — to move and sell truckloads of high-value product out of the distribution center and into what might be called alternative channels. Think Tony Soprano. With better paperwork.

So many times, it seems that thievery is discovered only after huge losses have been incurred over a long period of time. In another case we encountered, a chemical manufacturer for the automotive aftermarket became suspicious that product might be "leaking"

*Note: Ponzi schemes are investment scams having some similarities to pyramid schemes. They are named for Charles Ponzi, who prospered illicitly in the early 1900s.

out of its factory DC. In the end, its suspicions proved to be well founded. It turned out that thieves were taking a truckload of merchandise a day out of the DC and off the books through a scheme involving phony paperwork for phantom customers. But it took months of surreptitious observation and digging through paper and electronic files to come up with conclusive evidence and nail the individuals involved.

In another situation, no one in a catalog retailer's senior management ranks had even the remotest suspicion that a traffic manager of some 20 years standing might be on the take. But a routine fact-finding analysis, with no agenda other than assessing potential improvements, found carrier selections that made no sense. The manager was allowed to quietly resign and keep the money, though it seemed that the offense called for a pistol-whipping at the very least.

## An Organized Approach

In recent years, the impact of the Sarbanes-Oxley Act has been felt in the supply chain management arena, quietly requiring companies to put controls in place to prevent, identify, and detect fraud. PricewaterhouseCoopers (PwC), the public accounting and services giant, has published a white paper devoted to fraud schemes in the transportation and logistics sector. That white paper addresses not only the risks associated with financial reporting, but also the risks to a company's reputation and the legal and strategic implications of fraud. Ken Evans, the firm's U.S. transportation and logistics leader, has asserted that 45 percent of all companies have been victims of economic crime. (In the interest of full disclosure and in the spirit of Sarbanes-Oxley, we confess to being PwC alumni, having a predecessor firm as our consulting alma mater.)

PwC's five-step anti-fraud program is the usual straightforward, even dull, recitation, with the devil — as well as the excitement and the effectiveness — in the details. Its recommendations are as follows:

▪ Establish a baseline, preferably with a multi-disciplinary team, that includes the development of remediation plans.

▪ Conduct a risk assessment, which is not only an inventory but also a weighting of likelihood and seriousness.

▪ Evaluate controls design and effectiveness, with major roles and responsibilities for operating management.

▪ Assess residual financial-reporting risks, which link fraud risks to internal audit weakness and ineffectiveness.

▪ Standardize incident investigation and remediation processes that recognize that fraud will occur in the real world, and demand that the gaps must continuingly be filled.

In PwC's assessment, fraud and misconduct schemes can be classified into the following six categories:

▪ Financial statement manipulation, which can be sub-divided into improper revenue recognition and the over- or understatement of assets and liabilities. This is really the mother lode, encompassing such things as manipulation of estimates, over-accrual of rebates and receivables, understatement of liabilities, overstatement of receivables, sham transactions with related parties, overstating revenue, fictitious transactions, premature revenue recognition, revenue leakage, backdated and side agreements, and "round-tripping" transactions with no net economic benefit that can inflate earnings.

- Asset misappropriation, including cargo theft, fraudulent disbursements, cash skimming, industrial espionage, and "lapping" or theft of customer payments.
- Unauthorized receipts and expenditures, including bribery, tax evasion, improper labor practices, and fraud against employees (e.g., failure to fund pensions or pay insurance premiums).
- Aiding, abetting, or helping a third party commit fraudulent acts.
- Senior management fraud, including, in addition to involvement in all the above, conflicts of interest and insider trading.
- Disclosure fraud, including the intentional omission or misstatement of such items as channel stuffing, even if they conform to Generally Accepted Accounting Principles (GAAP), the usual gold standard for what practices are allowable.

We salute PwC for its work in this area. Its efforts could go a long way toward restoring accountants' reputation and credibility.

## New Disciplines

We have reached a point of understanding the nature, variety, and scope of supply chain fraud, and the linkages between its physical and financial components. It's time for a couple of forces to join together in fighting these crimes.

Forensic Accounting has been around for a long time, certainly since the days when Al Capone was jailed for tax evasion instead of murder. We see a need for a newer specialty that could be called Forensic Logistics and would entail the analysis of operations for evidence of and potential for bad behavior.

Putting these two together might put real teeth in efforts to thwart supply chain fraud.

# RISK MANAGEMENT

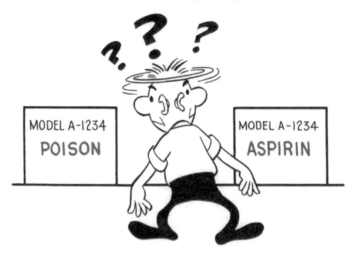

Men are men; they needs must err.
*Euripides*

A clever man commits no minor blunders.
*Johann Wolfgang von Goethe*

Don't ever take a fence down until you know why it was put up.
*Robert Frost*

How do you start a flood?
*Anonymous, but hopeful, insurance claimant*

## Identifying and Categorizing Risk

Risk management terminology entered our business lexicon at about the time that some-one discovered that "Risk Management Consultant" was a more dignified title than "Insurance Salesman." For a long time, we tended to think of risk management as an insur-ance thing. But that overlooks the risks for which insurance is either nonexistent or inad-equate as a solution. Before we think about how to compensate for actualized risks, we need to think long and hard about risk exposure.

In general, risks may fall into broad categories;
- Business continuity.
- Process interruption.
- Product loss or damage.
- Management and staff well-being.
- Product, process, and facility liability.

The real first step in risk management is to determine what risks we face, both in a global economy and in localized operations. The process is touched upon in Yossi Sheffi's book *The Resilient Enterprise.* As part of the process, management should grade each potential risk event according to both probability and severity. For example, the risk of flood in a given community might be low but would have severe consequences in the unlikely event that one were to occur. Other events, such as civil disturbance, while rare in the United States, could be considered high-probability events in some other geographies.

The exhibit at right illustrates one approach to identifying and grading, which will yield different results for different facilities. This example is skewed toward warehousing activity, but the model could easily be adapted to transportation, manufacturing or the overall supply chain network.

## Managing Risk

There are three ways to help control the risk of any loss:

- Insurance.
- Loss prevention.
- Contingency planning.

Nearly everyone has insurance, usually several levels of it. In supply chain operations, it is vital to recognize the significant differences in liability among logistics service providers, common carriers, and wholesale distributors.

Let's look at logistics service providers first. In the United

| Categories of Disaster | Probability* | Severity* |
|---|---|---|
| **Natural Disasters** | | |
| Flood | Slight | Extreme |
| Earthquake | | |
| Windstorm | | |
| Epidemic | | |
| **Chemical Disasters** | | |
| Fire | | |
| Contamination | | |
| Infestation | | |
| • Rodents | | |
| • Insects | | |
| **Operational Errors** | | |
| Product damage | | |
| Mis-shipments | | |
| Inventory discrepancies | | |
| **Human Disasters** | | |
| Employee malfeasance | | |
| Theft | | |
| • Burglary | | |
| • Pilferage | | |
| • Collusion | | |
| Work stoppage | | |
| • Strike at your warehouse | | |
| Strike at supplier or major customer | | |
| Death or disability of key executives | | |
| **Customer Failures** | | |
| Bankruptcy | | |
| Management change | | |
| Market change | | |
| Litigation | | |
| **Utility Failures** | | |
| Power outage | | |
| Disruption of water supply | | |
| Disruption of natural gas supply | | |
| IT/telecom failure | | |
| Mechanical breakdown – conveyors | | |
| Disruption of road access | | |
| Disruption of rail service | | |
| **Government Disasters** | | |
| Civil disobedience or riots | | |
| War or insurrection | | |
| Sanctions by OSHA | | |
| Sanctions for SOX violations | | |

*This will vary for each warehouse

States and in most nations whose legal codes are based on English common law, the warehouse service provider is a "bailee for hire"* and is therefore not responsible for product and cargo losses unless caused by operator negligence. This is the same concept that frustrates

*Note: A bailee is not someone emptying a boat that is taking on water, but a person who receives property from another, under contract.*

those of us who have suffered loss or damage in a parking garage or at the local dry cleaner. If product loses value due to an "act of God" or another disaster, you or your own insurer must pay for the loss.

By contrast, a common carrier — or a logistics service provider providing carriage — must insure products being transported. As for wholesale distributors, they typically own the products they store so they must insure them. It is critical to have good contract language when goods are consigned, technically owned by a supplier but resident on the property of a customer, to define insurance responsibility.

These conventions may not apply in international operations, particularly in multinational supply chain operations. It is vital to know how local legal systems treat responsibility for the safety and security of both stored and transported goods.

## The Alfred E. Neuman Syndrome — "What, Me Worry?"

It's too easy to shrug our shoulders and blithely assume that if disaster strikes, we're covered — insurance will pay for it. But that's not only foolish; it's short-sighted. We all have to do everything we can to prevent or minimize the effects of flood, fire, earthquakes, or any other disruption that might occur. Without vigilance and effort, insurance rates, which are high enough already, would go through the skylights. With sufficient neglect of the basics, our activities, like properties in severe flood plains or hurricane zones, could become essentially uninsurable.

We are being helped to do the right thing by preferred risk insurance carriers, who insist that their customers have comprehensive loss prevention programs. They also provide their own inspection services. And to keep their customers honest, they demand the right to make unannounced examinations of operations to check up on the readiness of fire protection equipment and the capabilities of plant emergency organizations.

## Contingency, Schmingency ...

Contingency planning is a longer-range, but mission-critical approach to addressing the unexpected and the unthinkable. The process consists of asking and thoughtfully answering a comprehensive list of "what if" questions such as:

- What if our top four executives die in a plane crash?
- What if our largest customer declare bankruptcy?
- What if we're hit with a million dollar OSHA fine following a fatal accident?
- What if a key supplier is crippled by a work stoppage?

Contingency planning can provide reasonable responses — and preventative measures — for an enormous range of disruptions and disasters. The scope of events transcends the supply chain and goes to the heart of corporate survival. But the process is truly useful only if it is completely comprehensive and soul-stirringly honest about possibilities and solutions.

## Resiliency

These points are discussed more fully elsewhere in this book (see the chapter on Resilience), but we think they bear repeating here. An important part of risk management is developing a resilient enterprise, one able to bounce back quickly from a disaster. As Dr. Sheffi has observed, companies looking to boost their resilience typically make it a point to build redundancy and flexibility into their operations.

Redundancy tactics might include amassing excess inventory or excess capacity. That strategy paid off for a prominent retailer when fire destroyed its distribution center in eastern Pennsylvania, and several other company DCs that weren't operating at full capacity were able to pick up the slack and maintain the flow of goods to stores in the region.

Flexibility might be supported through techniques in postponement and interchangeability. Postponement, as we've noted, comes in a number of flavors, including packaging, branding, and final assembly. An enterprise can keep going, nearly seamlessly, when one location has been shut down, if these activities can be accomplished at a DC *versus* a manufacturing facility or at a sister facility with a similar footprint and process flow.

## What Others Are Doing

In a survey of North American companies, 96 percent of respondents indicated that they consider risk management to be a moderate to high priority. We would ask why any organization would consider it merely "moderate" before concentrating on the 4 percent who will be out of business soon.

As for the approach they're taking to risk management, most companies now give more attention to loss prevention than to risk transfer through insurance. They have faced up to the reality that it's neither possible nor feasible to insure against everything. Even with insurance, putting rate escalation and loss of coverage issues aside, the likelihood of receiving insurance compensation for the full value of a loss and its associated costs is close to nil. Today's savvy manager has figured out that the avoidance of loss or disruption is far preferable to relying on insurance after the fact.

Asked to identify the business risks they currently face, the survey respondents cited government or regulatory sanctions and competitive threats. OSHA threats may be less likely or severe than they were a few years ago, but Sarbanes-Oxley (SOX) has raised the stakes in cost of compliance, scope of activities covered, and consequences of violation, elevating issues from the sphere of operations into the boardroom.

Any organization operating in the supply chain management world confronts risk in a competitive arena, either from the actions of others or from the failure to take the right actions internally. We can be outbidded on costs, outflanked on products, outmaneuvered on location, or outdone on technology.

Of property-related risks, survey respondents considered supply chain disruption and mechanical or electrical breakdown to be the most significant. We are betting that supply chain disruption would not have made the list as recently as five years ago. As for non-property-related risks, the survey respondents put labor issues and price changes at the top of the list.

## Too Many Eggs ...

Business threats don't necessarily take the form of fire, flood, or civil unrest, however. A leading contributor to business failure remains over-dependence on one or a few customers. This has affected suppliers, manufacturers, warehousing companies, transportation providers, 3PLs, and wholesalers.

The willingness of large players in the supply chain to abandon long-standing relationships for transient cost advantage in recent years has only heightened the risk. When the bough breaks, as the lullaby says, there is typically little chance of revenue replacement quickly enough to keep the cradle from falling.

Yet this is not an insurable business risk. Its avoidance is difficult and relies on marketing approaches that develop alternate products and channels or on the simple refusal to enter into a dangerous liaison in order to protect the long-term bottom line. Prudent management means recognizing the risks of putting too many eggs in one basket.

## Organizational Change

Never underestimate the power of relationships, particularly when it comes to supply chain operations. Friction-free interactions among suppliers, service providers, and customers are essential to the smooth flow of the contemporary supply chain. That said, relationships inevitably change. Key people retire or move on to new positions. Their replacements may not have the same values, motivations, or personalities.

Because these relationships inevitably change, there is a great risk of losing the business involved without focused planning. Among the tactics required for overcoming this risk are:

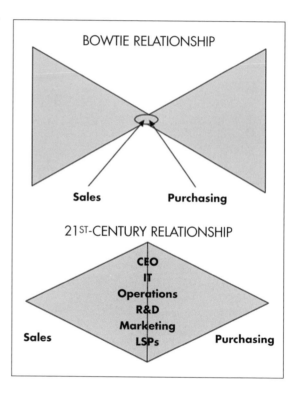

- Building business connections on a broader foundation than simply the relationship between buying and selling individuals; i.e., killing the "bow-tie" relationship.*

- Naming alternate relationship contacts for every functional customer interface to provide compatible points of communication for the customer throughout the organization

## Obstacles to Risk Management

Perhaps the biggest roadblock to effectively addressing risk remains optimism, the same trait that dooms many a project to disappointment. A hallmark of successful business leaders, particularly in the United States, is the belief that things will go right — that the things that might go wrong won't happen.

Contemplating snags, let alone disasters, isn't much fun. In fact, it's downright depressing. The active manager, focused on future achievement, will tend to avoid the process.

*Note: The bow-tie relationship is one in which the interests and communications of a large number of individuals and functions in dealings involving two companies get funneled through one individual on the selling side and one individual on the buying side. The opposite philosophy allows the several departments and people involved to communicate and solve problems in direct contact with one another.

"Insufficient time" was the most-cited excuse given in the referenced survey for a lack of disaster planning. But good managers will find the time for the important things.

Remember, risk management is important. Even when it deals with the unlikely, it is not dealing with the trivial. Consider the risks of doing nothing. The average corporation has a life span shorter than that of a dog. Even hundred-year business icons can find their lives abruptly cut short when risk of all sorts has not been managed.

Moving risk management to the top of the list of corporate priorities seems like a good way to extend an organization's longevity. Maybe active risk management, with frequent reassessments, is a good tool for building competitive advantage as well.

# SUPPLY CHAIN LITIGATION

If the laws could speak for themselves,
they would complain of the lawyers in the first place.
*Sir George Savile, Lord Halifax*

Lawyers are like morticians.
We all need one sooner or later, but better later than sooner.
*Eileen Goudge*

The trouble with law is lawyers.
*Clarence Darrow*

First, let's kill all the lawyers.
*William Shakespeare*

## Introduction

We Americans present a real paradox to the world and to ourselves. We are borderline lunatic optimists — whatever it is, it'll work, the future is always rosy, nothing can or will go wrong, and the other guy will do the right thing in the end. At the same time, we are obsessive litigants. We'll sue anybody for any kind of transgression, real or imagined.

Regrettably, the supply chain management world is not immune to this threat. In fact, entirely too many consultants and academics are spending too much time and making too much money as expert witnesses and advisors to lawyers in supply chain management litigation. There may be money in it, but it's not value-adding.

Is litigation really a topic for an overview of the fundamentals of supply chain management? Unfortunately, yes. Litigation is becoming increasingly common in our profession, and we fear it may become more so in future.

## Why Is There Litigation in Supply Chain Management?

We imagine that almost any element of supply chain interaction might generate enough heat to get a blazing lawsuit going. But the incendiary action is primarily confined to three arenas: Information Systems, Warehousing, and Transportation. It's not that these areas naturally attract evildoers or that other areas don't. But these are where billions of transactions take place and where customers are touched by outside parties, each and all presenting opportunities for things to go wrong.

And do they ever go wrong!

## Information Systems

You don't have to look far these days for accounts of information system projects gone wrong. For instance, there was the flawed enterprise resource planning (ERP) system implementation at a world-famous candy maker a few years back that prevented the company from shipping orders during peak season. Then there was the well-publicized ERP failure suffered by a prominent appliance maker, which also resulted in shipping delays.

Given the complex nature of today's information systems, any IT project will carry some risks. Those possibilities increase when the system requires modifications to be operational and fully useful to the purchaser. Warehouse management systems (WMS), which often require modification to fit into a client's environment, have traditionally been plagued with final-stage implementation glitches and delays.

In a recent case, a frustrated customer solved the problem by purchasing the source code from the software vendor, who was unwilling to complete the necessary modifications to its software package. That's an extreme solution, perhaps, but illustrative of possibilities on a road less-traveled.

In retrospect, software implementation problems shouldn't be a huge surprise. Nobody's got enough resources to do everything that needs doing — the vendors, the customers, or the consultants (although the consultants seem to have more resources than the others). There's so much to do — test, train, modify, train some more, and test again.

Small wonder that software vendors aggressively encourage implementing "vanilla" versions of packages with few modifications. IT management, once burnt and twice shy, will likely go along with this. The IT people can also be counted on to support the vendors' position that business processes should be changed to match software capability, rather than the other way 'round. These are the same people who implement the "safe" ERP modules like accounting, and never get around to the tough ones.

## Warehousing

There's so much that can go wrong in the warehousing world: failures to ship on time, the provision of sub-standard service to the most important customers, inventory inaccuracies, below-target fill rates, late shipments, shipping errors. And so on.

Ultimately, these failures constitute a breach of contract and provide the basis for lawsuits. Whose fault? Lawyers wrestle over that the question, abetted by their consulting and academic henchmen.

The customer, who has possibly been sued or fired by his own customer, wants to recover actual and punitive damages. The warehousing LSP maintains that the wounds were all self-inflicted or were never incurred.

At $500 to $800 an hour, their surrogates fight it out. At those rates, only the plaintiff and the defendant want to get it over with quickly.

## Transportation

The story here is much the same. There are plenty of things that can go wrong in transportation: late delivery, non-delivery, mis-delivery, shipment damage, or lack of capacity. As with warehousing, each of these opens up the possibility of litigation.

If a fourth party is involved, it faces particular risk. A fourth party that is responsible for managing the efforts of the other LSPs is liable for the performance on the part of the other players in the chain.

## News Flash! Another Set Of Deep Pockets Discovered!

Increasingly, consultancies are being looked at as being responsible for the consequences of bad advice, particularly if the firm is very large. Suing a solo practitioner only punishes the defenseless; going after a multinational behemoth raises the chances of the wounded party becoming whole.

This game gained popularity a decade or two ago when it was discovered that public accounting firms had large bank accounts. Now, otherwise successful consulting organizations are coming into the crosshairs. The most notorious recent example involves a British distributor and the consultant whose counsel managed to increase distribution costs and diminish service.

## Partners Don't Sue Partners

Oh yes they do! In fact, the closest relationships tend to become the most bitter when things go all pear-shaped, as our cousins in London say. It's a shame because the partnership-level relationships start off with the greatest promise, the highest hopes, and the warmest expectations for success.

## So, What Goes Wrong?

It usually comes down to expectations and communications. When salespeople oversell and a naïve buyer doesn't probe hard enough, the stage has been set for disappointment. When the buyer doesn't disclose *everything* about its products, processes, and customers, for example, the software or service provider is forced to react under stress and with insufficient resources.

When circumstances change and the parties insist on sticking to the letter of the contract instead of modifying it, things only get stickier. If provisions and processes for changing performance targets — and resulting penalties and bonuses — haven't been built in, jealousy over "easy money" or "impossible demands" can poison the working relationship.

When the service provider doesn't continue to provide unspecified "best-in-class" solutions, both parties will become frustrated when they inevitably discover that there are practical limitations to what can be achieved.

When the internal legal staffs take charge of the contracting process, and dense, incomprehensible, and rigorous language replaces flexible statements of intent, a budding relationship can be snuffed out.

When both parties are unrealistic about benefits, and mutually over-promise to top management, to customers, and or to employees, the relationship will eventually sour. Any of these constituencies can turn dangerous upon discovering that it's been fleeced.

We shouldn't have to say it. But entering into a software or service arrangement without a written contract is an open invitation to litigation.

## The Right Way to Fix Things

No, it's not by having the lawyers on speed-dial. The best "fix" is prevention. One key to preventing problems is to start off with mutual full disclosure and realistic expectations. Another is to acknowledge from the outset that problems may develop and disagreements may arise, and to make provisions for that contingency. That way, the wheels can be tightened as soon as they start to wobble.

Occasionally, the two parties will find themselves at an impasse. Here's where it is essential to have conflict resolution processes and responsibilities defined, in-place, and tested — well in advance of implementation. This approach requires that you establish broad working relationships throughout both organizations. If the relationship is important enough to both companies, include the CEOs in the mix.

But what if the two parties go through the conflict resolution process and are still unable to work out their differences? Is it then time to call in the attorneys? No, indeed. Here's where an unbiased consultant can assess the situation and deliver an unbiased opinion. The consultant can also facilitate negotiations toward a monetary and operational settlement that is fair to all.

This flies in the face of standard procedure in a litigious society, but it is a rational approach that saves both time and money. Sadly, despite the fact that we know better, some will still elect to sue, based purely on emotion.

## The Arbitration Alternative

Despite all the talk about arbitration, in our opinion, it's not much of an alternative. Arbitration simply provides an alternative arena in which the same combatants and surrogates battle to the financial death. The same law firms are involved. The same expert witnesses are involved. The arbitrator may not have an interest in a rapid resolution and the lawyers certainly don't. All that happens is that the drama is played out on a different stage.

## Another Alternative

Mediation, however, is a different story. People are beginning to recognize that mediation can offer a speedier, lower-cost alternative to litigation for resolving disputes. Contrary to some thinking, it is not an informal, feel-good process, but an organized approach to finding mutually satisfactory solutions.

As with almost anything else, mediation has its upsides and downsides. In addition to the time and cost advantages, mediation's upsides include its non-binding nature. That is, unlike arbitration, mediation does not require that the disputing parties accept the mediator's recommended solution.

But that same non-binding nature can also be a downside. Because the mediator has no real authority, closure cannot be reached without mutual agreement. Of course, if agreement cannot be reached, the options of arbitration and legal recourse are still open.

There are specialized organizations to provide general mediation services as well as some that focus on logistics and 3PL issues. We should note, however, the mediation doesn't necessarily eliminate the need for legal advice. In fact, it's always prudent to maintain legal support to underpin the mediation process.

## Summing up

We have made money as expert witnesses, but we still maintain that litigation is a costly, soul-searing, and ineffective way to resolve supply chain disputes. Building relationships the right way from the beginning goes a long way toward reducing the potential for supply chain litigation. Finding advisers to help sort out real — not judicial — responsibilities and consequences, and working from the beginning toward a fair negotiated settlement — those are what ought to replace the current debilitating wave of supply chain litigation.

# REGULATION AND DEREGULATION

The trouble with wedlock is there's not enough wed, and too much lock.
*Christopher Morley*

The marvel of all history is the patience with which men and women submit to burdens unnecessarily laid upon them by their governments.
*William E. Borah*

Government is a kind of legalized pillage.
*Elbert Hubbard*

You are remembered for the rules you break.
*Douglas MacArthur*

## In the Beginning

Back in the primordial mists of time, when no one had heard of "supply chains" and physical distribution was considered a revolutionary new concept, the buying and selling of transportation service was governed by federal regulation. Transportation wasn't alone, of course. Lots of things were regulated in those days.

In the realm of transportation, regulatory duties were divided up among several different bodies. There was the Interstate Commerce Commission (ICC), which oversaw the railroad and motor carrier industries. In the case of the railroads, the ICC approved rates and rail track extensions or abandonments. In the case of truckers, it determined what routes and territories specific trucking lines could serve, and it also set pricing.

There was also the Civil Aeronautics Board (CAB), which oversaw aviation. It determined what routes air carriers could fly and what they could charge.

Things were no different over in the telecommunications sector. Then, as now, the Federal Communications Commission (FCC) acted as guardian of the public airwaves for television and radio in content and bandwidth usage and assignment.

Throughout a large part of the 20th century, the business landscape was also dominated by a number of government-regulated monopolies, the best known being the telephone company commonly referred to as "Ma Bell." Other regulated monopolies include the local utilities that provide electricity, water, and natural gas for cooking and heating.

## Katie, Bar the Door!

But in the later part of the 20th century, the political climate began to shift. Under pressure from free-market advocates, the federal government began to re-evaluate its decades-old policy of economic regulation. Consumer advocates and big corporations seeking lower shipping costs kept the heat turned up high. And in the end, these and other economic pressures proved irresistible. In 1978, the government began dismantling the regulatory structure. And the rest, as they say, is history.

Air transportation was the first mode to be deregulated, and it's fair to say that for air carriers, it's been a decidedly bumpy ride. Since the industry was deregulated in 1978, we've witnessed the startup and subsequent failure of numerous new ventures, including People Express and Independence. We've also seen the failure of such venerable names in aviation as Pan Am and Eastern.

The remaining carriers have struggled to stay aloft. Delta, United, and USAir have all sought bankruptcy protection. Other traditional carriers have attempted to shore up their operations through mergers — examples include American/TWA and USAirways/America West. But there have been success stories as well. In recent years, brash upstarts like Southwest and JetBlue have entered the "airspace" with visionary new business models calculated to turn the industry on its ear.

For motor carriers, the wild ride began two years later with the signing of the Motor Carrier Act of 1980 (which deregulated the trucking business). Almost immediately, an industry-wide shakeout commenced. Operators who had grown complacent in the protected environment of regulation had no idea how to price their services and how to compete. Some under-priced themselves into bankruptcy. Those who tried to compete with those "always low price" carriers suffered as well.

Vestiges of the old regulated days can still be seen in the trucking industry. For example, it's still common practice among less-than-truckload (LTL) carriers to price their services at a variable discount percentage from a published "tariff." As for pricing in the industry overall, rates plummeted in the years following deregulation — sometimes to unsustainable levels. In recent years, however, rates have been steadily climbing, driven by increased demand, capacity shortages, and soaring fuel costs.

Over in the telecommunications sector, a similar story was unfolding. The national monopoly known as "Ma Bell" was broken up into smaller regional operating units, a manufacturing arm, and a research and development operation in 1982. Geographies and service offerings were opened to access by new competitors, at least to some extent. But mergers and divestitures have continued over the ensuing decades, as the surviving players try to figure out what combinations of talents and strengths will work in the modern marketplace. Prices are down and service has expanded, but contention and strife still rule.

## Unshackled, or Turned Loose Into a Hostile World?

That's not to suggest that where carriers are concerned, all the shackles have been removed. Deregulated does not mean unregulated — far from it.

There are a host of agencies, programs, regulations, and laws that define, direct, and limit what we can do in supply chain management. It should be no surprise that there is a lot of overlap, even competition, among the entities that have been charged through legislation with overseeing these activities.

As you read this, keep in mind that we're only describing conditions in the relatively free-wheeling United States. In Europe, supply chain organizations must wrestle with European Union regulations in addition to national, state, provincial, or departmental agencies.

## Sarbanes-Oxley

Of course, government regulations are by no means confined to transportation. There are plenty of regulations affecting other aspects of supply chain operations as well. Take Sarbanes-Oxley, for example. This act, passed in 2002, was designed to tighten corporate accounting standards and rein in accounting fraud following the collapse of Enron.

Sarbanes-Oxley, or SOX, establishes protocols for implementing and documenting accounting controls and for demonstrating compliance with its regulations. It also deals with issues of ethical transactions, whether domestic or international. In addition, it has implications for the conduct of import and export activities (see below).

Though Sarbanes-Oxley technically applies only to public companies, the reality is that public companies' partners and suppliers are often drawn into the compliance web as well. And by the way, under SOX, you are responsible for the actions of your suppliers as well as for your own.

As you might expect, Sarbanes-Oxley has its critics. Some businesses argue that the compliance costs are too high and the paperwork too cumbersome. A few have begun lobbying Congress to reconsider parts of the regulation.

## Import/Export

In a post 9/11 world, it's hardly a surprise that importing and exporting activities also come under government purview. The agency that comes immediately to mind when you think of international trade is the Bureau of Customs and Border Protection (CBP). But that's only the starting point as there's overlap, confusion, and competition in this area between federal agencies.

To complicate matters, both the rules and the regulatory bodies themselves have been in flux for the past few years. For example, Customs used to be an arm of the Department of the Treasury; now it's part of the Department of Homeland Security. Further complicating matters, some of Customs' historical functions are now divided between Customs and Border Protection, and Immigration and Customs Enforcement.

Congress has gotten into the act as well. Since the 9/11 attack, it has imposed several new laws aimed at securing the nation's borders against terrorism: the Container Security Initiative (CSI), the Trade Act of 2002, and the Bioterrorism Act of 2002.

In the meantime, CBP has taken some security-related steps of its own. In November 2001, it launched the Customs-Trade Partnership Against Terrorism (C-TPAT) as way to enlist cooperation from the private sector in safeguarding the borders.

And that's just the beginning. There are other import and export rules covering a multitude of areas: chemicals and toxins, wood packaging and pallets, computers and electronics, optics and imaging, arms and armament, food and agricultural products, commodities with quotas, and sanctioned nations, to name just a few.

Markings and labeling on shipping containers, advance notification of shipments, and other documentation and processes for cross-border movements all come under the purview of import and export regulation as well.

The reality is that import and export controls can involve as many as 12 agencies or divisions of the federal government. In addition to the CBP, agencies that have oversight over some aspect of foreign trade include the Department of State; the Directorate of Defense Controls; the Department of Commerce; the Bureau of Industry and Security; the Department of Homeland Security; the Bureau of Alcohol, Tobacco, and Firearms; the Nuclear Regulatory Commission; the Department of Energy; and the Food and Drug Administration.

## Occupational Safety and Health Administration (OSHA)

Established by the Nixon administration in 1970, the Occupational Safety and Health Administration (OSHA) has oversight of, well, occupational safety and health. OSHA, which was initially seen by many as an uninvited and particularly meddlesome guest, got off to a rocky start with industry. Things have quieted down since then, and today, businesses are more likely to view OSHA as a working partner than as a harsh overseer or tattle tale. The agency works closely with universities and other educational organizations in the establishment of standards and training.

The range of OSHA's interests is overwhelming. They begin with hazardous materials (see below). But they also include machinery and safety, hazardous energy sources, respiratory exposure and protection, ergonomics, musculoskeletal and nerve disorders, excavation and trenching, electrical standards, industrial hygiene, disaster site management and operations, health and wellness, behavioral safety, workplace violence, and construction and general industry. OSHA is also responsible for such equipment and items as ladders, scaffolding, cranes and rigging, walking surfaces, protective garments and equipment, welding, concrete and steel, tools, material handling, fire protection, and exits and entrances.

We should also note that besides the federal OSHA, there are individual state OSHAs as well.

## Antitrust

In the United States, antitrust regulation dates back to the Sherman Antitrust Act of 1890, which was passed to curb both the real and perceived excesses of big business at the time. Despite its roots in the 19th century, the legislation is still in effect today. In fact, it provided the basis for the 1980 breakup of AT&T.

The next hundred years saw the introduction of a number of other measures aimed at preventing restraint of trade. For example, 1914 brought the Clayton Antitrust Act and the establishment of the Federal Trade Commission. Government's antitrust powers were extended during Franklin D. Roosevelt's administration by the Robinson-Patman Act, which barred price discrimination by producers. The last revision occurred in 1976 with enactment of Hart-Scott-Rodino Act, which requires businesses (in some cases) to notify the federal government of their intent to merge.

In simplest form, these laws are meant to:
- Prevent or correct marketplace abuses in pricing or restraint of trade by a company that has grown too large and dominant.
- Disallow mergers and acquisitions that might create such a dominant entity that competition in an industry segment would be materially impaired.
- Forbid collaborative setting of prices and practices by ostensible competitors.
- Ensure equitable pricing and product access for all of a company's customers.

Exemptions to prevailing antitrust law are sometimes granted, notably to professional sports organizations.

## Labor Law

The Department of Labor (DOL) covers every imaginable aspect of life in the workplace, from the minimum wage to pensions and benefits. (OSHA is one of the DOL's agencies.) The department also has jurisdiction over workers' compensation, progressive discipline, and overtime, although these issues are also covered by agencies in the individual states.

In addition, the DOL oversees provisions of the Family and Medical Leave Act and the Americans With Disabilities Act, both of which have generated confusion, resentment, and misunderstanding in the business community.

Much of the Labor Department's traditional mission, including the control of child labor, is defined by the 1938 Fair Labor Standards Act. Training and education for workers facing the demands of the 21st century economy has become a recent priority.

## Union Organizing

The National Labor Relations Act, the law that covers relationships between and among employers, labor unions, and employees, is administered by the National Labor Relations Board (NLRB). The NLRB, through its Federal Labor Relations Authority, also has responsibility for the process of establishing — or de-establishing — union representation for workers and the procedures for collective bargaining process.

The provisions of the act and the decisions of the NLRB and its subordinate agencies can affect organizations and employees throughout the supply chain from drivers to warehouse workers, including clerical and other non-exempt salaried positions.

Modern employer and union relationships were significantly influenced — without legislation — when former thespian and union leader Ronald Reagan broke the PATCO (air traffic controllers) strike in 1981.

## Environmental Protection Agency (EPA)

Supply chain operations are also affected by a wide range of environmental regulations, which are overseen at the federal level by the Environmental Protection Agency (EPA.) Today, there are environmental regulations governing not just where and on what kinds of terrain a facility may be constructed, but also such matters as waste disposal, emissions, soil, ground water, rivers, and air quality. The EPA also controls activities and financing associated with the clean-up of hazardous waste sites. The agency has expressed an interest in recycling as well.

The EPA frequently works in concert with the Food and Drug Administration (FDA) and the National Institutes of Health (NIH). It also links to Homeland Security.

## Food and Drug Administration

If your company handles foodstuffs or pharmaceuticals, your supply chain's activities may fall under the purview of the Food and Drug Administration (FDA). That agency has rules governing the transport, handling, and storage of foodstuffs — linked to the Preparedness and Response (Bioterrorism) Act of 2002. Organizations and activities likely to be affected include third-party warehouses, brokerage deals, imported goods, cross-docking transactions, and vertically integrated trucking subsidiaries.

## Transportation

As noted earlier, the economic regulations governing the transportation industry were largely dismantled in the 1970s and 1980s. Still, the 1980 Motor Carrier Act (MCA) was really only partial deregulation, and industry experts estimate that supply chains could save an additional $28 billion a year if the trucking industry were fully deregulated. Similarly, airline deregulation is considered by many to be an unfinished business.

Although the federal government no longer exerts much economic control over the transportation industry, it continues to regulate safety. The Department of Transportation oversees the training and licensing of drivers and carriers as well as drug and alcohol testing. Though both the Interstate Commerce Commission and the Civil Aviation Board have been legislated out of existence, the DOT still includes a number of agencies. They include the Federal Motor Carrier Safety Administration (FMCSA), the Federal Highway Administration, the Federal Railroad Administration, the Maritime Administration, the Pipeline and Hazardous Materials Safety Administration, the Surface Transportation Board, the Federal Aviation Administration, and the Research and Innovative Technology Administration.

Along with the federal DOT and its agencies, there is also a network of state DOTs with their own regulations and agendas. This situation is similar to that of communications, in which state Public Service Commissions rule on rate increases, service offerings, and competitive access to the service delivery network. The state commissions also typically rule on matters affecting the partially deregulated gas and electric utilities.

## Hours of Service (HOS)

A highly visible and somewhat controversial regulation from DOT's FMCSA, known as the hours of service (HOS) rule, places limits on commercial motor vehicle drivers' work shifts. Among other matters, the regulations place restrictions on the following:

- The maximum drive tour following a minimum off-duty time.
- The maximum total consecutive work hours following off-duty time.
- The total maximum drive hours in a 7- or 8-day work period.

There are special provisions for short-haul drivers and for passenger-carrying drivers.

Many industry observers fear that these rules will exacerbate the current, extreme driver shortage; others maintain that well-managed fleets will suffer little harm. The issue has been complicated by a series of revisions and stays of implementation resulting from court challenges.

## Hazardous Materials (HazMat)

The federal government provides guidance and standards for all aspects of the handling of hazmat. The regulations can get quite arcane as there are many forms of hazardous materials. These include such obvious examples as nuclear, chemical, and biological agents, either as instruments of terrorism or in their more natural applications. Then there are toxic substances, flammable materials, and other corrosive or reactive products as well as materials that can cause environmental damage. Further, we need to consider issues for these items in their natural and usable states as waste.

The government has issued rules for hazmat storage, for hazmat transportation, for hazmat disposition, and for hazmat cleanup. A cottage industry has grown up around the need to provide hazmat training for emergency and incident response, site cleanups, protective equipment, decontamination, atmospheric hazards, testing and sampling, terrorism awareness, and chemical and biological agents.

OSHA is the most visible regulator in this arena, but there are others as well.

### Internal Revenue Service (IRS)
The role of the IRS is well understood, and we're not about to get into a discussion of its efficacy or its future. Suffice it to say that there are tax implications for many supply chain activities.

### It's Not Only the Embassy That's Been Bugged ...
The invasion of the United States by non-native insects has resulted in the implementation of phytosanitary regulations, in the form of ISPM 15. These are designed to embargo the entry of non-compliant wood packaging, including crates, pallets, and tie-downs.

### Take off Your Shoes and Put the Laptop on the Belt
The Transportation Security Administration (TSA) takes a real public relations beating in the popular press. But this unit of the Department of Homeland Security has responsibility for the safety and security of commercial cargo movement as well as for passenger movement throughout our transportation systems.

### In Conclusion
How can you keep up with all this? You can't. That's why it's smart to retain the services of the accountants and lawyers who do. They are dedicated specialists whose passion for the minutiae of regulation can be a life saver in an ever-changing regulatory landscape.

# GREEN SUPPLY CHAINS

Thank God men cannot fly, and lay waste the sky as well as the earth.
*Henry David Thoreau*

There is a sufficiency in the world for man's need but not for man's greed.
*Mohandas K. Gandhi*

Because we don't think about future generations, they will never forget us.
*Henrik Tikkanen*

We never know the worth of water till the well is dry.
*Thomas Fuller*

## How Green Was My Valley

Mention conservation and the environment to those of a certain age, and tree-huggers, flower children, and protest demonstrations spring to mind. But we've all come a long way since those days, for all the earnest anguish of Al Gore's *An Inconvenient Truth*. While the excesses of Greenpeace and PETA would have you believe that the world, particularly the business world, is populated by rapacious, soulless barbarians, the fact is that the supply chain world is getting serious about getting green.

And it's time for us all to pay attention.

## A Beginning Glimmer

For many of us, the mantra of "Reduce, Reuse, and Recycle" served as our introduction to the emerging green movement. At the consumer level, some of us took them more to heart than did others.

Then, the local trash haulers began to accommodate pickups of certain recyclable materials, sometimes subsidized by local governments. As is usually the case, the concept seemed to work when the economics of the process worked for the consumer as well as the hauler. With enough volume, it may work out for the local governments, too.

## Meanwhile, Back at Headquarters

It's no great surprise when enterprising politicians are able to locate a good parade to jump out in front of, and that's certainly happened with many things green — and not just in California. It *is* news when flinty-eyed C-level executives come over to the environmental side. Maybe this is for real after all.

For evidence of the growing interest in all things green, you need look no further than a sampling of the recent literature. Time Warner's *Business 2.0* has featured a 20-page section on business payoffs in green initiatives. *Global Logistics & Supply Chain Strategies'* November 2006 issue featured the "good for business" elements of green supply chain operations. The Council of Supply Chain Management Professionals (CSCMP) has devoted a full issue of *CSCMP Explores* to environmental sustainability.

*Business Week* carried "green" features in two successive months. The first touted green technology stocks in which to invest; the second focused on the United States' imperative to develop even more green technology or risk falling behind the market-driven European technologies that are helping to drive down carbon emissions.

*Newsweek* has carried similar content. So has *Time*. Imagine that — the popular press, the business press, and the trade press all going in the same direction.

## The Saudis Made Us Do It

Some would suggest that the cost of energy is driving our interest in thinking green. Maybe so. The price of oil and the cost of fuel — and excitement about future availability — change the economic equation of some critical supply chain elements. Business people will make what they think to be sound business decisions and future plans.

## Recent History

Just-in-time manufacturing and distribution have been premised on swapping low-cost, freely available transportation for high inventory cost. Offshore manufacturing in Asia demands fuel for both marine transport and longer over-the-road transport. Low labor costs in foreign countries are attractive if the cost of fuel is relatively low.

The business aspects of the Asia scenario get a little more complicated in the face of rising wages and growing affluence in the producing countries. But the primary concern is rising fuel and freight costs. As those costs rise and stay relatively high, the total landed cost piece for products becomes a factor in the decision whether to make goods offshore or close to the United States. If energy costs double, that could change the outcome altogether.

The addition of supply uncertainty to the equation, which adds more potential variability to supply chain performance, only makes the idea shakier.

So, here's where we seem to be. Inventories must necessarily increase — dramatically — to reflect realities in product delivery variability as well as the supply chain's length in both time and miles. Production of higher levels of inventory will also, by the way, consume more energy. Meanwhile, transportation costs, while not necessarily reaching new peaks every month, appear to be set at permanently higher levels. On top of that, the need to maintain customer service levels may drive the need for more distribution facilities to deploy inventories further forward in the chain. Of course, more resources will be consumed in the building and operation of those facilities.

Admittedly, not everyone is making wholesale changes to their supply chains — at least not yet. But more and more companies are eyeing developments cautiously and looking at alternatives. It's conceivable that the day may come — and it may not be far off — when offshoring to China no longer makes economic sense.

It's no wonder that tactical forces alone are driving hard looks at energy conservation of many kinds. But those organizations that are looking beyond knee-jerk reactions are beginning to think in strategic terms about supply chain construct and operation.

## Environmental Sustainability — Say What?

We think the term "environmental sustainability" really indicates a direction, more than an in-hand accomplishment, but some major players are getting into the act with far-reaching commitments. Wal-Mart has announced objectives of complete use of renewable energy, zero waste, and a product mix that sustains resources and the environment. Clearly, this initiative will require a long series of incremental improvements in facilities, fleet, operations, packaging, and sourcing.

## Global Considerations

We may look to Europe for a preview of coming attractions as that continent has already adopted significant environmental regulation. For multinational companies, European regulation is already influencing how green their behavior must become. Such initiatives as the Waste Electrical and Electronic Equipment Directive (WEEE) and Restriction of Hazardous Substances (RoHS) are forcing, in a positive way, both product design and material selection to consider environmental and health impacts. All this, plus mandated recyclable content in products of all levels of size and complexity.

## What Are People Doing?

The first step almost always involves energy efficiency. Maybe it's restructuring transportation to reduce fuel consumption. Maybe it's electricity usage management, through more efficient lighting, more efficient HVAC systems, or flexible management of heating and cooling in the warehouse. Maybe it's a reduction in materials that are major energy consumers in their own production.

Maybe it's a return to the days of fewer, larger orders to optimize transportation usage and cost. In all cases, long-lasting improvement begins with a clear and complete understanding of processes and decision points and gets legs through the attention of consistent and continuing measurement.

## What Are the Leaders Doing?

UPS, for one, has undertaken a number of programs designed to reduce its fleet's greenhouse gas emissions worldwide. Dell is pioneering a recycling program to improve and enlarge asset recovery. FedEx is rolling out hybrid trucks, with ambitious goals for particulate emission reduction.

Hewlett-Packard, with immense global sourcing and global sales, has developed a Social and Environmental Responsibility policy along with a supplier code that includes environmental activities. SC Johnson has, for years, carefully looked at — and significantly reduced — toxic substances in its products.

Sun Microsystems is restructuring its physical distribution network and at the same time, revamping product design, recycling, and end-of-life disposal processes. Timberland has developed a sustainability agenda that covers the use of energy, materials, chemicals, and systems. It has introduced water-based adhesives into shoe production and has begun recycling PVC as it moves toward zero PVC waste.

DHL and its parent, Deutsche Post are looking at biofuels and natural gas alternatives in fuel consumption, as well as working on greenhouse gas emission reduction and offering low-carbon (or carbon-neutral) shipping products. Even port authorities such as Long Beach are involved with programs to persuade tenants to adopt greener technologies and to construct green leases to help reduce diesel pollution.

## A Sustainable Supply Chain Model

The Council of Supply Chain Management Professionals (CSCMP) has synthesized the approaches of three major organizations into a unified system that links:

- Upstream elements
    - Supplier requirements
    - Code of conduct
    - Traceability and chain of custody
    - Returns policies
- Internal operations elements
    - Conversion and transformation
    - Logistics
    - Scrap and packaging recycling
    - Reverse logistics
    - Remanufacturing
- Downstream elements
    - Distributor requirements
    - Code of conduct
    - Traceability and chain of custody
    - Returns management
- Product development/stewardship
    - Design for environment
    - Lifecycle analysis
    - Packaging minimization
    - Product re-acquisition and disposal

## What Else Is Going on?

There are a host of initiatives devoted to a wide spectrum of environmental challenges, including hunger, epidemics, overfishing, and drug-resistant infections. Those that seem to be of the greatest interest to the supply chain community include:

- An interactive, renewable, smart power grid, with components of solar, wind, wave, methane from cattle, clean coal, and car power.
- Nuclear waste neutralization.

- Water purification.
- Waste disposal.
- Air and water purification and pollution prevention.
- Diesel to natural gas conversions.
- Emission-free nuclear power, wind farms, and reduced fossil fuel use.
- Oil independence.
- Varieties of hybrid technology.

## Is It Easy Being Green?

Of course not. But it's not as hard as it used to be. That's because the economic equation is definitely tilting toward the green side.

Look — this is no longer about the "thou shalt nots" of the regulators: Thou shalt not build a facility on wetlands. Thou shalt not leak nasty substances into the groundwater. Thou shalt not emit particulates into the air. It *is* about redefining and reconstructing the supply chains of the future.

# HEALTH, SAFETY, AND ERGONOMICS

Like a bad tooth and an unsteady foot is confidence in a faithless man in time of trouble.
*Proverbs 25:19*

Give a man health and a course to steer,
and he'll never stop to trouble about whether he's happy or not.
*William Shakespeare*

In nothing do men more nearly approach the gods than in giving health to men.
*Marcus Tullius Cicero*

The desire to take medicine is perhaps the greatest feature
which distinguishes man from the animals.
*William Osler*

## History Lessons

It is difficult to conceive the distance we have traveled in the realm of employee and worker well-being. In the early days of the Industrial Revolution, the employers who ran the factories, the mines, and what William Blake ominously referred to as "dark Satanic Mills" spared little thought for worker health, safety, and what's now known as ergonomics.

Men, women, and children were expected to put their backs into it and to be quick about it as well. Slacking and lollygagging were not tolerated nor were illness and injury.

Injury was an everyday hazard of employment — the responsibility of the worker. Illness was an unfortunate event, but it wasn't permitted to drag down production. There were always plenty of willing — even desperate — replacements for the consumptive and the lame. Anyone who couldn't pull his or her weight was out of work and out of luck. Social Security and health insurance had yet to be invented.

Beginning at the end of the 19th century and through the first half of the 20th, workers and their associations began to influence both public attitudes and governments. As a result, conditions began to improve in the areas of:

- Employer-provided health insurance.
- Disability insurance.
- Overall safety, both physical and environmental.
- Child labor.
- Working hours.
- Labor-saving devices.

Eventually, the federal government got into the act, although its initial attempts at regulation hardly got off to an auspicious start. Convinced that the government's initiatives were more about witch hunts than public policy, businesses generally dug in their heels. Although relations have improved over the years, decades were devoted to battles.

But something strange happened between the last final battle and the next final battle. At some point, it appears, industry had an epiphany. Management collectively began to figure out that having healthy workers, with all their body parts intact and relieved of undue physical and emotional strains, made good business and economic sense.

It's not that no one ever understood this. There have always been a few enlightened visionaries. And it's not that everybody gets the picture today. There are certainly still holdouts who will either get on board the Health/Safety/Ergonomics express or be left behind on the wayside.

## Health

The benefits of a healthy workforce are reasonably clear once the emotional and political positioning have been cleared off the stage. Healthy employees are absent less often. They are more productive, they don't drive up health insurance costs, and they tend not to die before their working careers are over.

Employers are seeing the value — not just the cost — of protecting workers from being contaminated by harmful materials in the workplace — particles, vapors, chemicals, byproducts, whatever. But they're not stopping there. With encouragement from their health insurers, many companies are actually promoting preventive and proactive care for their employees' general health. They are promoting prevention rather than blindly paying the high costs of reactive medical care. The next step has been to provide wellness programs, sometimes including company time in which to pursue them.

Such programs often are designed to influence behavioral factors in health, such as smoking, obesity, and substance abuse. They can include fitness activities as well as awareness and self-examination encouragement for a number of conditions. The smoke-free, drug- and alcohol-free, weapon-free working environment is now a commonplace in American business.

Some companies, reportedly including Wal-Mart, are approaching the problem by planning to hire healthier new employees. In contrast, PepsiCo gives cash to employees and spouses who complete online health risk assessments. It offers further cash awards for seminar and counseling attendance. But the movement is still going uphill, with many struggling to enlist employees in voluntary wellness programs.

All aspects of supply chain management benefit from contemporary approaches to improved individual health. So what if it's only enlightened self-interest? The movement represents a win-win proposition for employers, employees, governments, insurers, families, and eventually for consumers and product and service end-users.

## Safety

The rationale for safety is constructed in much the same way as for health. No sane executive wants workplace accidents. Exposures to unsafe situations vary widely among individual elements in the supply chain. The white collar employee doesn't face nearly the risks to his or her physical safety as those working in the distribution center, in the mine, in the factory, or in transportation. Employers that reduce their workers' exposure to unsafe conditions are seeing the payback.

In the dimension of physical safety, there are significant benefits to derive from doing the right thing. Look, it's no good to have people out because of injury or accidents. There are issues of long-term and short-term disability, workers' compensation, and, of course, lawsuits.

Beyond that, there is incredible cost tied up in finding less-experienced temporary substitutes or in the ghastly expense of recruiting and training permanent replacements. Finally, the returning worker may not be able to perform the same tasks he or she did before the accident or at least perform them at the same level.

The field of safety management has generated another cottage industry of specialized consultants. They develop plans and programs to organize corporate efforts to maintain safe and accident-free workplaces. Generally, such programs contain plans and streamlined, standardized processes for daily, weekly, monthly, and annual activities for defined areas of safety needs. They typically communicate:

- Who is responsible for what decisions, activities, and communications.
- How things are to be done.
- Where things — tools, controls, materials, etc. — are located.
- How often things need to be done (training, drills, inspections, tests, etc.).
- What equipment and processes are involved.

## The Public Weal

Another aspect of safety deserves more than passing mention. When the public is exposed to the effects of impaired workers, or of defective products that result from worker impairment, or of dangerous product content or environmental damage, the risks are nearly beyond counting. It's not merely the PR damage in the marketplace — it's about real money, involving sums with lots of commas.

The nightmares that keep management up at night may center on a truck driver who has gone 36 hours without sleep before plowing into a minivan full of kids. Or it could be the substance-impaired engineer whose locomotive takes out a school bus stalled at a grade-level crossing. These examples are only the outer limits. Sometimes the event in question is merely a fire and explosion generated by a mishap with a fuel truck. In fact, there are any number of more subtle consequences of safety gaps in supply chain operations.

Then there is the unfortunate practice of truck drivers' urinating into plastic containers to avoid the time loss of stopping for biological breaks, then pitching the used containers out the window. HOS rules didn't create this phenomenon, but they certainly don't make allowance for stops that do not include loading or unloading freight. We don't know if the incidence of "P-bombs" constitutes a health issue, a safety issue, or a regulatory issue, but it does deserve notice.

## Ergonomics

Curiously, OSHA proposed standards for workplace ergonomics as recently as 1999. The effort failed, and it raised concerns about the future of ergonomics. But to the amazement of some, the gratification of others, and the consternation of a few, businesses have apparently come to recognize the good business sense of good ergonomics without the visible hand of government intervention.

Sometimes, the lines between health, safety, and ergonomics blur, such as when white collar supply chain professionals deal with carpal tunnel issues that result from poorly designed keyboards and workstations. Or when continuous work with a computer monitor affects vision and leads to headaches. Or when chairs fail to provide correct lumbar and other back support.

We usually first think of ergonomics for its contribution to improved performance and productivity, and that's a legitimate perspective. But ergonomics actually contributes mightily to issues in health and safety as well. Beyond the white collar examples, which abound throughout the supply chain, a lot of work has gone into ergonomically designed tractor cabs. The professional drivers in these rigs need all the relief they can get in their long and kidney-jarring days and during their rest periods.

It is in the distribution center, though, that we can see the most direct applications of ergonomic designs, particularly for productivity advantage. But it's still enlightened self-interest; an ergonomically friendly workplace will yield not only higher productivity, but will also contribute to the longevity of a high-performance workforce.

## Ergonomics in the Distribution Center

The late Gene Gagnon, our friend and collaborator and the father of warehouse productivity management, provided many of the thoughts embedded in the discussion that follows. Here's a dose of ultimate reality in this always-timely topic: Ergonomics is difficult to describe.

If you ask the average person to define an accordion, you will usually get some hand motions that describe the contraption without telling you how it really works. Hand motions won't get the job done with ergonomics.

Some say that ergonomics is the science of designing work methods and tools for maximum human comfort. Others say that good ergonomics is the business of helping people work smarter, not harder. Still others define ergonomics as the arrangement of work to minimize the possibility of excess fatigue or personal injury. In fact, ergonomics involves all three, and more as described above.

In considering the process, you should begin with facility construction and then move on to look at hiring practices and every aspect of the layout. That means looking at buildings, equipment, training, and processes as you search for ways to improve the ergonomic impact of the workplace. To justify the necessary investment, weigh the cost of the ergonomics changes against the current cost of job-related injuries.

## The Motivators

Unfortunately, despite overall awareness of its importance, some managers consider ergonomics to be a smokescreen for staying out of trouble with the government. Negative feelings left over from past involvement seem to cloud attitudes toward the two federal agencies involved in workplace safety: the Occupational Safety and Health Administration (OSHA) and the National Institute of Occupational Safety and Health (NIOSH).

The two groups are separate and have somewhat different agendas. As part of the Department of Labor, OSHA acts as the policeman for proper safety standards in the workplace. NIOSH is part of the Department of Health and Human Services, and it produces guidelines and recommendations, rather than conducting inspections and policing violations. (See the chapter on Regulation and Deregulation.)

A major motivator for ergonomics should be the improvement of accident and safety records and the subsequent reduction of operating costs. Nobody likes accidents, and they are increasingly expensive. The average medical cost for a back injury is $30,000. As accident records improve, the costs for health insurance and workers' compensation should go down, helping ease the cost pressures felt throughout the supply chain.

But the most powerful motivating factor of all may be the potential to boost productivity. When the physical effort to do the job is reduced, the worker is more productive. When you arrange the workplace in a manner that reduces fatigue, your people will produce the same amount of work with less effort or even more work with the same effort. Therefore, they will move more units or pounds of cargo each day with no increase in work hours and no degradation in performance and quality.

## Improving Ergonomics

Many practical steps can improve operational ergonomics. For example, if there are two empty pallets on the floor beneath the first loaded pallet, the bottom case will be 8 to 12 inches higher than it would be otherwise. This reduces the risk of strain from leaning or bending down to the floor to pick up the lowest case.

Common sense in sequencing order-picking tasks will reduce walking or wasted time and motion. For example, if order picking is done in a "Z" pattern, the picker selects from one side of the aisle and then immediately selects from across the aisle. Other non-conventional sequences can deliver similar benefits.

Rotating jobs every few hours has at least three advantages. Job rotation allows workers to perform different tasks and minimizes the possibility that repetitive motion will cause injury. Second, it allows each worker to cross-train and develop new skills. Third, it reduces boredom on the job, which can degrade quality and safety.

Job-related injury is closely related to fatigue. Tasks should be designed for micro breaks, and workers should be trained to use these breaks to avoid fatigue and to plan ahead. Workers should stop moving periodically to study the remaining work and consider the best way to get the job done. In other words, they should have the opportunity and time to learn how to work smarter, not harder.

Uncontrolled overtime creates fatigue and contributes to injuries and accidents. Even planned and controlled overtime can yield diminishing returns and incur similar risks. Improved scheduling and appropriate use of part-time workers should be employed to reduce the amount and frequency of overtime work.

Avoid conditions that cause awkward or strained situations in the manual handling of goods. Twisting causes the worst strain, and it is particularly dangerous if it is done while lifting or handling cartons. Avoid situations that require the worker to stoop or to reach overhead while handling heavy cases. Remember that the jury is still out regarding the efficacy of back braces. Whether they work or not, they are no substitute for good ergonomics.

Arrange stock in the warehouse pick line to avoid an unnecessary amount of awkward motion. The fastest movers should always be stored in the "golden zone," which extends from the belt height to the shoulder height of the average individual. Items within this zone can be grabbed and moved without either stretching or bending. Special consideration should also be given to the location of oversize or overweight SKUs, even when they aren't the fastest movers.

There are five limiting parameters to consider in manual handling:
- The weight of the product.
- The product's dimensions.
- The height (or depth) of the product's location.
- The distance to reach and grasp the product.
- How frequently selection and movement motions are repeated.

## Training, Documentation, and Fitness

Have all of your order pickers been taught the best way to select product without wasted motion or undue fatigue? Are your supervisors sensitive to ergonomics so they know how to correct workers who are not following the best procedure? Training is absolutely essential, both for workers and supervisors.

Documentation is also important. Some companies use a methods checklist for order picking. The checklist provides both a training tool and a defense document if a company is vulnerable to citation from OSHA inspectors.

Proper slotting makes up another essential element of improved ergonomics. However, it is achieved only when management controls the putaway function so the fastest movers are always in the golden zone(s). The best warehouse management systems control the putaway function, and yet we still see too many warehouses where location of inbound material is not well-controlled. A complicating factor is that the population of "A" and "B" items may change frequently, and re-slotting can be hard work. But it must be done. The payoff is significant, and the risks of not doing it are equally so.

Exercise can be as important as training in the prevention of injuries on the job. Some warehouses — even entire companies — incorporate aerobic exercises into the daily routine. In one case that we've observed, management and office personnel as well as workers attend the exercise session, and 100 percent participation is expected.

## Be Proactive

There is a natural tendency for private-sector managers to resist the activities of government regulators. However, supply chain managers should not resist ergonomics programs — they should promote them. Preventing injuries and improving productivity are good for every business. Management should be an advocate for ergonomics, not because an OSHA inspector is watching, but because it will improve operations — usually at little cost.

Try to learn as much as possible about physical operations by observing the work and asking employees about how they're doing. The figure shown below will guide you in knowing what to observe.

Occasionally, you may encounter federal inspectors who are working from guidebooks

**Figure 4**
**Employee Observation Form**

Employee Name:_____ Employee I.D._____ Date:_____ Oberservers Name:_____
Area:_____ Shift:_____ Job Code:_____ Document Number:_____ Equip.#_____
Time: Start:_____ Actual:_____ Goal:_____ Previous Performance:____% Performance on this job:____%

**Questions For Employee**

| | | | |
|---|---|---|---|
| 1. | Does the job just completed represent your normal work assignment? | Yes | No |
| 2. | Do you feel you have the normal skills required to do the job just observed? | Yes | No |
| 3. | Do you feel you need additional training in the methods for this job? | Yes | No |
| 4. | Do you feel, while performing the job just observed, that you worked faster, slower, or | Faster | Slower |
| | equal to your normal work pace? Please explain._____ | Equal | |
| 5. | Do you feel the pace at which you worked was reasonable? | Yes | No |
| 6. | Do you feel that you could maintain that pace for an entire shift? | Yes | No |
| 7. | In your opinion, what could be done to create a more productive work environment? | | |
| | Comments:_____ | | |

**Questions For Observer**

| | | | |
|---|---|---|---|
| 8. | Were any equipment problems, barriers or significant delays encountered? | Yes | No |
| | Comments:_____ | | |
| 9. | Was the job function performed safely? Comments:_____ | Yes | No |
| 10. | Was the quality of work performed acceptable? Comments:_____ | Yes | No |

**THANK YOU FOR YOUR PARTICIPATION AND COOPERATION**

"I have reviewed this method observation with management."
Employee Signature:_____ Date:_____
Observer Signature:_____ Date:_____

and have little or no practical warehouse experience. If your management and your trade association are proactive in collaborating with OSHA to develop ergonomic guidelines, you should be able to avoid coming into conflict with the inspector or being cited for substandard ergonomic conditions.

Nobody really wants injuries or unsafe working practices, anymore. Good ergonomics offers a practical way to avoid both.

## The Traps

Paying attention to ergonomics requires constant vigilance. Unfortunately, it's all too easy to be lulled into complacency. And that can be costly, if not deadly. The following are the types of statements we've heard too often over the years and our response to them:

- "Yeah, yeah, we've heard it all before, and nobody's died yet." "Yet" being the operative word.
- "That's not heavy; it couldn't be a problem." Unless you don't know how to pick it up.
- "These little strains are all in a day's work." Right, and black lung disease is just an inconvenience.
- "Hey, it's only a strain — work through it." "Playing hurt" is for the NFL. Little aches can turn into chronic pains and big bills.
- "How can it be repetitive movement if you only do it a few times a day?" How about a few times a day for 35 years?
- "C'mon, we do that all the time." Try telling that to the widow's lawyer.
- "Where will we get the dough to go through all this ergonomic stuff?" Where will you get the dough to pay the $250,000 claim?

## In Conclusion

Some people consider ergonomics to be a dull topic. But we would argue that health, safety, and ergonomics are important and alive, and can be life-changing in a corporation's organizational experience. They are major factors in quality performance, operational productivity, and profitability — whether they are recognized as such or not.

# THE ROLE OF CONSULTANTS

Use me, O Lord — in an advisory capacity!
*Adlai E. Stevenson III*

When a man comes to me for advice,
I find out what kind of advice he wants, and I give it to him.
*Josh Billings*

Few things are harder to put up with than the annoyance of a good example.
*Samuel Langhorne Clemens*

A good scare is worth more to a man than good advice.
*Edgar Watson Howe*

## We're Consultants, and We've Come to Help …

Logistics service providers are not the only third parties lurking in the underbrush of supply chain management. The weeds are also full of management consultants.

And they don't stick to the weeds. They're everywhere. They're at every conference, seminar, and convention. They're on the Internet with Web sites, e-newsletters, webinars, and spam. They're in *all* the trade publications. They're speaking; they're writing; they're selling endlessly.

Who are they? What do they do? Do they help — or hinder? Do they really offer a value proposition? Where do they come from? And where do they go? Can they be killed with a silver stake through the heart? Can they be warded off with cloves of garlic?

## Some Perspectives

As for what they do, an old saw has it that a consultant is someone who borrows your watch, tells you what time it is, pockets the watch, and sends you a bill for it. In fact, the jokes are legion, and some are even repeatable in polite company. For example, there's the one about a brash city lad (always in the employ of one of the really big firms) who cleverly tells an old farmer everything he already knows, negotiating possession of a lamb as compensation, only to walk off with the farmer's dog.

Old hands talk about "management insultants." To be honest, there have been some spectacular failures in consulting projects, not all of which involved information systems implementations.

At its best, management consulting can be a noble calling. It's a high-minded endeavor, requiring enormous amounts of both talent and integrity as well as a strong sense of mission and urgency. At its worst, it is an embarrassment and a scandal.

Whatever your view, the emergence of supply chain management as *the* business focus of the new century has attracted consultants of every imaginable variety. Some have been at it for years, evolving along with the field. Others are new to the game, and they seem to think that adding supply chain management to the list of service offerings is enough to get on the playing field.

## The Difference Between Consultants and Advisers

There was a time when great care was taken to distinguish management consulting services from management advisory services. The distinction has faded with time. But the implication is that advisers provide feedback and informed opinion and that consultants take a more active role. Consultants make decision recommendations, acting on behalf of the client. They design and implement processes, facilities, and systems — in short, the hands-on work.

## Defining, Describing, and Seeking Clarity

Consultants come in all sizes, shapes, and flavors. Let's begin by trying to sort out some of the fundamental types. Consultancies offer a diverse collection of different business models as well as approaches to problem-solving. In general, a consultancy will take one of these forms, although shape-shifting is always a possibility.

## The Mega-firms

This category is made up of huge organizations with thousands of people. They may be partnerships; they may be corporations. They are increasingly multinational.

Many of the mega-operators have their origins in the giant public accounting firms. Several years ago, each of the so-called "Big Eight" U.S. public accounting firms had enormous consulting divisions. They generally attempted to be all things to all clients, and they would undertake consulting in any channel that held the promise of growth or profit, including public sector operations. As they created multinational accounting conglomerates, their consultancies likewise added the appearance of international capability, which tended to be more promise than practice.

Today, with mergers, acquisitions, and divestitures, their former consulting selves are barely recognizable. Accenture spun off from Arthur Andersen, which itself disappeared, thanks to Enron. KPMG became BearingPoint. Ernst & Young, itself a merged operation, folded in with Cap Gemini to become CGE&Y. PwC Consulting, a unit of PricewaterhouseCoopers (which itself was the product of a merger between Coopers &

Lybrand and Price Waterhouse), was acquired by IBM (after an attempted purchase by Hewlett-Packard) and has since disappeared as an entity. Deloitte Consulting, product of yet another merger and acquisition, retains its corporate identity but is legally a separate LLC entity.

The overall business model consists of a hierarchical, pyramidal organization, dependent on sales generation by a relatively small number of rainmakers to provide billable hours for large numbers of analysts and managers. Thorough methodology and process development is supposed to allow relatively inexperienced consultants to tackle complex problems in consistent ways.

This model has been likened to bringing in busloads of bright kids, who have been both indoctrinated into the corporate culture and provided with workbooks full of process descriptions and solutions. They must then hope to come across a client who is asking the right questions. Sometimes they become confused, and they begin to believe that the answers are more important than the questions.

Few of these were willing to bring in more seasoned, more highly experienced, more independent-minded, and more expensive old pros. It's not so much an age issue as a business model issue, abetted by a cultural conformity.

Some independent consultancies have become mega-firms. Some of the early leaders continue to prosper, while some others have fallen on hard times or have been sold off. Our favorite among them remains Booz Allen Hamilton, which has apparently flourished despite its unfortunate name.

## Big/Important, but Maybe Not Overwhelming

A small handful of firms concentrated on strategy, but took differing directions. Some tried their hands at tactics and implementation to grow the business, but struggled to bridge the gap. They remain successful in operational issues with strategic implications. Others took to taking equity positions and managing corporate operations.

Several entities focused on performance standards, productivity, and cost reduction. A few pioneers survive, but only just barely.

The business model tended to be based on the engagement of contractors, who are off the payroll as soon as they've completed their assignment. The permanent cadre comprises successful salespeople along with a handful of top executives.

There were dozens of others, the majority of which have disappeared. One of the biggest from days of yore was United Research, which has dropped off the map. But a few have survived. For example, the engineered standards and methodology-based consultancy H.B. Maynard remains an active player in the world of work measurement.

Some consultancies focused on operations such as manufacturing and logistics in the early days. One leader in the movement survived an unfortunate acquisition and has rebounded as a broad-based global consultancy. Others, including some specializing in physical distribution, have disappeared into the maw of history.

## Small/Mid-Sized

The small and mid-sized consultancies tend to be built upon limited, but deep, functional experience. They come and go, and wax and wane while they're here, but some have remarkable staying power. Too numerous to cite names, they can be local, national, or global in coverage. They may be franchises, or they may be real companies. They may affiliate with "stringers" in several locations, handing out business cards to anyone with a suit and a laptop. Or they may grow more organically.

Some achieve greater functional breadth through working partnerships with other consultancies and greater geographic coverage through multinational alliances.

They may follow the hierarchical organization model, or they be flatter partnerships with more hands-on consulting involvement from senior partners.

The supply chain field has spawned many of these operations, and many of them deliver cost-effective and sustainable results. Some are highly specialized, while others offer a broad range of supply chain strategy, planning, and execution services.

An early leader in the field of work measurement, engineered standards, and performance management was the late Gene Gagnon, whose work lives on as part of a large execution software company's offerings.

## Hanging out the Shingle

Next come the sole practitioners, and this is a difficult category to deal with. The solos run the gamut from internationally renowned specialists to prematurely retired managers to out-of-work inebriates. These sub-categories are not mutually exclusive.

Here's a clue — If the phrase "& Associates" appears in the company name, it's a sure sign of flying solo. Unlike in aviation, no lessons are required, and there is no meaningful certification and licensing process. The only barrier to entry in the consulting marketplace is a failure of nerve.

There are many, many really excellent one-man and one-woman shops. For the right kind of problem, they can often offer an on-target solution at the right price. The best of them recognize their limitations, and they are brilliant at enlisting other specialists to work on solving the fundamental problems.

The worst of them believe their own press clippings. Because of their egos, they hesitate to bring in people smarter than themselves to help deliver the right answers.

The recently unemployed complicate the picture considerably. They typically have no training and little real experience in being a consultant. They generally have no idea of how to price services or of what's involved in scoping and executing analyses and solution development. They often don't understand the subtleties of communications, client relationships, and selling. In general, they manage with the best of intentions to give professional management consulting a bad name.

The range of services the solos deliver is staggering. They cover everything from freight bill audits to supply chain strategies.

## Where Do the Academics Fit?

The short answer is in a category of their own. Many respected academics practice consulting on either an institutional or a private basis.

Often, their consulting contains a research component directed at a technical solution to a specific knotty problem. Sometimes, they are able to assemble study and research teams of students — graduate and undergraduate — to observe and assess operational problems and practices.

Other times, they might conduct and analyze industry surveys. Sometimes, they are called as expert witnesses in litigation as a well-known individual in any category might.

Several academics take the student research and analysis approach. Dr. Bernard J. LaLonde began the practice many years ago at Ohio State, and Dr. Walter Zinn continues the practice there today. Miami of Ohio's Dr. Tom Speh has been research director for the Warehousing Education and Research Council (WERC) for many years.

There are times when the right approach to a problem is to build a team with academic and consulting components. That way there's an effective blend of esoteric and practical solution elements.

## Turning the Ship in the Channel

Turnaround management specialists are not really consulting firms, although they employ many consulting techniques in their cost-slashing *blitzkriegs*. Two well-known leaders in the field have senior management with extensive cost management consulting background. They also manage either organic or affiliated investment partnerships that put their money where their mouths are.

The notorious "Chainsaw" Al Dunlap was neither a consultant nor a turnaround manager. But he often engaged management consultants to work though the details of cost-reduction opportunities. Dunlap, who has passed into the folklore of American business, parlayed his experience as an abrasive cost cutter in the paper industry into a cult of personality.

Early career misadventures, which included getting fired, debilitating downsizing, and accounting fraud, did not slow down his rise to self-attributed greatness. He went from lionized hero at Scott Paper to being Sir Jimmy Goldsmith's personal hired gun, then fell from grace at Sunbeam-Oster. There — surprise, surprise — he got fired. The surviving organization was debilitated, and there was a multi-million dollar settlement for — land o' Goshen! — accounting fraud.

## Litigation Support

Technically speaking, litigation support isn't really management consulting either. But many very senior consultants deliver litigation support. Usually this service consists of providing expert witness input for a case, which could take the form of testimony at trial, depositions, or written summaries of observations and conclusions.

These work products are frequently developed from a review of depositions, documents in discovery, personal visits and interviews, or all three. The apparent facts of the case are cast in the light of the expert's experience in either general or specific aspects of supply chain management.

Other roles, which may get a little nearer to consulting, include topical education for attorneys, collaboration on case strategy, deposition preparation for either attorneys or deponents, and offers of proof development.

From time to time, the mega-firms have set up litigation support units to provide resources for monstrously large and complex lawsuits such as *United States v. IBM*. These units typically last until the income stream dries up.

It is quite common for opposing experts in a case to be well-acquainted with one another and with their likely expert positions. The real pros are those who turn down a lucrative expert role when they are not persuaded of the merits of the case, or when a negotiated settlement would be both achievable and an obviously better solution for all parties.

## Clouding the Picture

For some reason, there's a peculiar notion out there that all business services ought to be considered consulting. In our view, that's ludicrous, but that's how we come to have Risk Management Consultants at insurance companies and Sales Consultants at automobile dealerships. Organizations whose revenue stream is derived from performing services — whether warehousing or running IT departments — aren't really consultants either.

The IT outsourcing company, EDS, the source of H. Ross Perot's billions, ventured into operational consulting through acquisition. The firm Accenture presents an interesting meld of service delivery and consulting. Real estate companies that do network design are a little frightening, and parcel companies that want to design supply chains raise some nagging questions of independence. LSPs are often guilty of delivering what are called consulting solutions as part of their business-getting activities.

Nothing against any of them. But at some point the solution has to lean toward their mainstream service offerings, doesn't it?

Despite some instances of vendors' actually charging money to recommend their own products, it is possible for a service provider to dispense honest, independent advice. We actually know of two, one in real estate and one in transportation. Here's the test: Does the "consultant" describe and offer up competitive alternatives to his own service?

## So, Why Do We Need These Consultants?

Lots of reasons. Here are some:
- Shortage of internal resources.
- Lack of specific internal experience.
- New geographic operations.
- New functional responsibilities.
- Need for independent review of operations, decisions, alternatives.
- Need for solutions outside of internal political dynamics.
- Desire for synthesis of multiple industry and functional experiences.
- Availability of experience with analytic or decision support tools.
- Exposure to experience with service providers.
- Experience with specific technology solutions — either software or hardware, or both.
- Knowledge of and access to best practices.
- Track record of creativity in solution development.

## What About Supply Chain Management?

So far, these points could apply to any element of an organization's operations. How do they apply to supply chain management specifically?

Good question. Our point is that supply chain management is not unique; it can benefit from the tactics and techniques applied across business operations. But there are some specific examples of applications within the supply chain community that illustrate areas in which real, honest-to-goodness management consultants can add genuine value:
- Creating a conceptual overall supply chain design.
- Designing a physical distribution network.

- Creating supply chain strategies for service and performance.
- Performance and practices diagnostics.
  - Overall supply chain.
  - Specific components: transportation, warehousing, sourcing and procurement, manufacturing integration, information technology, and supplier and customer relations.
- LSP/3PL evaluation, including selection, contracting, and management.
- Litigation support on either a plaintiff or defendant basis.
- Across-the-board or targeted cost reduction analysis and implementation.
- Transportation management analysis and improvement.
- Facility operations improvement.
- Facility retrofit and upgrade.
- Facility location.
- Software evaluation, selection, and implementation.
- Training and education in supply chain management concepts and components.
- Metrics design, implementation, and analysis.
- Supplier management programs.
- Process design and re-engineering.
- Due diligence on other studies.
- Performance management programs.

The list could be longer, but you get the drift. The trick is to find the right consultant for the right problem. Maybe a consultant can help with that task, too. Often consultants are asked to help evaluate other consultants' proposals or make recommendations.

## How Do You Select a Consultant?

What's important in a consulting relationship? Aside from competency, the real issues are chemistry, style, and comfort. If the organization is culturally welded to a mega-firm approach, it's usually pointless to open the bidding to a lot of solo practitioners. On the other hand, if the organization is confident and secure and wants to cut through the fog to get the answer, the solo practitioner can be marvelously time- and cost-effective.

If the problem has some size or complexity, the small or mid-sized firm, or a team of solo practitioners, can be the right way to go.

The ease of the working relationship, based on individual chemistry and style, is critical. Typically, you are going to be working with the consultant(s) for some time. If there's a style mismatch, tolerance wears very thin very quickly.

Competence can be evaluated from references and from experience. Experience means the stuff that the actual people on the job have actually done, hands-on, not the endless list of organizational qualifications.

There are a few additional points. As you evaluate the possibilities, look for a good listener, one who's more interested in you and your business than in his or her own credentials. Take that a step farther. Try to ferret out whether he or she is comfortable departing from the script when an unexpected subject pops up.

Finally, be sensitive to the consultant's sense of context, the ability to wrap a specific problem's solution in an appropriate setting of process design, information technology, best-in-class practices, integrated planning and operations, and corporate strategies. Not that every problem needs the universe to be analyzed before a solution can be considered.

Still, a good consultant can articulate when and to what degree these elements may be important.

How do you find consultants in the first place? For starters, use directories. The Council of Supply Chain Management Professionals (CSCMP) has one, but it is incomplete. Talking with industry peers or networking in your professional community can be good ways to find out about consulting professionals.

Check out the Internet, which is currently generating consulting contacts at a level undreamed of a few years ago. Anybody worth anything has a Web site. Be sure, however, to concentrate on Web site content versus gee-whiz site design and graphic effects. An emphasis on the superficial might be more revealing than the site owner realizes.

## A Grim Reality
Turnover in the field is incredible. The average consulting career is shorter than that of an NFL player, less than three years. The mega-firms chew 'em up and spit 'em out. It's a tough lifestyle; tough on the individual, tougher on families. The people who pretend to be consultants between stints of gainful employment help to drive up the statistics, too.

While inertia of motion may keep some larger firms going during tough times or market shifts, those same firms will not hesitate to downsize or redeploy people. The solo practitioner, however, faces almost no barriers to failure and contributes mightily to the turnover data. He or she may not have the financial resources to see things through or might not have the background to move with marketplace demands. The solo practitioner might burn out from the travel and workload factors that affect almost all management consultants at one time or another.

There are career consultants. Most bounce from firm to firm, a few years here and a few years there. Those who have successful small firms tend to stay in the game longer. Very, very few establish long careers at one organization.

So, the odds are heavy that the consultant you really liked last time is no longer at the same organization or even in the game.

## In the End
As much as we believe in the value and potential efficacy of consultants in building and improving supply chain excellence, it can be overdone. The normal company doesn't need consultants to answer *every* question. It might not need large numbers of them, if the consultant is inclined to leverage knowledge and experience through the efforts of internal teams.

It's a bit like those people on talk radio's "Dr. Laura," who answer their own questions before the call is over. The solution frequently lies within the company, and it may only need a little probing and direction to get on the right path.

*Note: One of the authors is a solo practitioner, and the other works in a small/mid-sized consultancy; both are alumni of one of the mega-firms.*

# PROJECT JUSTIFICATION AND MANAGEMENT

The best way to predict the future is to create it.
*Unknown*

Life has no limitations, except the ones you make.
*Les Brown*

Destiny is no matter of chance. It is a matter of choice.
It is not a thing to be waited for, it is a thing to be achieved.
*William Jennings Bryan*

Make no little plans; they have no magic to stir men's blood ...
*Daniel H. Burnham*

## Introduction

OK, it's time to knuckle down and do something about one or more of the many opportunities to improve your supply chain planning and execution. What's the best way to go about that? What's the secret to getting approval from the boss? Or from his or her boss? Good questions. Few of us have the freedom to operate without budgets. And fewer still have capital funding stuffed in our Christmas stockings without even asking for it.

Fact is, those of us toiling in the supply chain vineyard don't always have an easy time getting approval for our projects. Face it — we're not as sexy as the marketers, and not as sinister and mysterious as the IT people. We may not know how to phrase our propositions in persuasive ways. And we're entering a milieu in which the competition for funds is vicious, bordering on the unprincipled.

## First Things First

These key points from earlier chapters will help us to frame arguments and come home with the cash. At the end of the day, our challenge is to get more out of the following

218

assets:

- Facilities — space and velocity.
- People — time, numbers, and production.
- Inventory — turns/velocity and service levels.
- Rolling stock — trips, turnaround, and full miles.

We can call it leveraging assets, or return on assets, or utilization, or performance, or whatever we wish. But it all amounts to getting more done with the same or even less. The end game is simple: increase profitability and shareholder value.

As usual, the keys to supply chain project success are: time, money, resources, and the ability to leap tall buildings in a single bound.

With that in mind, doesn't it make sense to focus improvements and projects on asset performance that shows improved returns or increased profitability? When we want to undertake initiatives that will improve quality or increase customer service levels, shouldn't we translate those impacts into bottom-line results?

## The Language of Supply Chain Logistics

Don't forget that every manager has hot buttons, and your boss is no exception. It's up to you to take the core proposition out of the realm of impeccable logic and into the rough-and-tumble of politics and show business.

Play to your audience. Make sure your project pushes the boss's hot buttons on the way to the main points. You might shudder at the thought of being manipulative, but your project may not see the light of day if you don't push those buttons.

Start with what the boss gets measured on. Then follow up with whatever he or she measures others on. These might be headcount, budget, total supply chain cost, return on assets employed, inventory turns, return on investment, cost per unit, perfect orders, or order fill rate. Whatever they are, play them as if your project's life depends on them. It does.

Then it's time to think about the boss's boss's hot buttons. If the project is sufficiently big and robust, you're going to have to think about the things that make chief executive officers (CEOs) and chief financial officers (CFOs) get all sweaty.

Here's a slap in the face — they don't care anything about the language and arcane terminology we use in the everyday business of supply chain execution. Matter of fact, they'll lose interest almost immediately if you can't or don't couch your project's proposition in their language. Since C-level executives aren't going to take the time to understand your world, you're going to have to learn C-speak if you intend to communicate successfully with them.

## C-Speak?

In addition to touching all the bases on operational hot buttons, it's critical that you place the costs and benefits of your project in the context of the company's financial performance. It's vital to talk credibly about Return on Investment (ROI); Return on Assets (ROA); Earnings Before Taxes, Depreciation, and Amortization (EBTDA); Cash Flow; and the like. By the way, Discounted Cash Flow and Net Present Value generally don't come into play, given the duration of most of our projects.

Here's a tip. Even in the world of corporate finance, it helps to use pictures, charts, and graphs instead of columns of figures. Data can be mind-numbing, even to people who love data. And don't forget the DuPont model. This venerable tool has been used to demonstrate the effect of cost, asset, and revenue change on total corporate performance by generations of savvy managers (see the chapter of Supply Chain Finance and Accounting).

It's often useful to be able to present the benefits of a supply chain initiative with an Economic Value Added (EVA) perspective (see the chapter on Supply Chain Finance and Accounting). To illustrate with an oversimplification, the idea of a $1 million inventory that costs $250,000 a year to carry might or might not excite the top decision-maker. But the idea that it takes closer to $2 million in pre-tax dollars to build that inventory and between $400,000 and $500,000 in pre-tax dollars to carry it could tip the balance.

## The Foundation of Credibility

Being able to speak the language(s) of bosses and über-bosses gives you a major advantage in gaining approval, but all that hard work can be undermined if you have only sketchy knowledge of the underlying costs. You and your team have *got* to know each and every component of supply chain cost. That means inbound, outbound, facilities, inventories with all elements of carrying costs, acquisition and procurement, manufacturing, customer service, planning, and anything else that's part of your supply chain's execution and management.

Beyond that, you've got to demonstrate that you know the strengths and weaknesses of the data you're using to make the case for your project:

- Where is the data? (Sources, alternatives, and surrogates)
- What channels, customers, sources, transactions are included — or excluded?
- Is there tampering? (Billed but not shipped, holding open the books)
- How accurate is it? (Adjustments, error rates)
- What is the timing? (Update frequency, posting cycle times, cutoffs, closings)
- What portion of data profiles are real vs. artificial? (Deals, promotions, diversion, incentives, discounts)
- How clean is the nomenclature? (Names, ID numbers, family groupings, conversion maps — all subject to error and redundancy)
- How much junk is in the attic? (Discontinued, declining, kits, components)

## The Project Is Approved — Now What?

Congratulations! Now that you've caught the tiger by the tail, how are you going to survive the experience? Books have been written about project management (PM); we won't plow all that ground again. But there are a few key points to keep in mind:

- PM tools may vary with project complexity, but documentation is essential regardless of the size.
- Formality of the PM process will also vary with size and complexity, but all the bases need to be covered, even in small, simple efforts.
- The level of detail likewise varies by these factors and with corporate culture.
- Irrespective of tools, formality, and level of detail, make the measurement of status and progress simple and visible — to all stakeholders.
- Fix the problems, fix the people, fix the plan! Simply reporting what's wrong is no substitute for active project management. Only action counts. And don't duck for cover the first time stuff hits the fan.

• A communications plan is essential, with specific sequences for a project's various constituencies and target objectives for each.

• Project initiatives and planned outcomes *must* undergo a thorough risk assessment and mitigation process — before things get underway, and it's too late to stop the runaway train.

• Develop contingency plans and exit strategies; don't ever leave the house without a Plan B.

• Design and test the issues management and resolution process ahead of time; don't even think about waiting for the first fistfight to figure out how to handle problems.

## Why Is This Important?

If all you're doing is doing your job, that's not enough. Not today, and certainly not tomorrow. Everything you know, everything you are learning needs to be put into action — into projects — that will make a difference.

What's at stake? The future — both your company's and your own. The core questions get to be: Will your supply chain be a collection of cost centers or a customer-centric differentiator? A functional utility or a strategic asset? A necessary evil or a value chain contributor?

How well you can construct, sell, and execute initiatives that can move the needle of corporate supply chain performance will go a long way to developing the right answers to those questions.

## Going Forward

If you've read this far and haven't been persuaded that it's time to do something or do something different in how you approach, plan, execute, or assess your supply chain management activities, we've failed in our mission. Or at least,we haven't succeeded to the extent that we think we should have.

This is the most exciting time to be in the supply chain management business that we can recall in our combined 80 years in the field. No kidding. We're enthusiastic about hearing what the next generation has in mind.

If you're planning to take action or make changes based on what you've read here, please let us know. Write or e-mail us with your reactions and plans. We'll answer, pro or con. And good luck.

# AFTERWORD

All's well that ends well ...
*William Shakespeare*

The road is long from the project to its completion.
*Jean Baptiste Poquelin Moliere*

It ain't over till it's over.
*Attributed to Lawrence P. Berra*

Do not go gentle into that good night ... Rage, rage against the dying of the light.
*Dylan Thomas*

## Have We Come to the End?

For now we have. We hope you've enjoyed the journey through the world of supply chain management. We also hope you've found it useful — that you've learned things you didn't know before and that you can benefit from them in your business and professional lives.

But the journey isn't really over. In fact, it never actually is. Scope changes, definitions change, trends change — supply chain management will not stand still long enough for us to create the ultimate and permanent picture.

So, we'll need to revisit what we've put together here, to make sure that *The Fundamentals of Supply Chain Management* stays reasonably close to where the profession and practice are at the moment. Then we'll have to revisit it again.

That's part of what's behind our passion for the subject, which, like sunrises, are always striking and always different.

We're looking forward to the process, and to meeting you in these pages again.

In the meantime, let us know what you think — what worked, and what didn't, what rang your bell, and what didn't.


Art Van Bodegraven
avan@theprogressgroup.com
Powell, Ohio

Kenneth B. Ackerman
ken@warehousing-forum.com
Columbus, Ohio

222

# LAGNIAPPE

Lagniappe is a popular New Orleans term, indicating a little something extra. So, we leave you with just a few additional thoughts. They were too good to leave on the cutting room floor. Enjoy ...

On facility location:
The white man knows how to make everything, but he does not know how to distribute it.
*Sitting Bull*

On cost reduction:
Mere parsimony is not economy.
*Edmund Burke*

On outsourcing:
Executive ability is deciding quickly and getting somebody else to do the work.
*J.C. Pollard*

On human resources:
Remember that when an employee enters your office, he is in a strange land.
*Erwin H. Schell*

On strategy:
Not all those that wander are lost.
*J.R.R. Tolkien*

On risk management:
To do nothing is sometimes a good remedy.
*Hippocrates*

On customer service:
I have my faults, but being wrong ain't one of them.
*James R. Hoffa*

On the role of consultants:
No man ever listened himself out of a job.
*Calvin Coolidge*

On relationships:
We only make a dupe of the friend whose advice we ask ...
*Diane de Poitiers*

On communications:
Freedom of the press is guaranteed only to those who own one.
*A.J. Liebling*

On strategies:
The trouble with the world is that the stupid are cocksure
and the intelligent are full of doubt.
*Bertrand Russell*

In general:
Education is not preparation for life; education is life itself.
*John Dewey*

On materials handling:
Opportunity is missed by most people because it is dressed in overalls,
and looks like work.
*Thomas A. Edison*

On warehousing:
Properly speaking, such work is never finished; one must declare it so when,
according to time and circumstances, one has done one's best.
*Johann Wolfgang von Goethe*

On human resources:
By working faithfully eight hours a day,
you may get to be a boss and work twelve hours a day.
*Benjamin Franklin*

On speed:
Growth for the sake of growth is the ideology of the cancer cell.
*Edward Abbey*

On measurement:
I think that a society cannot live without a certain number of irrational beliefs.
*Claude Levi-Strauss*

On risk management:
The weak have one weapon: the errors of those who think they are strong.
*Georges Bidault*

On litigation:
To some lawyers, all facts are created equal.
*Felix Frankfurter*